EMOTION and EARLY INTERACTION

EMOTION and EARLY INTERACTION

edited by
Tiffany Field
University of Miami Medical School

Alan Fogel
Purdue University

LEA LAWRENCE ERLBAUM ASSOCIATES, PUBLISHERS
1982   Hillsdale, New Jersey   London

Lawrence Erlbaum Associates, Inc. Publishers
365 Broadway
Hillsdale, New Jersey 07642

Library of Congress Cataloging in Publication Data

Field, Tiffany.
    Emotion and early interaction.

    Bibliography: p.
    Includes index.
    1. Emotions in children.   2. Social interaction in
children.   3. Infant psychology. I. Fogel, Alan.
II. Title. [DNLM: 1. Emotions—In infancy and childhood.
2. Interpersonal relations—In infancy and childhood.
WS 105.5.E5 E54]
BF723.E6F5   155.4'22   82-7445
ISBN 0-89859-241-0   AACR2

Printed in the United States of America
10 9 8 7 6 5 4 3 2 1

Contents

Preface

As an area of psychological inquiry, the study of emotion is the ugly duck-ling. That duckling has paddled its way from infancy to adulthood, from imprinting to attachment, in the shadow of the proud swan of cognitive studies. While cognitive psychologists were making impressive theoretical and methodological pirouettes, students of emotion were publishing papers on the natural history of emotion expressions. Like any ground-breaking ethnography, the papers were filled with facts, gems of observational wisdom, most of which were unassimilated and therefore tedious and dif-ficult to read. Next to the elegance of a tightly designed and well controlled study of concept formation, the trick cameras of Eibl-Eibesfeldt and the complexity of the Facial Action Scoring System of Ekman must seem ugly indeed.

In the past few years the study of emotion has shed some of its infantile awkwardness, although it has yet to gain its full measure of respectibility in the scientific community. In the area of infancy, emotions are receiving in-creasing attention, in many cases by the standard-bearers of the cognitive approach to early development: Jerome Kagan, Michael Lewis, and Hanus Papousek, to name only a few.

Of course, the field of emotional development has always had its own in-digenous scholars who, in the recent past, have made major theoretical con-tributions to our understanding of emotions. Recent attempts to establish explicit links between emotional and cognitive processes seem to signal an increasing awareness of the importance of emotion as an organizing force in development.

Studies of both emotion and cognition have typically approached these subjects from a psychological view. Since these are patently intrapsychic processes, it has been assumed that it was enough to understand them by studying the individual subject. Even in those cases in which the emotion of interest was the feeling of love or attachment toward others, the construct has been measured primarily with respect to the individual.

Sroufe's work on attachment as an organizational construct, began to make us see that the quality of an infant's attachment to the mother could only be understood by observing the infant in the context of the mother in a particular setting. It may seem that these issues of context divert attention from an understanding of the substantive intrapsychic processes that one wishes to understand. But the recent data seem to suggest that it is impossible to fully appreciate the meaning and function of the infant's affective expressions unless we know the context in which they occur.

At an even more fundamental level, many investigators now believe that intrapsychic processes develop, at least in human infants, by virtue of the infant's transactions with the social environment. Concepts such as *person permanence, social cognition, social referencing, socialization of affect,* and *maternal regulation of infant arousal,* reflect a growing attempt to develop theoretical models to account for how feelings become structured, differentiated, and consolidated in relation to social transactions. We are still a long way from that goal.

This book is a collection of papers by investigators who have been attempting to integrate emotion and interaction processes in early development. None profess to have all the answers, yet each paper challenges us to question some of our notions about the boundaries between the individual and society.

We are not the first to address these complex issues. Whether we realize it or not, this work falls precisely in the tradition of James Mark Baldwin, George Herbert Mead, and Lev Vygotsky. If anything new is offered here, it is only with the blessing of a larger body of experimental and observational data, based on considerably more sophisticated methods than our eminent theoretical progenitors had at their disposal. In fact, the final section of this volume is devoted to a review of the recent methodological advances in the field.

In the first section we have included papers on the face-to-face interactions of infants and others during early infancy. These early interactions have become miniature natural laboratories in which many investigators have found a wealth of opportunities to study infant emotions and their development. The middle section of this book covers play interactions in older infants and toddlers. Here the methods and concepts are different due to the increasing complexity of the infant's behavior, and the increasing use of linguistic, in addition to non-verbal expressions of emotion.

In the first chapter, Malatesta provides us with a review of the literature and data from their own studies on facial expressions of emotion. These studies set the stage for the rest of the volume by providing the necessary natural history of expressions in the social context.

Fogel attempts a theoretical integration of a number of converging lines of investigation in the subsequent chapter. A model is presented that links the interactive process in early infancy and the development of arousal control later in the first year. The paper deals explicitly with emotion as a dynamic process that is enmeshed in the dynamics of the social interaction. Fogel suggests that much of the evidence for the interdependency of affect and interaction is derived from studies of natural and unnatural attempts to alter the flow of the interaction while observing the subsequent changes in the infant's emotional states.

The papers by Stoller and Field, by Tronick, Ricks, and Cohen, and by Field, each demonstrate the power of the interaction-variation paradigm in the study of emotional development. Stoller and Field have attempted to replicate earlier findings on the "still-face" interruption, adding some important methodological controls and some physiological measures. Tronick, Ricks, and Cohen discuss some other methods of perturbating face-to-face interaction, in particular, "depressed" maternal behavior, and they compare their results with those found in the still-face method.

Field's paper ends the first section of the volume with a theoretical integration of the results of these studies of interruption, as well as studies in which mother-infant interaction was compared with interaction with dolls, peers, fathers, and others. She presents a comprehensive model of the relationship between the activity level of the interactive partner and the ability of the infant to control affective arousal. All of the authors have attempted to make explicit the specific ways in which the behavior of the partner is related to the affective dynamics of the infant.

The next three papers carry these same themes over to the study of interaction with older infants. Demos provides us with a rich descriptive history of the range and complexity of expressive behavior in its natural context, a unique window into the ways in which emotion may become socialized on a day-to-day basis in the home. The Brooks-Gunn and Lewis paper fills in our descriptive canvas with data from developmentally delayed and handicapped infants. The authors' findings challenge our notions about the socialization of emotion by providing a glimpse of a distinctly different population. This section is concluded with a chapter by Lewis and Michalson that provides an important new theoretical framework for interpreting complex data on the infant's emotional behavior in a social context. They report research showing that older infants and toddlers are aware of the emotions of others around them, and they use the information contained in those expressions of others as a way of regulating their own emotional states.

The section on methodology covers a wide range of issues in the study of early interactions. Adamson and Bakeman debate the case for micro- versus macro-analysis, and discuss some of the philosophical issues that are raised in the task of coding dynamic, interactive data. Kaye offers us a hitchhiker's guide to the world of microanalytic investigation. He tells of its power and its inevitable pitfalls. It should be required reading for anyone who has the patience for using microanalytic methods.

The paper by Hannan provides us with a nice illustration of microanalysis as applied to the study of hand and finger expressions of emotion. The paper shows us the process of constructing a reliable and valid coding system for a class of affective displays that has received very little attention. Gottman, Rose, and Mettetal complete the volume with a discussion of a new and potentially useful tool for the study of dynamic-interactive data: time series analysis. Their presentation fosters a non-technical, intuitive understanding of time series concepts, and should serve as a primer for those who want to read further in that area.

We would like to acknowledge the Mailman Center for Child Development for hosting the symposium at which these papers were originally presented, and the Administration of Children, Youth, and Families and the National March of Dimes Foundation for their support of the symposium.

Finally, we would like to dedicate this volume to Silvan Tomkins whose work in this area has been inspirational to the contributors of this volume.

EMOTION and EARLY INTERACTION

EARLY INFANCY: FACE-TO-FACE INTERACTIONS

1

The Expression and Regulation of Emotion: A Lifespan Perspective

Carol Zander Malatesta
New School for Social Research

Several years ago I attended a conference at which R. D. Laing spoke. During the presentations of his paper, "Changes in the Human Life Cycle," Laing told a story that has remained with me over the years, and in which I find a metaphor for academic psychology. It seems that a young couple who had been living together for some time approached him after class one day. They asked if they might talk with him and get some advice on how to deal with their feelings. He looked at them and asked, hadn't they been doing that all along? They replied that they hadn't. They had wanted to wait until graduation.

In much the same fashion, academic psychology has managed to avoid dealing with emotions for several decades, although more recently this situation is changing. The reluctance of psychologists to deal with the "internal commotions" and their representations is connected, historically, not only with sociopolitical currents within psychology itself (Tomkins, 1981), but also with what we might regard as a common human ambivalence towards feelings. Emotions are linked to central motive states; they amplify drives (Izard, 1971, 1977; Tomkins, 1962, 1963, 1978). They make us feel good or terrible. They are powerful impeders or facilitators of interpersonal relationships. Consider the fact that every human culture has developed variously elaborate and subtle rituals for the regulation of emotional expressions. Rituals serve to restrain and refocus emotional energy. Certain rituals ensure that negative emotions are dampened or concealed to keep them from escalating and "getting out of hand." Other rituals serve to heighten or amplify positive feeling states and expressions. Because emotions can have both extremely positive and extremely negative consequences

1

for individuals as well as social relationships, there is great personal and social press to bring feelings under control.

In this chapter we take up the task of identifying the social processes promoting emotion regulation. The central questions are: How do individuals acquire knowledge about what's allowable and appropriate in the realm of emotion expression? Who teaches whom? What is the content of the instruction? Does it change with the age of the recipient? We feel that these are important developmental questions, questions that perhaps are best cast in a transactional and lifespan developmental framework. We begin by sharing some of the issues with which our laboratory has become concerned over the past few years and the results of our investigations. In the course of our discussion, we raise a number of additional questions and issues.

The research we describe spans several years. We began with the study of emotion expression in young infants and quickly realized we had to deal with the issue of how emotion expression becomes socialized. This led us to look at the interactive behaviors of mothers and infants. The infancy research propelled us to develop, and subsequently refine, a methodology for capturing the subtle kinds of social influence that appear to mediate the socialization of affect, or the adoption of "display rules," which can be considered part of a culture's rituals. More recently, the broader implications of this model and methodology have inspired a series of investigations that are more truly developmental, in the sense that they take up issues of change and continuity in the regulatory aspects of emotion expression. In an earlier paper (Malatesta, 1981a) we distinguished between the public, or expressive, and the private, or experiential, phenomenological aspects of emotion. This is a distinction we continue to emphasize, and, in the course of the chapter, attempt to reconcile as a feature of human emotional development.

The first section of this chapter provides some background for the discussion of emotion socialization. It is followed by a report of two empirical studies of affect socialization in infancy as well as preliminary results of another study geared to a description of developmental trends in the experiential and communicative aspects of emotion during the adult years. The chapter concludes with a consideration of lifespan models of emotion regulation and some suggestions for future research.

BACKGROUND

One of the oldest controversies within the field of emotions research has been the issue of whether emotional expressions are learned or innate (Oster & Ekman, 1978). Do we acquire emotional expressions in the context of learning situations while growing up, or are they prewired from the start, only requiring maturation for their manifestation? A series of cross-cultural studies conducted within the past 15 years strongly suggest that there are certain basic or fundamental human emotions (Ekman & Oster, 1979), and that they are accompanied by characteristic facial expressions (Izard, 1971, 1977; Tomkins, 1962, 1963) and perhaps vocal expressions as well (Malatesta, 1981b). Adults from various cultures show the same facial expressions under similar incentive conditions, and report experiencing the same emotions. People from different cultures also tend to label photographs of facial expressions in the same way. However, there is a good deal of individual variation superimposed on the universals (Ekman, 1972, 1973). People are capable of exercising voluntary control over the expression of their feelings. They can adopt masks and conceal their true emotions. Assumedly, this skill is acquired gradually over a period of years, so that by adulthood it is well established. However, this is *not* to say that masked feelings have become extinguished. If you think you have outgrown your emotions, Donald Hebb once remarked, consider: When was the last time you told your neighbor what you *really* think of him or her?

This gets us to the heart of the matter. There are both formal as well as functional aspects to the emotins—surface or representational qualities, and underlying feeling states. A good degree of discrepancy can exist between the two aspects. Several years ago, Paul Ekman and Wallace Friesen coined the term "display rules" to capture the idea that there can be distance between feelings and expressions. Display rules are those unspoken but tacit "norms" that govern the degree and manner of concealment of our emotions in particular circumstances.

Broadly speaking, there are three kinds of display rules: cultural, gender-related, and personal rules. Cultural rules are those that are specific to a particular culture and are practiced by most of the members of that culture. In fact, not to practice the indigenous cultural display rules is to appear "inappropriate" and to risk censure as a crazy person. For example, in our culture, bereaved persons display their grief overtly; distress is signaled in the oblique configuration of the brows and in the flaccid, downward-turning corners of the mouth. In other cultures, however, sorrow may be masked by a smile, as part of a ritualized means of dealing with strong emotion (Kleinberg, 1935).

Sex-related display rules are those that govern gender-specific codes of behavior (Fujita, Harper, & Wiens, 1980; Harper, Wiens, Fujita, & Kallgren, 1981). These rules are apparently acquired in the course of growing up. Research indicates that there are gender-related rules operating among children as well as adults (Buck, 1977; Fujita et al., 1980; Weitz, 1976; Zuckerman & Przewuzman, 1979). Situational factors apparently interact with sex-related rules governing the expression or inhibition of overt affect displays (Harper et al., 1981), but one of the most consistent findings concerns the sex-differentiated use of the smile. For women, the smile seems to be an all-purpose mask. Children clearly sense this because they evaluate a woman's smile differently than a man's (Bugental, Kaswan, & Love, 1970; Bugental, Kaswan, Love, & Fox, 1970; Bugental, Love, & Gianetto, 1971). They are less likely to attribute authenticity to a woman's smile. And, in fact, women's smiles quite frequently do conceal sentiments other than pleased feelings or friendliness. There are other ramifications, as well. The female affinity for smiling sets a base rate for women as a class of people. Women who smile less frequently than the norm will be regarded as peculiar or unfriendly, and they may suffer various social consequences.

Personal display rules are those that are learned within the context of a particular family. They can be learned casually and unconsciously, or in highly pressurized situations. Much learning is of the casual sort and involves simple observational learning. A good deal of this kind of learning occurs in early childhood. In the first place, cultural rules that normally dictate the concealment of emotion are more relaxed in the context of family. Infants, especially, have good opportunity to observe full-blown categorical facial expressions because mothers typically present highly articulated facial emotional expressions to their infants in the course of face-to-face interaction (Stern, 1974; Trevarthen, 1979). The opportunity to observe such expressions is not trivial. A recent review of the literature on infant imitation (Malatesta, in preparation) indicates that infants can and do copy what they see and hear. They are capable of imitating the pitch of the human voice and the muscular patterns of facial expressions. Infants show quite specific featural changes in response to a model's changes—brow, lip, and tongue movements—and they accommodate their responses over time to match a model, all without self-observation or reinforcement. Thus, young infants are capable of adopting the vocal and facial mannerisms of anyone with whom they spend a good amount of time; they are capable of adopting the emotional postures of others, and simple observational learning is all that is required. Second, it is probable that parents teach their children about the appropriateness of certain facial responses to classes of events, and the particular instruction may be quite idiosyncratic. One parent may display highly articulated disgust in the context of a son's failure at a task, whereas another may display reproach or anger. These styles of reacting may be imitated directly or stored for later "deferred imitation." Over time, such characteristic reactions will leave an imprint.

Once a behavioral mode of expression has become well learned and habitual, it tends to be enacted more or less unconsciously; it becomes incorporated into the personality, so to speak. These personalized modes of expression may find reification on the face with age. As the body ages, the face becomes lined and wrinkled. This is a slow but cumulative process. The interesting thing is that everyone's face ages somewhat differently. Part of this, of course, is genetically determined. There are individual differences in underlying bone structure, form and distribution of striate musculature, resiliency of the skin, and so forth. However, as Darwin suggested, lifelong experiences can alter the pattern of wrinkling beyond the genetic predisposition. In a similar vein, Haviland (1980) suggests that one's "background affect" or general mood may leave an enduring impression on the face in the form of "crystallized affect." Although this has yet to be demonstrated empirically, informal observation would seem to support the notion. It is easy to see how such crystallization could come about. A person who continuously experiences contempt towards others, for example, will hold the facial muscles in a pattern of tension quite different from someone with a less disdainful attitude. Similarly, a characteristically sanguine, outgoing person will tend to use the facial muscles differently than will a person who is a chronic worrier.

A person may also learn to *withhold* certain feeling states. For example, a child's response to a volatile family situation may be to inhibit his or her own facial expressions—to freeze the face into a mask-like state of indifference, or to freeze particular regions of the face that communicate certain categorical classes of feelings. This can lead to the selective absence of wrinkling in a part of the face, as in the case of one 70-year-old man whose face had the normal number of lines and creases for a man his age, with the exception that the brow region was singularly clear and unfurrowed. This man had simply never used the upper portion of his face expressively. It is perhaps not coincidental that he grew up in a family in which everyone took great pains to avoid provoking the father, who was highly unpredictable and volatile. Displays of anger and excitement were especially harshly punished. As a boy, then, this man learned to inhibit facial changes that normally convey anger and excitement while in the presence of his father, and, as is typical of other kinds of learning occurring under highly charged circumstances, it became a well-learned and generalized response bias. Such personal display rules are idiosyncratic and interesting in their own right. They are a window on individual personality.

It should be obvious from the foregoing that there is tremendous plasticity in the realm of emotion expression, though this plasticity is bounded by certain rules. Developmental psychologists may well question how such rules are acquired in the course of growing up. How do people learn these display rules? Do other people tell them what to do and what not to do? Do parents, for example, tell children not to laugh when someone else is embarrassed? Or do they communicate this proscription nonverbally? It is our hunch that both verbal and nonverbal messages are important organizers and socializers of affect expression. In the past, psychologists have focused almost exclusively on verbal commentary. And yet, it may be that nonverbal messages carry equally important weight. In some cases, nonverbal messages may carry special impact. They are subtle and diverse, as reflected in many of our colloquial expressions. We "frown on" something we don't like, or "turn our nose up," or give someone "the cold shoulder." Because nonverbal messages operate at a primitive emotional level, both in communication and reception, and because they can be extremely subtle, they are difficult to defend against, especially because they frequently operate out of range of awareness. One can form the "impression" that another dislikes him or her, and yet be unable to identify the source of the impression. In such states of uncertainty, there is little a person can do.

As an area of research that has been neglected, and yet so important for understanding interpersonal dynamics, the nonverbal socialization of emotion expression would seem ripe for study. However, as Ekman and Oster (1979) point out in their review of the literature on facial signaling, there has been very little in the way of objective information on the kinds of social feedback individuals receive for their emotional expressions.

In order to examine this questin in our own laboratory, we decided to focus on the nonverbal dyadic communication that goes on between mothers and infants during face-to-face play (Malatesta & Haviland, 1982). We developed a methodology we hoped would be sensitive to the kinds of subtle influence we expected to be occurring. Our own previous research with mothers and infants as well as anecdotal accounts in the developmental literature led us to hypothesize two key mechanisms in the socialization of emotion: modeling and selective reinforcement. We guessed that mothers modeled facial expressions of emotion to their infants quite regularly and that they selectively responded to the infants' facial expressions in a contingent fashion. Because these expressive interactions might be very fleeting, we wanted permanent records that could be coded at a later date using a fine-grained level of analysis. In the following sections our empirical questions are defined, the methodology is discussed, and the data from our first two studies are reviewed.

THE EMPIRICAL QUESTIONS

There were four questions that appeared to be central to an articulation of mutually influential behaviors and socialization for display rules:

1. First of all, what are the types and frequencies of facial expressions that mothers and infants display to one another and, more importantly, what are the contingencies between these expressive behaviors? Is there any evidence that mothers are promoting, nonverbally, the adoption of certain kinds of expression that might reflect local cultural ideals of expressive behavior? Do mothers teach their children to become less overt and more positive in expression in accord with the displays considered acceptable in

this culture (Izard, 1971, 1977; Malatesta, in prep.; Tomkins, 1962, 1963)?

2. Are there any sex-related differences in the patterns of expressions exhibited by male and female infants? Do mothers show selectivity in the ways in which they respond to their sons and daughters that could be considered "instruction" in gender-related display rules?

3. Can we detect measurable changes in infant emotion expression within a relatively short period of time, and how might such changes reflect the influence of maternal nonverbal behavior? Do infants come to resemble their mothers, facially, over time? That is, is there any evidence of the adoption of personal, or familial, display rules?

4. At the more global level, do the nonverbal behaviors of the mother, as measured by tests designed to tap emotional traits such as empathy and anxiety, predict change in infant emotional or temperament traits over time? What are the consequences of particular patterns of maternal responding over the long run?

In order to explore the first three questions, samples of the behavior of mothers in face-to-face play with their infants were required; to ensure that a wide range of infant expressions would be obtained—negative as well as positive expressions—both a play and a separation–reunion episode were included. These episodes were videotaped for objective coding of facial behaviors. To address the fourth question, mothers also filled out the Infant Behavior Questionnaire (Rothbart, 1977), which contains scales for certain emotional behaviors, and measures of mothers' emotional traits were obtained. The subjects were followed longitudinally to obtain another rating of infant temperament traits. Change in infant traits was then evaluated as a function of maternal expressive behaviors (as measured in the laboratory) and maternal emotional traits.

Procedure and Analysis of Data from Study 1

Sixty mothers and their 3 to 6-month-old infants participated in our study (Malatesta & Haviland, 1982). Each mother-infant pair was videotaped while they played together before our cameras. Output from the two cameras trained on the mother and infant were fed into a special-effects generator for a split-screen image. We later added a digital time display for coding timed behaviors. After the end of the 16-minute session, mother and infant returned home. Mothers completed and returned infant and maternal temperament scales via mail. These measures included the Infant Behavior Questionnaire (IBQ), a measure of maternal empathy (Mehrabian & Epstein, 1972), the State-Trait Anxiety Inventory (Spielberger, Gorsuch, & Lushene, 1970), and the Emotionality Scale of the EASI Temperament Survey (Buss & Plomin, 1975).

Videotapes were coded by judges trained on the Maximally Discriminative Facial Movement Coding System—Max of Izard (1979). Tapes were coded for instances of anger, fear, sadness, joy, interest, surprise, pain, knit brow, and brow flash. We coded mother and infant individually and then we looked at the patterns of contingency. Six months after the laboratory visit, mothers were mailed another copy of the Infant Behavior Questionnaire to fill out and return.

Results of Study 1

Infant Expressions

The data indicated that infants as young as 3 months of age are capable of emitting a wide variety of categorical expressions including anger, pain, interest, surprise, joy, sadness, knit brow, and brow flash. They are really very expressive. Table 1.1 shows the relative frequencies of the various expressions. Young infants are also very labile in their emotional expressivity.

TABLE 1.1
Means and Standard Deviations (in Parentheses) of Expression
Frequencies per Infant and Mother during 6 minutes of Interaction[a]

Expression	x̄ Infants	x̄ Mothers
Interest	5.98 (4.2)	8.83 (8.80)
Enjoyment	8.97 (8.33)	22.55 (11.28)
Surprise	3.38 (5.65)	7.75 (8.24)
Sadness	2.30 (3.29)	.80 (1.92)
Anger	6.83 (6.14)	.28 (1.22)
Knit Brow	10.95 (10.02)	2.37 (4.25)
Discomfort/Pain	2.83 (3.79)	0
Brow Flash	4.42 (2.94)	6.03 (7.38)

[a] Adapted from Malatesta & Haviland, 1982.

Their expressions change at an average rate of once every 8 seconds. We find that the main developmental change taking place between 3 and 6 months is a reduction in knit brow and pain expressions, which reflects the reduction in crying and predistress states. We also find that there is a reduction, overall, in the rate at which infants change their facial expressions. The rate at 3 months is one change per 7 seconds; by 6 months, it is one change per 9 seconds. Why do infants undergo such a reduction in rate change and move in a direction of greater stability of state? We suspect it has to do with maturational factors as well as with what the mother does. There is evidence that mothers engage in certain practices that serve to reduce infant lability, as discussed further in the next section.

The types of emotion expression are very similar for males and females. Infant males and females emit approximately the same rates of joy, sadness, surprise, anger, pain, knit brow, and brow flash. However, infant females show significantly more interest expressions, as coded by an objective scoring system.

Maternal Expressions

There are two striking findings with respect to maternal emotion expression. First of all, in comparison with the data on infants, we find that mothers display a more restricted range of expression. Table 1.1 allows a comparison of mothers' and infants' expression types and frequencies. As indicated, mothers tend to express mainly positive emotion—joy, interest, surprise, and the positive signal of brow flash (a greeting or agreement signal). There were no instances of discomfort/pain expressions and only very limited amounts of sadness or anger. As an aside, we mention one Danish mother who had volunteered for our study and was actually filmed before we decided to delete her tape from the study. Her pattern of facial play was so different from that of the other mothers in the study we suspected that we might be tapping cultural differences. This mother made "sad" or "concerned" faces at a far higher rate than any other mother we had taped. We have no idea whether this was an idiosyncratic bias or a cultural one, but it does suggest that it might be important to get some cross-cultural data using a similar paradigm. The second major finding is that for the overall sample of mothers, the profile of emotion expression remains relatively unchanged over time. Mothers of 3 month olds show the same relative profile as mothers of 6 month olds in terms of types and frequencies of emotional expressions, with the exception that mothers of 6 month olds show a reduction in the amount of brow flashes.

Within-Pair Analyses

Maternal contingent responses. Mothers were found to emit the same kinds of expressions to males and females when we just looked at maternal expressions without reference to what their own infants were doing. Quite another pattern emerges when we consider contingent responses. One of the most striking observations was the immediacy with which mothers responded to changes in infant affect expression—less than half a second lag. There were two kinds of contingent response. Mothers who did not ignore their infants' expressions either imitated them—that is, gave matching facial responses—or gave dissimilar responses. For example, a mother might show a mock surprise face in response to an infant's expression of anger. We found that there are sex differences in this realm of responding. Sequential lag analysis (Sackett, 1979) indicated that mothers tend to match more male expressions and show more dissimilar responses to female expressions. Mothers thus appear to be engaged in more of a "dialogue" with their daughters. They are also showing more variety in their contingent emotional responses to their daughters than to their sons. Mothers also respond more contingently to the smiles of older sons (versus daughters).

Mother-infant pattern similarities. It was obvious from viewing the videotapes, even before coding was performed, that mothers and infants showed great similarity in terms of their use of certain regions of the face and even in certain types of emotional expression. Some mother–infant pairs were brow oriented—that is, they showed fluidity in brow movements and less use of mouth movements; others were mouth oriented. It appeared that mothers and infants shared commonalities in the ways they used their facial muscles that were dyad specific. Correlational analysis was used to substantiate these impressions. Even with instances of maternal imitation of infant expressions deleted from the data set, there were a number of strong correlations. Highly significant mother–infant correlation included use of the brow region, mouth region, and reciprocal smiling; sadness and surprise expressions were marginally correlated. When we looked at the strength of the correlations for 3 and 6 month olds separately, we found stronger correlations with the 6 month olds and their mothers, suggesting an increase in familial expression patterns.

In summary, we find that infants and mothers show striking similarities in their use of the facial muscles and in making emotional expressions. In light of literature indicating that infants have the capacity to imitate facial expressions (Malatesta, in preparation), we are inclined to believe that our 3 and 6 month olds had learned to accommodate their facial expressions to resemble those of their mothers. An alternative explanation is simply that there is a genetic loading to signaling preferences, a possibility we do not rule out at this point.

Summary of Study 1 and Implications

Two very important findings emerged from the first study. First of all, we have demonstrated that the affect of young infants, at least as measured by their facial expressions, is not "undifferentiated," thus supporting mothers' impressions (Emde, 1980) and refuting Bridges (1932). Infant affect takes categorical form and is highly labile. It is also worth mentioning that male affect seems to be especially labile. Although the difference is only a trend in the present study, we have since found a strong sex effect for lability of expression in another study of infants ranging in age from 6 months to a year and a half. In addition, some of our colleagues who do work with infant rats and monkeys report, informally, that the same may be true of the young males of these species—they appear to be more excitable and labile. This suggests that there may be some very basic sex-linked biobehavioral differences between males and females in the realm of emotion expression. These observations, of course, must be tested more formally.

Secondly, mothers appear to be actively shaping infant affect. This impression is supported by two lines of evidence:

1. Modeling: Mothers, at least middle-class American mothers, restrict their demonstrations of affect to the positive emotions. Because negative affect is contagious (Malatesta, in preparation), it makes sense for mothers to steer clear of such demonstrations, even of the mock kind. In fact, mothers of 2 month olds who were instructed to display brief negative expressions towards their infants had extreme difficulty in doing so; this suggests a built-in inhibition (Lewicka, 1981). The modeling of positive affect serves both to demonstrate socially acceptable display behavior, and at the same time to probably enhance the child's adoption of positive affect via contagion.

2. The other way in which mothers exert nonverbal influence over infant affect is by the way in which they respond to infant expressions. Mothers make immediate, contingent responses; to a certain extent, patterns of contingent responding vary with the sex of the child, suggesting that mothers may be promoting the regulation of emotion along gender lines. Because the lag between infant expression changes and maternal changes is within the most optimal range for "instrumental conditioning," we hypothesize that differential learning may be taking place.

In summarizing this first study, we note that there are changes occurring in emotion expression during early infancy that are indicative of instruction in facial display. Mothers were found to behave in ways that could easily be construed as attempts to moderate the emotional expressions of their infants. The next study was inspired by the finding that there were indeed differential patterns of maternal responding, sex effects, and individual differences. It seemed clear that the next step should involve attempts to measure the consequences of this differential responding. We hypothesized that mothers respond differentially to males and females because male and female infants have differing biobehavioral states to begin with (Haviland & Malatesta, 1981), even though these differences may be marginal at first. Mothers also probably encourage the adoption of sex-appropriate behavior, although when the infant is young, the effect may be quite subtle. We anticipated that sex differences in patterns of emotion expression would become more pronounced with infant age. On another level, we expected that individual differences in contingent responding and certain temperamental traits in mothers would predict differential stability or change in infant temperament qualities and emotional patterns. The second study involved a longitudinal investigation of infant temperament traits with maternal behaviors and traits as predictor variables.

Study 2

Six months after mothers had completed the first temperament-scale rating they were mailed a second copy of the scale to fill out and return. Thus we ended up with two scores for each infant on each of six temperament-scale dimensions: fear, anger, positivity, activity, soothability, and duration of orienting. Changes in infant temperament were assessed against a backdrop of maternal styles of interaction as well as infant and maternal temperament and emotional traits. The hypotheses and results of the study are enumerated here:

1. We made a basic assumption about contingent responding—that the mother responds to infant facial changes with changes of her own in order to influence the child by drawing the child into a prevailing state of positivity. The theoretical literature has stressed the importance of maternal contingent responding in promoting optimal infant development (Ainsworth, Bell, & Stayton, 1971; Bell & Ainsworth, 1972; Sroufe, 1979). Thus, we hypothesized that the mother's level of contingent responding to infant facial expressions would predict gains in infant positive emotion. That is, we anticipated that mothers who exercised a good deal of contingent responding to emotional signals would have infants who showed substantial gains in positivity, even with initial differences in positivity covaried out. We found that mothers who showed the highest rates of contingent responding at Time 1 had the most positive infants at Time 2 (6 months later). Although the difference does not quite reach significance, it was in the predicted direction. Examination of individual scores indicated that there is probably some kind of ceiling effect for infants who are very positive from the start.

2. Mothers of males and females use different types of contingent responding—that is, more dissimilar responses around girls, and more matching or imitative responses around boys. We hypothesized that these differences are related to the greater lability and irritability of males (see Haviland & Malatesta, 1981, for a review of the literature). If boys are more labile and more readily upset, mothers should refrain from using much variability in their contingent responding. Restraint in the use of variability around males makes sense if mothers wish to promote optimal positivity. We therefore predicted that mothers of boys who were particularly high in the use of matching would have sons who were more positive than would mothers who showed moderate or low levels of matching. Correspondingly, we anticipated that an opposite trend would hold for girls. In accord with the assumption that mothers engage in the use of dissimilar responses with their daughters because this playfulness is not punished by infant irritability and crying and is in some way positively reinforcing to girls, we predicted that mothers of girls who ranked high in the use of dissimilar expressions

would have girls who would show substantial gains in positivity when measured 6 months later. The data for boys showed a nonsignificant trend in support of the hypothesis. The prediction for girls was confirmed and the difference was significant.

3. Maternal anxiety has been linked in the developmental literature with negative developmental outcome, both theoretically and empirically, although not with very young infants (Anders & Weinstein, 1972; Davids, 1968; Kulka, 1968). We therefore predicted that our more highly anxious mothers would have infants who would be most likely to rank low in positivity at the 6 months' follow-up. This prediction was confirmed. The positivity levels of infants having low anxious mothers were significantly different from those having moderately anxious mothers.

4. Infant temperament traits are normally characterized by a high degree of stability (Rothbart & Derryberry, 1981). We were interested in taking a close look at those infants whose scores on the various temperament traits changed radically within the 6-month period of assessment. We rank ordered the infants in terms of their original scores and also in terms of their follow-up scores. Selecting those infants whose ranking relative to the rest of the sample shifted three quartiles up or down from T1 to T2, we examined the characteristics of their mothers. Table 1.2 summarizes the results of this analysis. As indicated, there were seven infants who satisfied this stringent criterion. When we examine the emotional traits and contingency scores of the mothers of these atypical infants, a pronounced pattern emerges. Infants who by Thomas and Chess (1977) criteria showed signs of becoming "difficult" in that they became more negative or withdrawing (less positive, less active) all had mothers who ranked medium to high on anxiety, medium to high on emotionality, medium to low on empathy, and medium to low on contingency. On the other hand, the two infants who became more amenable, moving up three quartiles on activity and soothability (Babies C, G), both had mothers who were medium to high in empathy, and who were low in anxiety. Baby G showed the most improvement, moving up three quartiles on soothability, down one quartile on fear and two on anger, and up slightly on positivity (rank 7 to rank 17), remaining essentially the same on the other traits. This boy's mother was medium on emotionality and contingent responding, but high on empathy. Baby C, who went up from seventh lowest in activity to 48th, and also went up one quartile in positivity, had a mother who was medium in empathy, low in emotionality and contingent responding, and low in anxiety.

The foregoing pattern of results indicates that there is a *constellation* of maternal traits and behaviors that are associated with infant temperament change rather than a single all-encompassing maternal variable. This is not surprising. In the mother–infant relationship, both partners bring unique, individual differences to bear in interaction with one another. The impact

TABLE 1.2

Emotional Traits and Behaviors of Mothers Whose Infants Moved Three Quartiles Up or Down on Temperament-Traits Rankings Relative to Total Sample of Infants

	Infant Temperament Traits and Change Scores				Maternal Characteristics (Trait Rankings)		
Baby	Time 1 Rank	Time 2 Rank	Temperament Trait	Emotionality	Empathy	Anxiety	Contingent Responding
A (3-month male)	10	49	Fear	Medium (23)	Medium (25)	Medium (34)	Low (2)
B (3-month female)	2	48	Fear	(Medium) (19)	Low (15)	High (39)	Low (13)
C (3-month female)	7	48	Activity	Low (6)	Medium (26)	Low (8)	Low (5)
D (6-month female)	46	6	Activity	Low (2)	Low (2)	Low (13)	Medium (34)
E (6-month female)	49	6	Duration of orienting	High (40)	Medium (22)	Medium (26)	Medium (28)
F (3-month male)	47	8	Soothability	Medium (28)	Medium (19)	High (49)	Low (10)
G (3-month male)	7	48	Soothability	Medium (23)	High (46)	Low (11)	Medium (26)

14

of a particular maternal variable will necessarily vary depending on the original constitutional make-up of the individual child.

In summary, Study 2 indicates that maternal expressive behaviors as measured by a fine-grained level of analysis of contingent patterns of behavior within a relatively limited laboratory session can predict changes in infant expressive (emotional) behavior 6 months after initial assessment. Maternal emotional traits are also associated with changes in infant temperament traits, although at this time it is not clear what the behavioral analogues of these traits are.

Summary and Implications of the First Two Studies

In the foregoing studies we begin to discern the parameters of social influence in the mother–infant relationship. Mothers "speak" to their infants in nonverbal as well as verbal ways. The nonverbal language is rich in emotional expressivity, is contextually meaningful, and is contingent on the infant's on-going behavior. To all appearances babies are very responsive to these emotional messages. The emotional messages of mothers have an attention-arousing function as well as an attention-maintaining function (Field, 1977; Francis, Self, & Noble, 1981; Malatesta, 1980). We hypothesized that the effect of these behaviors is cumulative and that they exert a powerful influence on infant expressive behavior. In fact, a longitudinal follow-up of a moderately large sample of infants substantiated this. Differences in the way mothers responded nonverbally to their infants were found to predict infant emotional change. This leaves us with a model that says that significant socialization of affect occurs within nonverbal channels. We are, to be sure, looking only at the mother–infant relationship, perhaps a unique kind of dyad. Nonetheless, this process probably goes on throughout development, and in ever-widening circles of social influence. In fact, a recent study from the literature on nonverbal communication (Brauer & DePaulo, 1980) suggests that even adults acquire certain types of nonverbal sensitivity and styles of communication in the course of specific dyadic relationships. This should come as no surprise to anyone who has ever caught him- or herself using the gestures and mannerisms of a close friend.

ON-GOING STUDIES

The direction our research has now begun to take is three-pronged. First of all, in terms of lifespan developmental patterns, we have begun to collect basic descriptive data on the types and frequencies of emotional expression people display in interaction with one another—in interaction with partners of the same age, same sex, opposite sex, or different age. For example, in one study, using an ethological paradigm adapted by Lockard (1980), students trained in expression coding have been deployed to observe humans in what could be considered a natural habitat—shopping centers and malls—in order to record the incidence of certain types of nonverbal behaviors.

Second, we are looking at sequential patterns of interaction as a means of getting at the continuing socialization of affect. It is likely that there are age- and sex-related "norms" that govern the mode of nonverbal emotional communication, and that these norms act as rules that may be found in ritualized interaction. Goffman (1967) comments on these kinds of emotion-related rituals in his book *Interaction Ritual:*

> It is plain that emotions play a part in these cycles of response, as when anguish is expressed because of what one has done to another's face, or anger because of what has been done to one's own. I want to stress that these emotions function as moves, and fit so precisely into the logic of the ritual game that it would seem difficult to understand them without it. (Even when a child demands something and is refused, he is likely to cry and sulk not as an irrational expression of frustration but as a ritual move, conveying that he already has a face to lose and that its loss is not to be permitted lightly. Sympathetic parents may even allow for such display, seeing in these crude strategies the beginnings of a social self.) In fact, spontaneously expressed feelings are likely to fit into the formal pattern of the ritual interchange more elegantly than consciously designed ones [p. 23].

Although Goffman does not specifically address the issue of how such rituals may vary as a function of the interactants' age and sex, this would seem to be an important consideration in attempting to construct the "grammar" that governs nonverbal language and emotion expression.

Let us consider the variable of age. As children acquire the ritualized modes of expression "appropriate" to them, we may expect that the basic structural rules are modified in certain ways through childhood, adolescence, and early adulthood. In fact, a study by Hottenstein (1977) indicates that adults use more partial versions of facial expressions than do children. Elsewhere we have referred to this fractionation of expression as "miniaturization" (Haviland & Malatesta, 1981).

With advanced age there is the possibility of other kinds of changes in facial–emotional expressivity. Do the interactive rituals acquired in a lifetime of interacting with others break down in old age, or do they become more stylized and perhaps more rigid? There is virtually no literature that addresses this issue. However, we know that age norms pervade the culture. As Neugarten, Moore, and Lowe (1973) have pointed out, there are fairly well-defined age norms and age constraints evident in matters of dress, in timetables for ordering major life events, and in social behaviors. It seems unlikely that age proscriptions should be limited to dress patterns and related matters. With respect to the emotional domain, children are frequently admonished to "grow up." Once they are grown up, they may be reminded to "act your age." However, we have yet to identify what age-related display rules may be operating within our culture and how such display rules are communicated and reinforced. There are a host of related questions: What are the age norms and age constraints experienced by members of our culture? What is the degree of constraint on expressivity as perceived by different age individuals? Do older people place the same degree of constraint on their own behavior as do others—do they ascribe more or less importance to age norms than younger individuals? What is the relationship between expressive behavior and the experience of subjective emotional states? Are the two aspects congruent, are they disjoint? We know that people acquire the ability to mask their true sentiments, to put distance between what they feel and what they express. Is there the same amount of distance during adolescence as, say, during old age?

These questions concerning the relationship between expressiveness and phenomenology are the center of focus of our third major research endeavor. We are interested in parsing the relationship between expressive and experiential emotional behavior at different stages in the life cycle. There are presently two opposing viewpoints concerning the transitivity and importance of facial expressivity and emotional experience. The "facial feedback hypothesis" maintains that subjective emotional experience proceeds from proprioceptive feedback from the muscles and nerves of the face during states of emotional arousal. Those who oppose this position maintain that other bodily cues, such as those stemming from the viscera and autonomic nervous system, as well as cognitive factors, are more important in the subjective experience of affect. (For a more elaborate discussion of these positions see Buck, 1980, and Ekman, Friesen, & Ancoli, 1980.) The *developmental* implications of the facial feedback hypothesis have yet to be considered. With respect to our foregoing discussion of age-related changes in the overtness of emotional expression, we noted that there is some evidence that the facial expressions of individuals become miniaturized as they mature. If we take the facial feedback hypothesis in *sensu stricto,* we are led to predict that the subjective experience of emotion in adults, and perhaps especially in older individuals, may be less focused or intense than is the case for children. Is there any evidence that this is the case? A recent review of the theoretical and empirical literature (Malatesta, 1981a) disclosed that older individuals are viewed as having impoverished affectivity both in terms of overt expressivity and in phenomenology. However, as pointed out in the review, the studies upon which such assumptions have been based are quite flawed from a methodological point of view.

We have begun our own initial exploration into these and related issues concerning emotional development qua development or process. To conclude this chapter we discuss the preliminary findings of a study recently completed by our team of investigators. The study consisted of a survey administered to a large sample of individuals of various ages. The intent was to gather information concerning the perception and retrospection of emotional experiences in people of different ages. The survey instrument was designed to measure not only the kinds of emotional experiences people have, but their intensity of feeling and their consciousness of age norms for the expression and concealment of certain classes of emotion. To our knowledge, this study represents the first attempt to measure *categorical* emotions (cf. differential emotions theory), in adults across the lifespan, using a direct self-report format. Earlier studies measured more global constructs such as degree of "satisfaction" or "happiness" (viz. Cameron, 1975; Harris & Associates, 1976). The limitations of this kind of approach become obvious as we examine some of the findings of the present study.

ADULTS VIEW THEIR EMOTIONAL LIVES

Before we describe the study population, let us consider the questions that guided the study. A first question was: Is there any evidence that people are aware of age- and sex-related display rules for the expression of emotion? Given such awareness, is there differential sensitivity or responsivity to norms or proscriptions as a function of age or sex? Is there a drift towards negative affect with age as predicted by theory and the accumulated findings of previous research? (See review by Malatesta, 1981a.) Is there increasing "lability" in emotion expression towards the end of the lifespan as portrayed in the classic works of literature (deBeauvoir, 1972) and as suggested by theoretical formulations of psychologists (reviewed by Malatesta, 1981a)? What is the relationship between a person's dominant mood states and his or her perception of the world?

As indicated previously, the present study involved the use of an affect survey instrument. A large-scale pilot study provided interesting leads that encouraged a larger, more ambitious study. Although the data from the larger study are not yet fully analyzed, they appear to conform to the earlier findings from the pilot study. Here, we report the results of the pilot data.

The subjects were white middle-class individuals from suburban communities. They ranged in age from 18 to 84. The survey questionnaire consisted of scaled Likert-type items as well as several forced-choice items and open-ended questions. Several items dealt with respondents' awareness of and agreement/disagreement with the desirability of concealing emotions. A typical item was "A man (woman) my age shouldn't show anger when he (she) feels it." Similar items tapped other emotions including fear, sadness, happiness, interest/excitement, shame, and disgust. Age and sex differences in response to these questions were clearly in evidence, and they appeared to be affect specific. Analysis of variance disclosed a linear age effect for the affects of anger, sadness, happiness, interest, disgust, and shame, with older subjects showing more agreement than younger persons that people their age should hide such feelings. However, there were no age differences for the affect of fear/anxiety. In terms of sex differences, males showed more agreement than females that anger, sadness, fear, and interest should be concealed, but there was no difference between males and females in terms of how much they felt that happiness, disgust, or shame should be concealed. This pattern of results indicates that there is general sensitivity to display rules for the expression of emotion, that the degree of agreement/ disagreement with statements about the concealment of emotion varies with the sex and age of the subject, and that display rules appear to be organized around certain *types* of emotion, rather than emotion per se.

Another part of the survey asked subjects to choose, from a set of emotion terms, which emotion they recall having been most discouraged from showing while growing up. Fear was the most frequently chosen emotion, and sadness the least frequently chosen. When asked to identify the emotion they thought most people *ought* to conceal, the modal choice was anger; fear and sadness were the *least* frequently chosen affects. What can we make of these findings? For the moment, let us assume that our respondents' retrospective accounts accurately reflect the socialization experiences of white, middle-class individuals who have grown up in the first half of this century. Our data indicate that few of these people, as children, were discouraged from showing sadness. As adults, very few chose sadness as an emotion they thought should be concealed. On the other hand, most people recall having been discouraged from showing fear/anxiety as children, but do not themselves, as adults, feel that fear/anxiety should be concealed. The intriguing question is whether these latter results represent a rejection by the respondents of their own socialization experiences concerning the display of fear, or whether in the culture at large there are different sets of values concerning how overt one may be about certain types of feelings depending on whether one is a child or an adult.

There was another interesting finding that has bearing on the issue. A factor analysis of 41 items from the survey yielded a seven-factor solution. One was a factor we labeled "Anxiety." This factor consisted of a cluster of items regarding the frequency of experiencing fear/anxiety, the inhibition of feelings, and avowal of a childhood characterized by emphasis on hiding feelings. In other words, people whose childhood was characterized by a strong emphasis on hiding feelings report that they greatly inhibit the expression of their emotions; they also experience a great deal of anxiety. The opposite relationship holds for persons who experienced little emphasis on hiding their feelings. If we take these results at face value, we must entertain the possibility that early experiences with proscriptions concerning emotion expression have an important and enduring impact on adult emotional life. This is a thesis we are continuing to examine and attempting to cross-validate in our studies.

SUMMARY, INTEGRATION, AND CONCLUSION

By way of conclusion I would like to spell out what I feel to be the two most important points emerging from our studies.

In the first place, the results of all three studies underscore the importance of using the typological approach in the study of emotions and emotional processes. This approach is relatively new in psychology (although Darwin introduced the notion over 100 years ago). During the earlier part of this century, the dimensional model of emotion held sway, led by the work of Lindsley, Magoun, and Spencer, among others. This model claimed that all emotional experience could be located somewhere on a continuum of activation, arousal, intensity, hedonic tone, or other general polar scale. The more recent typological model, best exemplified by the work of Izard (1971, 1977), Ekman (1972, 1973), and Tomkins (1962, 1963, 1981) among contemporary investigators, stresses the differential signal value and phenomenology of discrete classes of emotional events. The utility of this approach is clearly illustrated by the findings of the three studies discussed in this chapter. It is our conviction that the typological approach will continue to teach us important things about individual variability in emotion expression, personality, and interpersonal dynamics.

Second, our studies clearly indicate that the expression of emotion is subject to social influence and that the impact is probably substantial. Social influence appears to operate at two levels—the global and emotion-specific levels. Let us consider further the nature and impact of social influence on emotion expression.

There is evidence that individuals, in growing up, become organized around certain classes of emotion, that some emotions have more saliency than others. People respond to some emotional signals with greater reliability or immediacy than to others. They experience certain mood states more frequently than others. How do we account for these individual differences? Constitutional or temperament factors probably play a substantial role. One's life circumstances, such as living in a state of poverty or frequent contact with adversity, will also necessarily alter one's emotional perspective and manner of viewing the self and the world. However, another powerful dynamic, one that has rarely been treated in more than a superficial manner in the psychological literature, is emotion socialization. The term itself, "emotion socialization," has only recently entered the vocabulary of psychologists. And in terms of understanding the parameters and dynamic mechanisms involved in this kind of socialization, we have barely begun to scratch the surface.

In the present chapter we focused on two questions related to emotion socialization: How do people learn the cultural and familial rules governing the expression of emotion? How do the rules change with age? These are both process-oriented questions that lend themselves to the construction of developmental models. Taking into consideration the results of studies from our own laboratory and field experiments, as well as the research from other laboratories, let us conclude this chapter with an outline of the processes we hypothesize to be involved in emotion regulation developmentally.

We know that mothers model facial expressions of emotion to their infants and that they respond selectively to their infants' own expressions. They also make verbal references to their infants' affective expressions, but it is the mothers' facial expressions, their tone of voice, and the infants' feeling states that comprise the most salient aspects of the interchange for preverbal infants. (See Malatesta, in preparation, for further discussion of the processes involved at this stage of development.)

Beyond infancy, a parent's verbal instructions will carry greater and greater impact. We suspect, however, that facial gestures and tone of voice remain important sources of information concerning acceptable behavior. Children imitate and copy others all through childhood. In addition to observational learning, children receive differential attention to their own emotional expressions, depending on the personalities of their parents and significant others. Certain classes of emotin can become more or less salient in the child's life not only via direct parental punishment or reinforcement but by the parent's failure to acknowledge certain expressions in the child or the parent him- or herself. For example, the sex-role literature indicates that children learn both masculine and feminine roles but that they code one set of behaviors as negative and the other set as positive, depending on their own sex. A child may observe, for example, that his father never displays sadness, but that his mother does. The sense that "sadness" is not masculine may be further reinforced by the observation that father never uses this term, although his vocabulary does contain other affect-related words. In fact, Greif, Alvarez, and Ulman (1981) have demonstrated that parents use differential emotion terminology in telling stories to their children depending on the sex of the child and sex of the parent. Greif (1981) also reports that children reference their parent's face when emotional scenes are being described.

Although there has been little research on the emotions of adults (outside of the clinical literature) and virtually nothing concerning the mechanisms that constrain and direct the emotional expressions of adults, our own investigations indicate that both verbal and nonverbal social influences are very much a part of the control of overt emotional expressions. It is likely that the regulation of emotion in adults contains more elements of consciousness and intentionality than is the case with children. Adults are also more socially skilled and can exert more mutual control in the flow of interaction. As such, there may be more day-to-day, contextual, and social variability in the emotional expressivity of adults, at least in the public sphere. In addition, the overt aspects of emotion will be more transactional, and more truly interpersonal in the dialectic sense, during the adult years.

In old age, we speculate, there may be greater contextual stability in patterns of overt emotional expressivity. In the first place, old age brings with it a reduction in the diversity of social contacts for most people. Second, over the years, preferential patterns of responding may become so well established that they become completely interiorized and automatic. Finally, older people appear to perceive more social disapproval of the overt expression of a variety of emotions (with the exception of fear) than do younger individuals. Whether these perceptions exert an actual influence on the older person's behavior has yet to be determined.

We have begun to investigate these and related questions in our own laboratory. A lifespan perspective and typological approach to the study of emotion appears to be an especially promising way to proceed in the investigation of emotional/personality dynamics. It is our hope that this approach will ultimately enable us to parse a more complete picture of the transactional and transpersonal aspects of emotional development.

REFERENCES

Ainsworth, M., Bell, S., & Stayton, D. Individual differences in strange situation behavior of one-year-olds. In H. Schaffer (Ed.), *The origins of human social relations.* London: Academic Press, 1971.

Anders, J. F., & Weinstein, P. Sleep and its disorder in infants and children: A review. *Pediatrics,* 1972, *50,* 312-324.

Bell, S. M., & Ainsworth, M. D. S. Infant crying and maternal responsiveness. *Child Development,* 1972, *43,* 1171-1190.

Brauer, D. V., & DePaulo, B. M. Similarities between friends in their understanding of nonverbal cues. *Journal of Nonverbal Behavior,* 1980, *5,* 64-68.

Bridges, K. B. Emotional development in early infancy. *Child Development,* 1932, *3,* 324-341.

Buck, R. Nonverbal communication of affect in pre-school children: Relationship with personality and skin conductance. *Journal of Personality and Social Psychology,* 1977, *35,* 225-236.

Buck, R. Nonverbal behavior and the theory of emotion: The facial feedback hypothesis. *Journal of Personality and Social Psychology,* 1980, *38,* 811-824.

Bugental, D. E., Kaswan, J. W., & Love, L. R. Perception of contradictory meanings conveyed by verbal and nonverbal channels. *Journal of Personality and Social Psychology,* 1970, *16,* 647-655.

Bugental, D. E., Kaswan, J. W., Love, L. R., & Fox, M. N. Child versus adult perception of evaluative messages in verbal, vocal and visual channels. *Developmental Psychology,* 1970, *2,* 367–375.

Bugental, D. E., Love, L. R., & Gianetto, R. M. Perfidious feminine faces. *Journal of Personality and Social Psychology,* 1971, *17,* 314–318.

Buss, A. H., & Plomin, R. *A temperament theory of personality development.* New York: Wiley, 1975.

Cameron, P. Mood as an indicant of happiness: Age, sex, social class and situational differences. *Journal of Gerontology,* 1975, *30,* 216–224.

Davids, A. A research design for studying maternal emotionality before childbirth and after social interaction with the child. *Merrill-Palmer Quarterly,* 1968, *14,* 345–354.

deBeauvoir, S. *The coming of age.* New York: G. P. Putnam's Sons, 1972.

Ekman, P. Universals and cultural differences in facial expressions of emotion. In J. K. Cole (Ed.), *Nebraska symposium on motivation* (Vol. 19). Lincoln: University of Nebraska Press, 1972.

Ekman, P. Cross-cultural studies of facial expression. In P. Ekman (Ed.), *Darwin and facial expression.* New York: Academic Press, 1973.

Ekman, P., Friesen, W. V., & Ancoli, S. Facial signs of emotional experience. *Journal of Personality and Social Psychology,* 1980, *39,* 1125–1134.

Ekman, P., & Oster, H. Facial expressions of emotion. In M. R. Rosenzweig, & L. W. Porter (Eds.), *Annual review of psychology* (Vol. 30). Palo Alto, Calif: Annual Reviews, 1979.

Emde, R. N. Levels of meaning for infant emotions: A biosocial view. In W. A. Collins (Ed.), *Development of cognition, affect, and social relations. Minnesota symposia on child psychology* (Vol. 13). Hillsdale, N.J.: Lawrence Erlbaum Associates, 1980.

Field, T. M. Effects of early separation interactive deficits, and experimental manipulations on infant-mother face-to-face interaction. *Child Development,* 1977, *48,* 763–771.

Francis, P. L., Self, P. A., & Noble, C. A. *Maternal imitation of their newborn infants: Momma see, momma do.* Paper presented at the Biennial Meeting of the Society for Research in Child Development, Boston, April 1981.

Fujita, B. N., Harper, R. G., & Wiens, A. N. Encoding-decoding of nonverbal emotional messages: Sex differences in spontaneous and enacted expressions. *Journal of Nonverbal Behavior,* 1980, *4,* 131–145.

Goffman, E. *Interaction ritual.* New York: Anchor Books, 1967.

Greif, E. B. Personal communication, Boston University, 1981.

Greif, E. B., Alvarez, M., & Ulman, K. *Recognizing emotions in other people: Sex differences in socialization.* Paper presented at the Biennial Meeting of the Society for Research in Child Development. Boston, April 1981.

Harper, R. G., Wiens, A. N., Fujita, B. N., & Kallgren, C. Affective-behavioral correlates of the test of emotional styles. *Journal of Nonverbal Behavior,* 1981, *5,* 264–267.

Harris, L., & Associates, Inc. *The myth and reality of aging in America.* National Council on the Aging, Washington, D.C., 1976.

Haviland, J. M. Personal communication, Rutgers University, 1980.

Haviland, J. J., & Malatesta, C. Z. A description of the development of sex differences in non-verbal signals: Fantasies, fallacies and facts. In C. Mayo, & N. Henley (Eds.), *Gender and non-verbal behavior.* New York: Springer-Verlag, 1981.

Hottenstein, M. P. *An exploration of the relationship between age, social status, and facial gesturing.* Doctoral dissertation, University of Pennsylvania, 1977.

Izard, C. *The face of emotion.* New York: Appleton-Century-Crofts, 1971.

Izard, C. E. *Human emotions.* New York: Plenum, 1977.

Izard, C. E. The maximally discriminative facial movement coding system (Max). Newark, Del.: University of Delaware, 1979.

Kleinberg, O. *Racial differences.* New York: Harper & Row, 1935.

Kulka, A. M. Observations and data on mother-infant interaction. *Israel Annals of Psychiatry & Allied Disciplines,* 1968, *1,* 70–83.

Lewicka, M. Personal communication, University of Delaware, 1981.

Lockard, J. S. Studies of human social signals: Theory, method and data. In J. S. Lockard (Ed.), *The evolution of human social behavior*. New York: Elsevier, 1980.

Malatesta, C. Z. *Determinants of infant affect socialization: Age, sex of infant and maternal emotional traits*. Doctoral dissertation, Rutgers University, 1980.

Malatesta, C. Z. Affective development over the lifespan: Involution or growth? *Merrill-Palmer Quarterly*, 1981, *27*, 145–173. (a)

Malatesta, C. Z. Infant emotion and the vocal affect lexicon. *Motivation and Emotion*, 1981, *5*, 1–23. (b)

Malatesta, C. Z. The ontogenesis of human social signals: From biological imperative to symbol utilization. In preparation.

Malatesta, C. Z., & Haviland, J. Learning display rules: The socialization of emotional expression in infancy. *Child Development*, 1982, *53*.

Mehrabian, A., & Epstein, N. A measure of emotional empathy. *Journal of Personality*, 1972, *40*, 525–543.

Neugarten, B. L., Moore, J. W., & Lowe, J. C. Age norms, age constraints, and adult socialization. In B. L. Neugarten (Ed.), *Middle age and aging*. Chicago: University of Chicago Press, 1973.

Oster, H., & Ekman, P. Facial behavior in child development. In A. Collins (Ed.), *Minnesota symposia on child psychology* (Vol. 11). Hillsdale, N.J.: Lawrence Erlbaum Associates, 1978.

Rothbart, M. K. Infant Behavior Questionnaire. Eugene, Ore.: University of Oregon, 1977.

Rothbart, M. K., & Derryberry, D. Development of individual differences in temperament. In M. E. Lamb, & A. L. Brown (Eds.), *Advances in developmental psychology*. Hillsdale, N.J.: Lawrence Erlbaum Associates, 1981.

Sackett, G. P. The lag sequential analysis of contingency and cyclicity in behavioral interaction research. In J. D. Osofsky (Ed.), *Handbook of infant development*. New York: Wiley, 1979.

Spielberger, C. D., Gorsuch, R. L., & Lushene, R. E. Manual for the state-trait anxiety inventory. Palo Alto, Calif.: Consulting Psychologists Press, 1970.

Sroufe, L. A. Socioemotional development. In J. D. Osofsky (Ed.), *Handbook of infant development*. New York: Wiley, 1979.

Stern, D. The goal and structure of mother–infant play. *Journal of the American Academy of Child Psychiatry*, 1974, *13*, 402–421.

Thomas, A., & Chess, S. *Temperament and development*. New York: Brunner/Mazel, 1977.

Tomkins, S. *Affect, imagery, consciousness, Vol. 1: The positive affects*. New York: Springer, 1962.

Tomkins, S. *Affect, imagery, consciousness, Vol. 2: The negative affects*. New York: Springer, 1963.

Tomkins, S. Script theory: Differential magnification of affects. In H. E. Howe, Jr. (Ed.), *Nebraska symposium on motivation* (Vol. 26). Lincoln: University of Nebraska Press, 1978.

Tomkins, S. S. The quest for primary motives: Biography and autobiography of an idea. *Journal of Personality and Social Psychology*, 1981, *41*, 306–329.

Trevarthen, C. Communication and cooperation in early infancy: A description of primary intersubjectivity. In M. Bullowa (Ed.), *Before speech*. Cambridge, Eng.: Cambridge University Press, 1979.

Weitz, S. Sex differences in nonverbal communication. *Sex Roles*, 1976, *2*, 175–184.

Zuckerman, M., & Przewuzman, S. Decoding and encoding facial expressions in preschool-age children. *Environmental Psychology and Nonverbal Behavior*, 1979, *3*, 147–163.

2 Affect Dynamics in Early Infancy: Affective Tolerance

Alan Fogel
Purdue University

The infant's emotional behavior and development have become subjects of interest for an increasing number of developmental psychologists. Newborns seem to possess most of the basic emotional expressions that are seen in adults (Charlesworth & Kreutzer, 1973), although the muscle movements of the face that produce these expressions are not nearly so well defined in infants as in adults (Oster, 1978). Most investigators seem to agree that the experience of emotions in infants starts out as rather global and undifferentiated and becomes more differentiated into discrete affects as a function of age (Bridges, 1933; Emde, Gaensbauer, & Harmon, 1976; Spitz, 1965; Sroufe, 1979). The infant's facial expressions do not always carry with them the same emotional experience as they might for an adult. In fact, the quality of the emotional experience related to a particular expression changes even within the infancy period. Sroufe (1979) has shown that the infant's smile at 9 months reflects a good deal more cognitive sophistication and awareness than the smile of recognitory assimilation at 3 months.

Although much is still to be gained from studies of emotion expressions and their changes over age, this chapter attempts to address the issues of how sequences of emotion expression are organized. Rather than asking if or how expressions occur, the approach here is to ask about whether emotions are likely to occur in predictable, repeatable sequences. Can a single emotion last indefinitely, or is there an inevitable hedonic alternation? And what accounts for developmental changes in the quality of the infant's affective experiences?

These questions grew out of previous research on infant-mother interaction in which investigators became aware that infants often proceed through a predictable sequence of increasing involvement culminating in positive affect expressions when in the presence of a sensitive, interacting adult (Brazelton, Koslowski, & Main, 1974). Since this ground-breaking study investigators have been studying the social dynamics and developmental course of early face-to-face interaction. In addition to finding certain predictable patterns of affect expression, it was discovered that face-to-face interaction had a fairly well-defined developmental course. It begins with the onset of eye-to-eye contact at about 6 weeks (Robson, 1967), reaches a peak between 8 to 12 weeks during the ascendance of social smiling, and declines after the third month as the infant becomes interested in inanimate objects. In this last phase, the infant uses the mother as a means to explore the object world. Face-to-face play does not end after 3 months. The mother and infant usually achieve a highly synchronized interaction, but the amount of joint attention during face-to-face play declines after 3 months (Kaye & Fogel, 1980). Because this period of face-to-face interaction is associated with the transition from obligatory attentional patterns to more voluntary control over attention, with the transition from internally generated to externally generated smiling, and with the development of arousal self-regulation in general, it serves as a natural laboratory for the study of emotional development.

Our previous studies on face-to-face interaction have shown the importance of explicitly including time (elapsed, real time) in our analysis (Fogel, 1977, 1979, 1980, in press; Kaye & Fogel, 1980). These studies have shown that structure can arise from the time intervals between events (as in a bout or run) as much as from the type of events that occur. All of these papers were exploratory attempts to chart the temporal dependencies of behavior of mother and infant in interaction.

In this chapter I propose a theoretical model that seems to account for the observed sequences of infant affect expression during face-to-face interaction. This theoretical model is an attempt to describe the nature of the infant's "free-running" affect dynamics as well as the response of the infant to maternal behavior during social interaction. This is not a structural theory of the infant's cognitive or affective functions, but rather a description of the process of affect generation in real time. There is reason to think (Kaye, 1980) that developmental explanations based on extrapolations from structural models may not be as valuable as the use of process or functional models of the individual. I attempt to show how a theory of sequential processes of affect within the interaction can lead to an explanation of social and emotional development over repeated interactions.

My arguments are directed primarily at face-to-face interaction during the first 6 months of life, so I make no claim for the generalizability of the model proposed. Nevertheless, the theoretical literature from which the basic premises are drawn covers a wide range of phenomena across ages, situations, and species. Suggestions are provided to indicate how such a model might be applied to the understanding of a number of other aspects of emotional development in infancy, most notably the development of secure attachments. There is, however, no reason to expect that the developmental principles that seem to work in the first 6 months of human life continue to function in the same way as the child gets older.

AFFECT DYNAMICS IN ADULTS

Emotional phenomena are a part of the fabric of our experience: the primitive and the sublime of personal existence. It is little wonder that philosophers and psychologists have been unable to agree on a definition of emotion. Is emotion to be found in the expressive movements of the skin and muscles (Darwin, 1872), or in the consciousness of those movements (James, 1890)? Perhaps emotion is powered by the "discharges" and "firings" of the central nervous system (Tomkins, 1962), or in the psychological "arousal" produced by those discharges and felt as pleasant or unpleasant (Young, 1961)? Or is emotion the cognitive interpretation and evaluation of perceptual inputs or visceral changes (Arnold, 1960; Schacter & Singer, 1962)?

One can find situations in which any definition seems correct, and they may all be correct: Each may refer to phenomenologically distinct categories of existence. These phenomenological levels—arousal and expressive movements, awareness of arousal, and conceptualization of categories of awareness—can be thought of as different perspectives on the same phenomenon. Recent data, from social psychology, developmental psychology, and ethology, suggest that these various levels of experience may interact with each other. For example, the evaluation of a feeling experience can lead to changes in that feeling, and changes in feeling states can lead to alterations of cognitive conceptualizations (Izard, 1971).

Magda Arnold (1960) addressed this issue only briefly in her work on emotion. In a section entitled "The Residual Effects of Emotions," she writes, "feeling attracted, we see only the attractive side; feeling repelled, we center all our attention on the distasteful aspect [p. 182]." Arnold spoke of "emotional attitudes" related to particular objects or events: The fact that one continued to feel the same way about something each time that thing reappeared. Her ideas can be encompassed under a classical conditioning model in which the emotion becomes the unconditioned response. The model does not predict emotional sequences over time as much as it predicts a constancy of emotion on repeated exposures to the same or similar situations. Children's acquired fears would be an example of this phenomenon.

"Affect Dynamics" is the title of a chapter on this subject by Silvan Tomkins (1962). In it, he provides a number of hypotheses about affect sequences.

1. The reduction of any negative affect is "rewarding" and this reward can motivate future attempts to reduce the negative affect. Conversely, the reduction of any positive affect is "punishing."

2. Reduction of negative affect is an activator of enjoyment, and the intensity and duration of the joy is proportional to the intensity and duration of the prior negative affect.

3. Interruption of a positive affect will result in distress or aggression, the intensity of which depends on the intensity and duration of the positive affect as well as on the suddenness and intensity of the interruption.

4. Every affect is an activator of itself, creating longer-term emotional states, or moods.

Tomkins justified these hypotheses by appeals to innate response biases of the individual: the spontaneous generation of an aftereffect that is hedonically opposite to the original affect, when that original affect is reduced or interrupted.

In another section of the same chapter, Tomkins describes how two different affects, existing simultaneously within the individual, may produce a resultant affect. His reasoning relies upon the notion that there are three basic kinds of affect: those for which the density of neural stimulation (arousal) is increasing (interest, excitement, fear), those for which the density of neural stimulation is decreasing (enjoyment, joy), and those for which the density of neural stimulation remains constant (anger, distress).

Tomkins proposes three principles that apply to competition between these three types of affects.

1. Constant density affects will prevail over decreasing density affects. This means, according to Tomkins, that enjoyment is a "luxury" response, one that is the "most vulnerable to exclusion."

2. When there is competition between increasing density affects and constant density affects, the former will prevail for short periods, but the latter will prevail over longer periods of time. Excitement may sometimes prevail over distress conditions, such as hunger and fatigue, but as soon as the source of excitement fades, the distress comes into awareness.

3. Continuing novelty will favor increasing or decreasing affects over constant density affects.

Tomkins' major contribution is to think of discrete affects—enjoyment, anger, distress, and so on—as the result of fluctuations in the density of neural stimulation, making the theory a dynamic one. The concept that affects can compete with and modulate each other, simply by some kind of summation of arousal levels, is also extremely useful for understanding the multiple ways in which emotions change and flow together.

Another theorist who deserves mention here is Carroll Izard. As a student of Tomkins, Izard championed the notion of discrete affects. Izard argued that each affect was a separate and discrete unit, and that there was no theoretical reason to assume that any one should necessarily follow any other (Izard, 1971). He did concede, following Tomkins, that one affect might amplify or attenuate another, and that at times affects can be observed to occur in alternating sequences. An example of the latter is the attachment-exploration system in which interest in the environment alternates with fear of loss of mother. Izard recognized that many affects have polar opposites, an insight he owed to Darwin (1872), but he did not hypothesize opposing aftereffects of stimulus interruption.

Nowlis (1965) has suggested that there may be "configurations of activity," or "moods," that have a systematic and lasting effect on a person. Nowlis found 12 mood factors, among them aggression, anxiety, concentration, affection, sadness, and elation. He postulated that there was a hierarchy of emotional states within the person. At the most fundamental level were the basic emotions; as defined by a number of authors, these are interest, excitement, fear, surprise, enjoyment, shame, anger, and distress (Ekman, Friesen, & Ellsworth, 1972; Tomkins, 1962). Sequential configurations of these emotions made up the next level of Nowlis's emotional hierarchy: moods. One might suppose that within a mood state only a specific few transitions between the basic emotions are observed, thus suggesting sequential rules. Nowlis never really makes this explicit, nor have other students of mood (Wessman & Ricks, 1966). These workers have approached mood phenomenologically, without attending to the series of component affect states that comprise the mood. The final level of the hierarchy is temperament, defined as the types of moods a person is likely to feel and the tendency to change mood states. Some moderate correlations have been observed between measures of mood and measures of personality, suggesting that, within a given individual at least, there may be preferred transitions between mood states.

Sequential patterns of emotion have been noted in a small number of research studies. These studies suggest that measures of personality, achievement, and emotion may vary as a function of the person's emotional state prior to the measurement. For example, prior evaluations of threat can influence subsequent evaluations of a situation, as in one study in which subjects were shown a 5-minute film rated as having "intermediate" threat value immediately after they had seen either a highly threatening film or a nonthreatening film. The former subjects were significantly less threatened by the intermediate threat film than were the latter subjects (Krupat, 1974). Messick (1965) found that the general depression engendered by the assassination of President Kennedy had a significant effect on how people evaluated themselves in personality tests. Compared to a testing 3 months after the assassination, subjects tested the day after were more indifferent and yielding, more conventional, and more dogmatic and extreme in expressing their opinions. Affect induction has been another method of investigating the effect of emotion on subsequent perception and cognition. Masters, Barden, and Ford (1979) found that children's cognitive performance was significantly lowered if they received a negative induction as compared to a positive induction.

Perhaps the most comprehensive theory of affect dynamics is Richard Solomon's *opponent-process theory,* an explicit attempt to deal with the "Temporal Dynamics of Affect" (Solomon & Corbit, 1974). Solomon noticed that when a strong species-specific unconditioned stimulus (UCS) is presented, regardless of whether that stimulus has hedonically positive reinforcement value (as a moving mother duck to a duckling) or hedonically negative reinforcement value (as an electric shock or during a parachutist's first free-fall from an airplane), the termination of the USC produces in the subject an opposing hedonic state that may last minutes or hours. Thus, the removal of the moving mother causes the duckling to experience distress, whereas the successful completion of the parachute jump produces a long-lived state of euphoria in the trainee. If A and B are opposing affects, then one observes the sequence (baseline state—State A—State B—baseline state) (Solomon, 1980).

Solomon reports the results of various studies showing that the time course of the A and B states has a characteristic form. At the onset of the UCS, there is a sharp rise in the subject's arousal level. This peak of arousal can be either hedonically negative or hedonically positive, depending on the nature of the UCS. The peak is followed by a gradual decline in the intensity of the A state, although the rate of decline depends on the nature of the UCS and the susceptibility of the organism to it. When the UCS is terminated, the organism responds with a decline in the intensity of the original hedonic tone and an increase of arousal having the opposite hedonic tone. This opponent B state also has a peak followed by a decline. According to Solomon, observations of B states have revealed that they tend to linger for considerable periods of time. After the removal of the mother, ducklings can be observed to exhibit prolonged periods of distress, even though the mother may have been present for only a relatively short period. Once a parachutist returns safely to earth, he or she experiences a long-lived state of exhilaration (Solomon, 1980).

Solomon posits the existence of two underlying processes, a and b, which are hedonic opposites. The manifest A and B states are hypothesized to be the summation of the a and b processes, both of which operate simultaneously. Whereas Tomkins describes the underlying processes in terms of increases or decreases of the density of neural stimulation, Solomon proposes a psychochemical process to account for the existence of *b* processes. He cites evidence showing that when an organism is under any kind of stress, whether from positive or negative arousal, the brain secretes opiate-like substances called endorphins. Such substances act to lessen the effect of the original stress, hence the gradual decline in the intensity of the *A* state over time. The presence of the increased endorphin level in the system at the time of the termination of the UCS would explain the peak in the opponent process, followed by a long-lived decline in the *B* state as the endorphins are assimilated.

Both of these theories could be tested by using appropriate measures of physiological arousal, such as heart rate or respiration. Solomon suggests injecting an opiate antagonist prior to stimulation as a way of retarding endorphin secretion, thus reducing the effect of the *b* process. Although the process of infant development may be illuminated by casting the problem in terms of physiological or chemical substrates of behavior (Field, Chapter 5, this volume), a good deal of progress can be made by ignoring the substrate and concentrating on the behavioral and psychological aspects of opponent processes: Can such dynamics be observed to occur?

Assuming that Solomon and Tomkins are correct that the interruption of intense affective states will be followed by equally intense opponent states, a number of problems still remain that can only be solved by behavioral studies. One of those problems has to do with the nature of the UCS. Not all stimuli produce intense affective responses. It is important to find out which do and which do not for any given individual at any particular age. The second problem is that there are many types of "positive" affects and many types of "negative" affects. Solomon and Corbit (1974) list a number of the possible combinations. For dogs experiencing an electric shock, fear may be followed by euphoria when the shock is turned off. Excitement and happiness engendered by the presence of a loved one may be replaced by loneliness or distress. Each particular stimulus may produce a different initial affective state, and the opponent state may be a resultant of the type of stimulus and the intensity and quality of the original affective reaction. The opponent-process theory only describes the temporal changes in the intensity of arousal, but it does not account for the qualitative aspects of the affective experience. A synthesis of opponent-process theory and discrete-emotions theory is required if we are to fully account for affect dynamics.

In a further elaboration of the model, Solomon describes a process whereby the quality of the affect in the *A* and *B* states changes as a function of repeated exposure to the UCS. According to the model, *b* processes become strengthened by use and weakened by disuse. In some cases this means that the *A* state becomes less intense over repeated stimulations whereas the *B* state becomes more intense. One example is imprinting in ducklings. During the first few presentations of the mother, the duckling shows pleasure and excitement while she is there and shows distress cries of short duration when she is removed. After many presentations of the mother, the duckling shows moderate amounts of pleasure while she is there, but when she is removed, the distress cries are of much longer duration than during the initial separations.

Another example shows how both the intensity and the quality of the affects may change over repeated presentations. After the first few encounters with a loved one, human adults show ecstasy, excitement, and happiness with that person and loneliness when not with that person. After many encounters, the A state becomes one of security, comfort, and contentment, whereas the B state includes emotions such as distress and grief responses (Solomon & Corbit, 1974).

Epstein (1967) has observed similar phenomena occurring for the anxiety responses of novice and experienced parachutists. For the novice, anxiety slowly builds before the approaching time of the jump. Often, in the early stages of anxiety build-up, the novice jumper uses a number of forms of psychological defense, including denial of the anxiety, but these defenses often give way to visible tremors, vomiting, and other overt manifestations of fear as the time of the jump draws near. Experienced jumpers, Epstein found, feel a peak of anxiety hours before the jump, and as the time of the jump approaches, their anxiety level falls. According to Epstein, this shift of anxiety backward in time allows the jumper to gain control over his or her voluntary movements so that he or she can successfully execute and enjoy the jump. Thus, over repeated experiences, the jump shifts from having a high arousal value to having high cue value for the jumper. Epstein reports that some experienced jumpers never seem to be able to control their anxiety levels and continue to show highly labile prejump arousal curves.

The model that Epstein proposes is that repeated exposure to highly arousing situations leads to the individual's mastery of self-control over the arousal and thus permits the development of more adaptive responses. The model is similar to that of Solomon in that the repeated exposure to highly arousing situations leads to a change in the temporal patterning of arousal as well as to a change in the quality of the affective state that is experienced in the presence of the arousing stimulus.

AFFECT DYNAMICS IN EARLY SOCIAL INTERACTION

These theories of affect dynamics leave one wondering whether they can be applied to enhance our understanding of infant development. Solomon and Epstein are clearly talking about very highly arousing stimuli—jumping out of an airplane, receiving electric shocks, having sexual intercourse—all of which seem to be beyond the range of experience of the human infant. If this theory is to apply at all, we would need to find comparably intense affective experience in infants. I believe that intense affects are commonplace in early infancy; that young infants are probably closer to their emotions than at any other point in later life. As adults we have developed a considerable set of defenses that shield us from becoming overwhelmed with our emotions. In fact, we rarely face the kind of intense emotion experienced by the novice parachutist, and if we did, Epstein has shown that it does not take us long to develop coping responses to lower our level of arousal.

Infants, on the other hand, experience rather profound and intense states of distress, fear, enjoyment, and excitement, depending on their age and the situational context. Adult investigators may have fallen into the trap of adultomorphizing the infant's emotional states, so that we tend to see them as less intense than they may be for the infant. In what follows, I hope to demonstrate that the early stages of the mother–infant face-to-face interaction create intense states of excitement and pleasure in young infants, and that an opponent-process model can add to our understanding of sequencing of affect during face-to-face interaction when combined with other models of infant affect, most notably the tension-release model of Sroufe and Waters (1976). The tension-release model seems to be suitable for periods when the infant experiences moderate levels of arousal. Sroufe (1979) has argued that the development of arousal tolerance is poorly understood. The theory proposed here postulates the existence of opponent processes for high arousal levels, a process that may lead to the ultimate development of tension-release processes for moderate arousal levels.

Affect Sequences During States of Moderate Arousal

The regulation of arousal has been viewed as the primary goal of mother and infant during early face-to-face interaction (Brazelton et al., 1974; Stern, 1974). Infants seem to strive not to reduce arousal to zero, but to maintain optimal levels of engagement with the mother. Mothers, for their part, adjust the content and timing of their behavior in order to facilitate the infant's maintenance of an optimal arousal state. This idea of a homeostatic, or deviation-correcting, system has received a good deal of support from recent studies on face-to-face interaction.

Brazelton et al. (1974) provide a clinical description of the mother–infant interaction in the early months of life. They show how the mother attempts to carefully adjust the timing of her behavior to follow the natural cycles of the infant. As the infant begins to gaze towards the mother, the mother begins to increase her level of involvement, gradually building up to a peak of excitement that culminates in a smile. The smile is followed by a relative decline in the infant's engagement, during which time the mother reduces her stimulation level. Similarly, Fogel (1977) and Kaye and Fogel (1980) found that mothers tended to reduce their facial expressiveness when the infants were gazing away from the interaction, and to increase their expressiveness when the infants were gazing at them. In a more recent study, we noted that the mother's expressiveness tended to inhibit the 2 month old's gaze state changes. When the mother was expressive, the infant was less likely to change gaze state (at or away from the mother) than when the mother was not expressive (Fogel, in press).

In order to account for the interdependence of the mother's activity and the infant's attentiveness, Tiffany Field has proposed an *optimal-stimulation* model of affect and interaction (Field, 1977, 1980, Chapter 5 this volume). According to this model, if the adult provides either too much or too little stimulation, the infant will withdraw from the interaction. The amount of stimulation that is optimal depends on the characteristics of the particular infant: his or her tolerance for stimulation, internal thresholds for arousal, maturity of arousal self-control mechanisms. So long as the mother can maintain the infant within his or her optimal range of arousal, one sees the regular cycling of gazing and smiling that have been described by Brazelton and his colleagues.

The most comprehensive theory on infant affect during moderate arousal is that proposed by Sroufe and Waters (1976). According to their data, the infant's arousal levels, as measured by heart-rate changes, can be observed to fluctuate regularly, rarely straying either too far above or too far below some optimal level. These fluctuations are characterized by the gradual build-up of affective tension, followed by the release of that tension. Tension-release cycles can be seen in newborns during quiet sleep, and they can be observed in older infants during quiet alert periods. Sroufe and Water's concept of tension is equivalent to the concept of arousal in this chapter, although they have contributed to our understanding of arousal processes in infancy by suggesting that tension can be psychologically generated: It is only a purely physiological response during the first month of life.

Sroufe and Waters (1976) found that the alternation of heart rate over time could be systematically related to behavioral changes. Release of tension tended to be followed by smiles, whereas tension increase was associated with attentive behavior. This fits very neatly into the descriptions of Brazelton et al. of the infant's sequences of affect during optimal face-to-face interaction: a cyclic alternation of smiling and gazing. Sroufe and Waters suggest that the smile serves the adaptive function of allowing the infant to control the level of internal arousal and thus remain engaged in the relationship. The smile also communicates to the mother that the infant is involved with her at an optimal level.

Affect Sequences During States of High Arousal

The description of the function of smiling given by Sroufe and Waters is similar to the description given by Epstein of experienced parachutists' ability to control their prejump anxiety. After many jumps, parachutists learned to displace their anxiety backward in time from the jump. This allowed them to focus on the important cues necessary to execute and enjoy the jump, rather than on the arousal. The jumpers had not eliminated the high arousal levels, they had simply found a way to internally regulate the timing of their arousal states in relation to a crucial environmental event.

Because the leap from infant smiling to parachute jumping may be a bit abrupt, let me state where I am going in the form of an hypothesis. The ability of infants to use smiling to maintain engagement with the mother during optimal arousal states may be preceded, developmentally, by a situation in which the arousal caused by maternal stimulation was highly intense. So intense, in fact, that like the anxiety of the novice jumper, the infant's arousal level must have precluded any continued enjoyment or engagement with the mother. The infant's ability to remain engaged with the mother during a period of optimal arousal may be a developmental achievement that begins with becoming overwhelmed by intense positive arousal, and culminates with the ability to control the level of arousal through tension-release mechanisms.

Developmentally, we would first expect to find that the infant's initial attraction to the mother's face is highly charged: Smiling should be coupled with nearly overwhelming excitement. This intense excitement would lead to an increase of arousal beyond the limits of the optimal range, and would culminate in a relatively rapid shift to gaze away, or possibly even distress. After many interactions we might expect to see a lessening of excitement at the first approach of the mother, and a more even distribution of smiling and continued engagement throughout the interaction session.

During the course of this process, the infant is learning how to control his or her own behavior in relation to the mother. The goal is not so much to maintain optimal arousal: That only comes later. The goal at first is to learn to tolerate the intensity of the arousal, to develop appropriate regulatory or "ego" functions that allow the infant to maintain engagement, while at the same time to experience the enjoyment of the interaction.

According to Solomon, this process does not involve learning in the strict sense of conditioning. The infant does not learn to smile at the mother as a specific conditioned stimulus. Rather, the mother is, from the beginning, a highly arousing unconditioned stimulus. Due in part to the mother's sensitivity in managing these initially extreme expressions of excitement and the subsequent withdrawal that they generate, the infant develops increasing *affective tolerance* for high arousal. This idea of affective tolerance is similar to habituation, but the results of the two processes appear to be quite different. In habituation the infant seems to lower arousal as well as expressive responses to stimuli by effectively tuning out the stimulus. Affective-tolerance processes allow the infant to maintain moderate levels of internal arousal while remaining engaged with the stimulus. Solomon (1980) likens the process of affective tolerance to the process of drug addiction and drug tolerance. A psychoactive drug can, during the first few administrations, create rather exalted states of euphoria. After many administrations, the individual feels "high" and content, but not as overwhelmed as the first few times. Because the levels of the active components of the drug remain unchanged over repeated administrations, Solomon has concluded that there is a change in the psychophysiological ability to tolerate the drug levels. That tolerance is observed in the form of changes in the quality and timing of the individual's affect displays.

This model seems to fit well with the model presented by Field (Chapter 5, this volume). High-risk infants may have a minimally developed tolerance for arousing stimuli. They are likely to withdraw in situations that seem optimal for normal infants. Field suggests that parents learn to reduce their levels of stimulation in order to find the high-risk infants' optimal range. It may be fruitful to consider high-risk infants using high arousal, rather than moderate arousal, models. Epstein (1967) suggests that the best way to help children develop affective self-control is to provide small doses of stimulation when a more usual dose might be overwhelming. Over repeated occasions, the child will gradually learn to tolerate increased levels of arousal.

Affective Tolerance and Attachment

A natural concomitant of affective tolerance is *addiction* to the UCS. This has been used to explain imprinting in ducklings and addiction to such things as drugs and sport parachuting (Solomon, 1980). According to Solomon, the addiction to the UCS comes about in the form of an acquired motivation. This new motivation—the desire to be near the imprinted object, for example—can be explained using the dynamics of affective-opponent processes. The high intensity of positive arousal in the presence of the UCS is followed by a high intensity of negative arousal when the UCS is absent. One becomes addicted by a motive to avoid the unpleasant aftereffects as well as a motive to seek out the positive. This differs from classical conditioning because there is no conditioned stimulus. The infant does not learn to display the same behavior to some other stimulus; rather, the timing and quality of the affective arousal changes in relation to the same stimulus.

Can a tolerance-addiction process also be used to explain human attachment? An addiction model of attachment is very attractive for a number of reasons, the most important of which is that the process establishes a clear link between the infant's affect and attachment. The idea of affective tolerance may explain how maternal sensitivity in the first 6 months, a variable that has been demonstrated to correlate strongly with the 1 year old's security of attachment (Ainsworth, Blehar, Waters, & Wall, 1978; Clarke-Stewart, 1973), is linked to later attachment. The mother's ability to adjust the amount and timing of her stimulation may be directly implicated in the process by which infants learn to control arousal. The tolerance-addiction model further proposes that the mother's behavior will be different during early, high arousal situations than during the periods when the infant is able to maintain moderate arousal levels. Studies of attachment must also include a consideration of intensely arousing states of negative affect. Tolerance for distress states, again in conjunction with maternal responsiveness, could lead to predictions of an infant with an increasing ability for self-comforting, decreasing demanding behavior, and more security.

Because the tolerance-addiction model of attachment predicts a two-phase process—one in which the parent serves to help regulate high-intensity arousal, and a later one in which the parent is involved in a more facilitative or reciprocal role when the infant can maintain moderate arousal—it has similarities to psychoanalytic views of parenting. Most writers speak of such a two-phase process. Spitz refers to the early maternal function as being the infant's "external ego" (Spitz, 1965), and similar themes have been developed by Mahler, Pine and Bergman (1975) and by Winnicott (1971).

Many of the ideas that have been discussed in relation to high-intensity affects have the ring of Freudian theory. High arousal states are similar to drive stages in which the infant must initially attempt to reduce the stimulation. Although the sight of the mother is not a drive in the psychoanalytic sense, the intent is the same: reduce arousal. Furthermore, the development of the ability to gain increasing control over highly arousing situations can be equated to ego development, the ego being the consortium of coping, defense, and adaptive functions of the individual. Ego functions serve the aim of controlling arousal in highly charged situations.

I believe that psychologists began to be disillusioned with psychoanalysis when it was discovered that most of adult functioning seemed to work on an optimal-stimulation model, rather than on a drive-reduction model (see, for example, White, 1963). The optimal-stimulation models that were cited earlier reflect our modern, western preoccupation with optimal functioning and self-fulfillment. And these models very adequately describe an important range of infant functioning. However, let us remember that the prototype of the drive-reduction model for Freud was not the adult, but the young infant.

I am not proposing a return to classical psychoanalysis, but rather to a recognition that young infants regularly experience highly charged emotional states that often overwhelm them. The only counterparts in adult functioning are those rare times in our lives that we too become overwhelmed. I am suggesting that with infants we need to deal explicitly with high arousal processes, and that the successful integration of high arousal states by the infant may result in developmental changes in the quality and timing of affective sequences, in the development of arousal-regulation mechanisms, and in the acquisition of emotionally meaningful relationships with objects and with people.

A Model of Affective Tolerance

The ideas that have been developed in the preceding sections have been represented in Fig. 2.1. We presume that the infant starts out in some encounter with a highly arousing unconditioned stimulus. In early infancy this

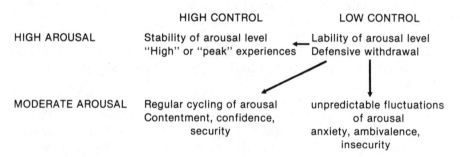

SELF-CONTROL OVER AROUSAL
(EGO)

	HIGH CONTROL	LOW CONTROL
HIGH AROUSAL	Stability of arousal level "High" or "peak" experiences	Lability of arousal level Defensive withdrawal
MODERATE AROUSAL	Regular cycling of arousal Contentment, confidence, security	unpredictable fluctuations of arousal anxiety, ambivalence, insecurity

FIG. 2.1   Model of the relationship between self-regulation and arousal. Infants are presumed to move from a state of high arousal and low self-control to one of the other states as a function of organimic and environmental parameters.

usually means the sight of the mother, a nipple in the mouth, hunger, or fatigue. It is also assumed that the infant has preadapted response systems that can process the stimulus and create the arousal, but that there is little self-control over the timing or intensity of the arousal, once it has begun. Examples are overwhelming excitement or overwhelming distress. The system does not self-correct; it simply responds. This state is represented by the upper right portion of Fig. 2.1. Depending on the infant's level of built-in arousal tolerance, on the type of stimulus presented, and on the ability of the parent to regulate the presentation of the stimulus in small doses, the infant may take one of three possible developmental paths, as depicted in Fig. 2.1. In the "normal" course of events, most infants progress along the diagonal: They develop an increased tolerance for the affective arousal and begin to display self-regulated modulation of arousal about an optimal level. They transform an experience of overwhelming excitement to one of contentment or pleasure, an experience of overwhelming distress to one of security or confidence.

One could also imagine extremely well-controlled infants who are able to tolerate very high levels of arousal, although this may come somewhat later in the first year (see upper left corner of Fig. 2.1). The high arousal, high control cell of the Figure may represent states leading up to and including laughter, because laughter is presumed to require a considerably higher arousal level than smiling (Sroufe, 1979). It may also describe developmental changes in infants' responses to pain, separation, hunger, and other highly arousing events having a negative hedonic tone.

Failure to develop affective tolerance may lead the infant to remain on the right-hand side of Fig. 2.1, showing a continued withdrawal from arousing stimuli and a persistent insecurity even during moderate states of arousal. The implications of this model for the development of insecure and secure attachments should be clear from the preceding discussion. It should be pointed out, however, that the model suggests that there may be factors other than the parent's responsiveness that account for later attachment security/insecurity differences. Individual variations in attachment might arise, according to the tolerance-addiction model, because of differences in parental sensitivity to the infant's need for external support to help control highly arousing states, or because of insufficiencies in the infant's own arousal "immune system." The latter refers to possible malfunctions of physiological mechanisms (e.g., endorphin secretion) that are hypothesized to underlie the affective-tolerance process. This model may suggest new approaches to old problems of accounting for individual differences in the security of the infant's tie to the mother.

RESEARCH RELATING TO AFFECTIVE TOLERANCE IN YOUNG INFANTS: THE CASE OF FACE-TO-FACE INTERACTION

The study of affect dynamics requires a somewhat different approach to data than has been employed heretofore. Most of the research on early face-to-face interaction has used summary measures, such as the frequency and duration of smiling over a whole interaction session, or contingency measures. In order to test hypotheses related to the affective-tolerance theory, we need to look at the behavior of the infant as a function of elapsed time. Although contingencies take elapsed time into account, they do so in only a limited way. The contingency asks whether there is a before–after relationship between two behaviors. A measure of contingency is in fact a summary score because it compiles all instances of each behavior across the session, regardless of the actual time of occurrence of those behaviors. In what follows, these methodological issues should become more clear.

Evidence for Opponent Processes During Face-to-Face Interaction

The intent in these sections is to show that early face-to-face interaction can be understood using an affective-tolerance model. That means that we must first demonstrate that the mother is a highly arousing stimulus for the infant. One way that this can be done is to monitor the infant's heart rate during the course of interaction. Tiffany Field has found that for 3 month olds, interactions with the father and mother elicited higher levels of heart rate and more gaze aversion than interactions with a mirror or a doll (Field, 1981). Field also found that a mother who exhibited spontaneous interactive behavior elicited higher heart rate and more gaze aversion than an imitative (and presumably less active) mother, or an animated or still doll. This effect was seen for both term and preterm infants at 3 months (Field, 1979). The increased levels of gaze aversion coupled with the high levels of heart rate suggest that the mothers were highly arousing and that the infants did not have the ability to control their own states of arousal long enough to remain engaged in the interaction.

Another indication of a highly arousing stimulus would be the existence of an opponent affective process of high intensity. The opponent process could be observed by removing the stimulus and watching for the development of an affective state of opposite hedonic tone from the original. In an attempt to do this, I looked at the behavior of 2 month olds as their mothers left the room following a 2-minute interaction (Fogel, 1980). When their mothers turned and left, infants quieted and visually tracked the departing mother. Some infants reached in the direction of the mother's exit, but few showed any measurable distress. Although infants were more likely to show the pattern (quieting, tracking, reaching) following an interaction with their own mother than after an interaction with a female adult stranger, this behavior could hardly be thought of as representing an opponent state.

There could be at least three explanations for this finding. The first is that face-to-face interaction is not highly arousing, and therefore does not produce a strong opponent response when terminated. This seems to contradict the findings of Field and prompts a search for another explanation. A second possibility is that the sight of the mother is so arousing to the infant that the infant can maintain engagement for only a brief period of time: when the mother first enters the room. Two minutes later, when the separation actually occurred, the infant was no longer aroused and hence the departure was of little consequence. A third possibility is that the departure of the mother has no real meaning for an infant who does not possess an object concept.

As we see in the next section, infants do become highly aroused right at the beginning of an interaction, and this arousal tapers off after a short time. But it is also true that the infants do not have an object concept, so that we cannot decide between these two possibilities as an explanation for the lack of negative arousal during departure without further study. The obvious experiment is to have the mother leave the room at the point when the infant is highly aroused, right at the beginning of the interaction session.

Although this study has not been done, a similar procedure has yielded results consistent with an opponent-process model. Instead of having the mother leave the room, some investigators have asked the mother to cease her interaction. The "still-face" procedure required mothers to stop talking or moving and simply to look at their infants for a short time. During the still-face period, infants often made some attempts to look and to smile at the silent mother; however, these attepts were soon replaced by an increasing amount of gaze aversion and reduction of positive affect (Tronick, Als, Adamson, Weise and Brazelton, 1978).

We have replicated this effect in our laboratory in two separate experiments (Fogel, Diamond, Langhorst, & Demos, 1981; Fogel, Hannan, & Demos, in preparation), and it has been replicated in Tiffany Field's laboratory by Sherilyn Stoller (Stoller & Field, Chapter 3, this volume). In these three studies, however, a third condition was added in which the mother resumed her interaction with the infant following the still-face condition. According to the opponent-process theory, the opponent, or b process, is thought to be slow to decay, and, according to Solomon (1980): "b processes, though interacting with a-process arousers, retain their integrity in time and are not destroyed, discharged, or terminated when a processes are superimposed on them in time [p. 705]." One example of this is that rats showed less inhibition of drinking following an established conditioned stimulus (CS) for shock if that CS came immediately after another CS for shock (LaBarbera & Caul, 1976). We therefore hypothesized that the infant's response to the mother following the still face would be less positive than before the still face, making the assumption that the opponent process engendered by the still-face procedure would carry over to affect the infant's subsequent behavior to the newly animated mother.

These hypotheses were confirmed in all three studies. There was a significant reduction in smiling and a significant increase in crying in the resumed interaction compared to the initial interaction. In each of these studies, the interruption of the mother's behavior was initiated near the beginning of the interaction, suggesting that 2 month olds are highly aroused by the interaction situation, at least for a short time.

Evidence for Affective Tolerance During
Face-to-Face Interaction

In order to confirm the notion that young infants experienced high arousal states at the beginning of an interaction, it was necessary to look at the infant's behavior as a function of elapsed time in the interaction. The affective-tolerance theory suggests that during the first few weeks after the infant initially becomes attracted to the mother's face, there will be a peak of positive arousal right at the beginning of the interaction, followed by a period of low arousal without social engagement. At this stage (see Fig. 2.1), the infant is either highly aroused by the mother or else is not engaged for long periods: The infant has very little self-control over the arousal and is easily overwhelmed to the point of withdrawal. The tolerance model further predicts that with increasing exposure to the mother over days, weeks, or months, the infant will learn to lower arousal to a more optimal level and to continue to maintain a positive engagement with the mother for a longer time in the session. Emde et al. (1976) have suggested that infants' early behavior fits a "discharge" or "homeostatic" model, whereas later there is a trend towards self-control in maintaining contact with the stimulation.

In order to look more closely at these processes, I took data from a recent study (Fogel, in press) and reanalyzed it from an elapsed-time perspective. Twenty infants between the ages of 7 and 13 weeks were observed interacting with a female adult stranger and with their mothers. There were few effects of order of presentation or of adult, so the data were pooled across all 40 interaction sessions, each lasting 2 minutes. The sessions were divided into 30-seconds epochs and the number of gazes, smiles, and cries were counted for each of the epochs. The results are shown in Fig. 2.2. According to expectations, there were significantly more gazes, smiles, and cries in the first 30 seconds of the interaction than in any of the remaining epochs. Because 25% of the total number of gazes, smiles, or cries can be expected to fall in the first 30 seconds by chance, the observed frequency in the first 30 seconds was compared to the expected frequency using a chi-square multinomial test (Hollander & Wolfe, 1973). For gaze, the chi-square value was 18.00, $p < .001$, for smile, chi-square was 15.26, $p < .01$; for cry, chi-square was 11.44, $p < .01$.

These data show that infants tended to smile during the first 30 seconds more often than at any other time. This suggests that the highest arousal was at the beginning of the session, and that infants in this age range were not capable of maintaining visual engagement, nor of sustaining positive affect with the adult over the entire 2-minute period. Crying presents a somewhat different picture because there were about as many cries during the second 30 seconds as during the first, which may indicate that a typical response to the initially high arousal levels is gaze aversion followed by cry-

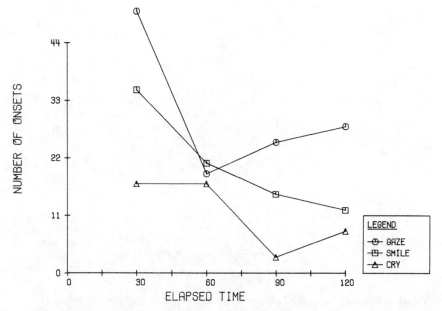

FIG. 2.2 Changes in the number of onsets of gaze, smile, and cry as a function of elapsed time during face-to-face interaction with adults. The sample consists of 40 2-minute interactions made up of 20 infants who each interacted with mother and an adult female stranger.

ing. These results are consistent with the findings of Field (1979, 1980, and Chapter 5, this volume) and with the affective-tolerance theory as outlined in this chapter.

Another way to examine elapsed-time behavior is to look at durations of events, rather than their frequencies. The durations of smiles and cries do not vary considerably, but gaze at mother can range from a few seconds to a few minutes. Fig. 2.3 shows the mean duration, across all interaction sessions, of the first gaze of the session, the second gaze, and so on, up to the fifth gaze in the session. These data corroborate those of the frequency analysis: The first gaze of the session tends to be the longest, with a mean duration of 30 seconds compared to a mean of about 12 seconds for subsequent gazes.

Infants in this age range are just beginning to become involved with visual exploration of the mother's face and are just beginning to show high arousal with regard to the face-to-face interaction situation. A more conclusive test of the affect-tolerance theory would be to show a systematic change in these elapsed-time curves over age. Specifically, one would expect that the infant's gaze would become more evenly distributed over the session, showing continued involvement with the interaction. In addition, we would expect to find more smiling during the entire interaction, and a

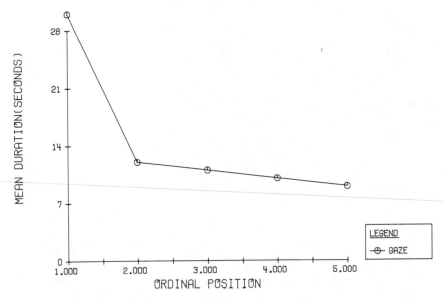

FIG. 2.3   Mean duration of gaze as a function of the ordinal position of the gaze episode in the session, using the same sample of subjects as in Fig. 2.2.

reduction of crying, suggesting that the infant has learned to manage arousal. Whereas high arousal states can be seen in the rapid falling off of smiling and gazing over time, moderate arousal (and hence self-control of arousal) should show up as a tension-release process: There should be higher frequency of smiling, and smiling should be organized into bouts of repeated smiling. Repeated smiles, smiles alternating with relaxation of the face, would be indicative of an optimal level of arousal that is maintained by a cyclic regulatory mechanism of the kind described by Sroufe and Waters (1976).

Developmental shifts of this kind were found for two infants who were observed weekly from birth to 6 months. For the first 3 months, each infant interacted with his (J.) or her (H.) mother while sitting in an infant seat placed on a table. The infants were also observed in face-to-face interaction while seated on the mother's lap. The lap observations started at birth and continued until the eighth month. Each interaction, whether lap or seat, lasted 5 minutes and was videotaped using a split-screen method. Details of the procedure and coding methods can be found in Fogel (1981). The data presented here cover from birth to 6 months, and concern the infant's gaze direction and facial expression. Categories of facial expression are given in Table 2.1. Reliability across categories was .83 proportion of agreements. Gaze was simply coded as either at or away from the mother.

If we look at the total frequency and duration of gaze and at each of the facial-expression categories, one finds trends as a function of age (Table

TABLE 2.1
Categories of Facial Expression[a]

Category	Description
Cry	Burst-pause and continuous cry vocalizations
Whimper	Low-intensity sobbing sounds or precry sounds
Frown	Mouth corners turned down, sometimes with brow knitting
Rest	The absence of any of the other expressions on this list
Mouthing	Lip smacking, mouth opening, "O"-shaped mouth, tonguing, chewing
Pucker	Puckered lips, sucking, compressed lips
Hand to mouth	Any contact between the hand and the mouth
Object in mouth	Any contact between an object, the mother, or the infant's clothing and the mouth
Smile	Full smiles with mouth corners up and mouth open, and "incipient" presmiles with mouth closed and partially up-turned corners
Laugh	Smile accompanied by laughter

[a]Other functional categories were included in the coding process. These were yawn, spit up, and cough. Due to their low frequency of occurrence, they were not included in the analysis.

2.2). None of these findings is the least bit surprising. There is an increased likelihood that infants will smile and laugh more often and for longer durations as they get older, with a corresponding decrease in the likelihood of crying and frowning. These infants were likely to increase the rate, but decrease the duration of rest mouth, a pattern that suggests a possible alternation between rest and other expressions related to tension-release cycles. The infant's mouth is also more likely to be occupied by objects as reaching

TABLE 2.2
Kendall Correlations of Rate and Mean Duration with
Age of Infant

Category	Infant = J. (N = 22)		Infant = H. (N = 16)	
	Rate	Mean Duration	Rate	Mean Duration
Cry	-.08	-.15	-.61^c	-.71^c
Frown	-.27^a	-.56^c	-.18	-.24
Rest	.34^b	-.53^c	.51^b	-.25
Mouthing	.22	-.13	.47^b	.17
Pucker	.16	.21	-.18	-.56^b
Hand in mouth	.46^b	.25	.21	.07
Object in mouth	.39^b	.36^b	.46^b	.48^b
Smile	.50^c	.33^a	.46^b	.42^b
Laugh	.52^c	.47^b	—	—
Gaze	-.38^b	.32^a	-.41^b	.45^b

^{a} $p < .05$.
^{b} $p < .01$.
^{c} $p < .001$

and grasping become more sophisticated with age. Both infants showed an increase in mean gaze duration, but a decrease in gaze frequency.

In order to look at age trends in the likelihood of a particular behavior's occurring at the beginning of the interaction, each session was divided into five 1-minute epochs. Fig. 2.4 and 2.5 show the changes in the proportion of smiles, gazes, and cries that occurred during the first 2 minutes of the interaction. Fig. 2.4 shows the data for the lap interaction, Fig. 2.5 shows the seat interaction. Note that the expected value of this variable is .40, because 40% of the onsets of any single behavior could have occurred in the first 2 minutes by chance.

Looking at the lap interactions (Fig. 2.4), the first few weeks are dominated by crying, although there does not appear to be any systematic tendency for cry to occur at the beginning of the session. For infant H., half

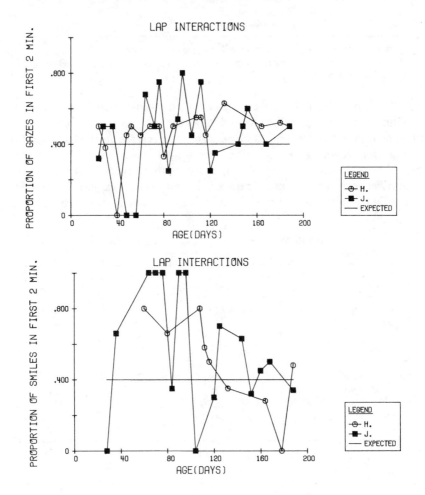

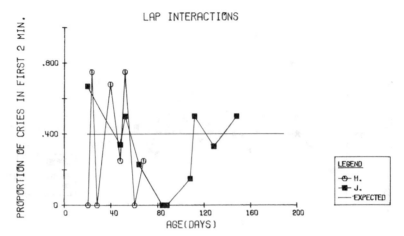

FIG. 2.4   Proportion of onsets during the first 2 minutes of an interaction for the case-study data. These data represent face-to-face interaction while the infant is held on the mother's lap.

of the sessions are above chance and half are below chance, and the same holds true for infant J. Of greater importance is that crying tends either to occur near the end of the session or not at all as gaze and smile begin to occupy the first 2 minutes. This occurs during the period from approximately 40 to 100 days.

This period appears to be a time of high intensity of positive arousal for the face-to-face interaction. Smiling is most likely to occur during the first 2 minutes (five out of six sessions for J.; five out of five sessions for H.). During this period, gazing also tends to occur more often during the first few minutes (seven out of eight sessions for J.; nine out of ten sessions for H.).

After 100 days, both infants show a more even distribution of smiling over the session, and their gazing, although hovering about chance level, tends to occur more often during the first few minutes.

Similar trends can also be observed for the seat interaction, but one can see that the period of high arousal peaks somewhat earlier, between 36 and 50 days for both infants. This may be because the mother has fewer opportunities to arouse the infant in the seat. The peak of early smiling for the seat may represent arousal due primarily to distal–visual stimulation. High arousal in the lap may be due more to proximal–tactual–vestibular stimulation.

According to the affective-tolerance model, we should expect to see an increase in the number of bouts of repeated smiling, smiles alternating with nonsmile expressions such as rest and mouthing, after 100 days. This is extremely critical for the affective-tolerance model: There should be few tension-release cycles as long as arousal remains high. The more even

TABLE 2.3
Trill Patterns for J.

Age (Days)	Type of Trill	Number of Trills	Number of Smiles or Laughs per Trill	Number of Lone Smiles or Laughs	Total Number of Smiles and Laughs
21		0	0	0	0
25		0	0	0	0
28		0	0	1	1
36		0	0	7	7
45		0	0	0	0
57		0	0	0	0
64		0	0	2	2
70		0	0	1	1
77		0	0	2	2
84		0	0	3	3
91		0	0	7	7
98		0	0	6	6
105	smile-mouthing	2	2	8	12
112	smile-mouthing	0	0	3	3
119		1	3	5	8
126		0	0	9	9
144		0	0	6	6
147		0	0	2	2
150	smile-laugh-rest	2	3	12	18
155	smile-rest	4	3	1	13
171	laugh-rest	1	5	1	6
189	smile-mouthing	6	3	1	19

tion are shown in Figs. 2.7 and 2.8. The data have been broken down into three age groups: 0 to 7 weeks, 7 to 13 weeks, and 13 to 27 weeks. Only infant H. shows a tendency to have a longer first gaze after 7 weeks of age. This is true for both the lap (Fig. 2.7) and the seat (Fig. 2.8). It is hard to know what these individual differences might mean, but it seems that, regardless, both infants displayed developmental trends in the number of onsets during the first 2 minutes, trends that are consistent with the affective-tolerance model.

SUMMARY

This chapter reviewed a number of theoretical and descriptive accounts of affect dynamics in adults and in infants. As a result of this review, an attempt was made to build a model of the development of affect sequences during early mother–infant face-to-face interaction. The model predicted systematic developmental shifts in the time of occurrence of affect expres-

TABLE 2.4
Trill Patterns for H.

Age (Days)	Type of Trill	Number of Trills	Number of Smiles or Laughs per Trill	Number of Lone Smiles or Laughs	Total Number of Smiles and Laughs
25		0	0	0	0
31		0	0	0	0
40		0	0	0	0
46		0	0	1	1
60		0	0	14	14
67		0	0	0	0
74		0	0	0	0
80		0	0	5	5
87		0	0	5	5
108		0	0	13	13
111		0	0	7	7
116		0	0	4	4
132	smile-rest	1	2	2	4
164	smile-mouthing	5	4	8	28
178	smile-rest	1	2	4	6
188		0	0	15	15

TABLE 2.5
Kendall Correlations of Trill Measures with Age

Measure	Infant J. (N = 22)	Infant H. (N = 16)
Number of trills	.55[a]	.47[b]
Number of smiles or laughs per trill	.57[a]	.47[b]
Number of lone smiles and laughs	.23	.46[b]

[a] $p < .001$.
[b] $p < .01$.

sions during interaction. In particular, the model predicted that there would be an initial phase of high-intensity affect characterized by infant smiles and gazes at the mother immediately at the beginning of an interaction. This would be followed by a period of withdrawal from the interaction due to the infant's inability to regulate the high arousal intensity. This high-intensity phase in the development of face-to-face interaction was hypothesized to develop into a phase in which the infant can better regulate the arousal caused by the mother's presence. In this second phase, the infant's control over the arousal is represented by the presence of tension-release cycles: repeated bouts of smiling and laughter.

These developmental changes can be explained by a theory of affective tolerance. According to this theory, developed by Epstein (1967) and by

GAZE,   0 - 7 WEEKS,LAP

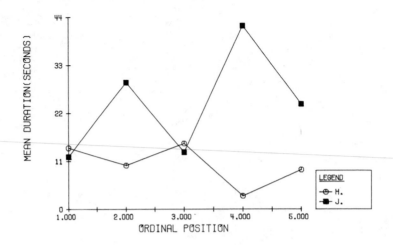

GAZE,   7 - 13 WEEKS,LAP

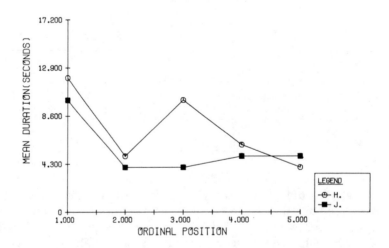

Solomon (1980), individuals who are exposed initially to a highly arousing unconditioned stimulus (usually a species-specific stimulus) eventually come to reduce the intensity of the arousal while at the same time maintaining engagement with the stimulus. This change is thought to occur by means of the development of a psychophysiological tolerance for the arousal, accompanied by the development of an "addiction" to the unconditioned

GAZE, 13 - 27 WEEKS,LAP

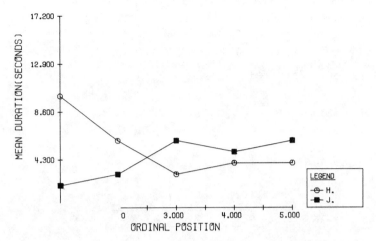

FIG. 2.7   Mean duration of gaze as a function of the ordinal position of the gaze episode for the lap interactions.

stimulus. This affective-based process is different from learning, in which the individual associates the original emotional response to a conditioned stimulus or in which behavior is shaped by an outside reinforcing agent. In the case of affective tolerance, there are changes in the quantity and quality of the affective response to the UCS.

Although this chapter explored the idea of affective tolerance as it relates to early face-to-face interaction, the addiction process that is thought to accompany the tolerance process was not systematically explored. In addition, theory directs attention to elapsed-time processes that have been ignored in past research on early interaction. Measures of behavior as a function of time may yield more valid measures of individual characteristics of infants than have been obtainable in the past. Explorations of real-time dependencies may provide a clearer link between affective development and the development of the infant's attachment to others.

ACKNOWLEDGMENTS

This study was funded, in part, by a grant from the National Science Foundation (BNS-77-14524). I would like to thank Virginia Demos, Tiffany Field, Kenneth Kaye, and Daniel Stern for their comments and suggestions on earlier versions of this chapter.

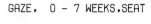

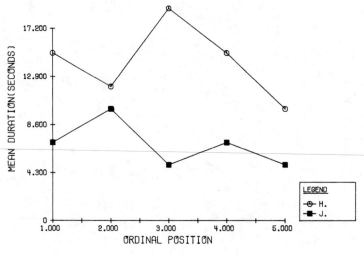

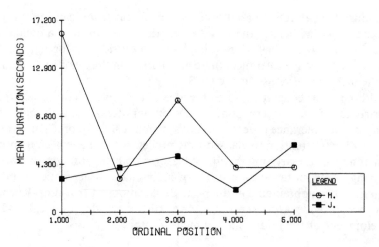

FIG. 2.8   Mean duration of gaze as a function of the ordinal position of the gaze episode for the seat interactions.

REFERENCES

Ainsworth, M., Blehar, M., Waters, E., & Wall, S. *Patterns of attachment.* Hillsdale, N.J.: Lawrence Erlbaum Associates, 1978.

Arnold, M. *Emotion and personality.* New York: Columbia University Press, 1960.

Brazelton, T. B., Koslowski, B., & Main, M. The origins of reciprocity. In M. Lewis, & L. Rosenblum (Eds.), *The effect of the infant on its caregiver.* New York: Wiley, 1974.

Bridges, K. M. B. A study of social development in early infancy. *Child Development,* 1933, *40,* 36–49.

Charlesworth, W., & Kreutzer, M. Facial expressions of infants and children. In P. Ekman (Ed.), *Darwin and facial expression.* New York: Academic Press, 1973.

Clarke-Stewart, A. Interactions between mothers and their young infants: Characteristics and consequences. *Monographs of the Society for Research in Child Developoment* (Serial No. 153), 1973.

Darwin, C. *The expression of the emotions in man and animals.* New York: Appleton, 1872.

Douglas, J., & Tweed, R. Analyzing the patterning of a sequence of discrete behavioral events. *Animal Behavior,* 1979, *27,* 1236–1252.

Ekman, P., Friesen, W., & Ellsworth, P. *Emotion in the human face.* New York: Pergamon Press, 1972.

Emde, R. N., Gaensbauer, T. J., & Harmon, R. J. Emotional expression in infancy. *Psychological Issues,* 1976, *10*(1), Monograph 37.

Epstein, S. Towards a unified theory of anxiety. In B. Maher (Ed.), *Progress in experimental research* (Vol. 4). New York: Academic Press, 1967.

Field, T. Effects of early separation, interactive deficits and experimental manipulations on infant–mother face-to-face interaction. *Child Development,* 1977, *48,* 763–771.

Field, T. Visual and cardiac responses to animate and inanimate faces by young term and preterm infants. *Child Development,* 1979, *50*(1), 188–194.

Field, T. Interactions of high risk infants: Quantitative and qualitative differences. In D. Sawin, R. Hawkins, I. Walker, & J. Penticuff (Eds.), *Current perspectives on psychosocial risks during pregnancy and early infancy.* New York: Brunner/Mazel, 1980.

Field, T. Gaze behavior of normal and high-risk infants during early interactions. *Journal of the American Academy of Child Psychiatry,* 1981, *20,* 308–317.

Fogel, A. Temporal organization in mother–infant, face-to-face interaction. In H. R. Schaffer (Ed.), *Studies in mother–infant interaction.* London: Academic Press, 1977.

Fogel, A. Peer vs. mother directed behavior in 1- to 3-month-old infants. *Infant Behavior and Development,* 1979, *2,* 215–226.

Fogel, A. The effect of brief separations on two-month-old infants. *Infant Behavior and Development,* 1980, *3,* 315–330.

Fogel, A. The ontogeny of gestural communication: The first six months. In R. Stark (Ed.), *Language behavior in infancy and early childhood.* New York: Elsevier, 1981.

Fogel, A. Early adult–infant face-to-face interaction: Expectable sequences of behavior. *Journal of Pediatric Psychology,* in press.

Fogel, A., Diamond, G., Langhorst, B., & Demos, V. Affective and cognitive aspects of the 2-month-olds' participation in face-to-face interaction with its mother. In E. Tronick (Ed.), *Joint regulation of behavior,* Baltimore: University Park Press, 1981.

Fogel, A., Hannan, T., & Demos, V. Infant's responses to "still-face" interruption: A replication and clarification of recent findings. In preparation.

Hollander, M., & Wolfe, D. *Non-parametric statistical methods.* New York: Wiley, 1973.

Izard, C. *The face of emotion.* New York: Appleton-Century-Crofts, 1971.

James, W. *Principles of psychology.* New York: Henry Holt, 1890.

Kaye, K. The development of skills. In G. Whitehurst, & B. Zimmerman (Eds.), *The functions of language and cognition.* New York: Academic Press, 1980.

Kaye, K., & Fogel, A. The temporal structure of face-to-face communication between mothers and infants. *Developmental Psychology,* 1980, *16,* 454–464.

Krupat, E. Context as a determinant of perceived threat: The role of prior experience. *Journal of Personality and Social Psychology,* 1974, *29,* 731–736.

LaBarbera, J., & Caul, W. An opponent-process interpretation of postshock bursts in appetetive responding. *Animal Learning and Behavior,* 1976, *4,* 386–390.

Mahler, M., Pine, F., & Bergman, A. The psychological birth of the human infant. New York: Basic Books, 1975.

Masters, J., Barden, C., & Ford, M. Affective states, expressive behavior, and learning in children. *Journal of Personality and Social Psychology,* 1979, *37,* 380–390.

Messick, S. The impact of negative affect on cognition and personality. In S. Tomkins, & C. Izard (Eds.), *Affect, cognition and personality.* New York: Springer, 1965.

Nowlis, V. Research with the mood adjective check list. In S. Tomkins, & C. Izard (Eds.), *Affect, cognition and personality.* New York: Springer, 1965.

Oster, H. Facial expression and affect development. In M. Lewis, & L. Rosenblum (Eds.), *The development of affect.* New York: Plenum Press, 1978.

Robson, K. The role of eye-to-eye contact in maternal–infant attachment. *Journal of Child Psychology and Psychiatry,* 1967, *8,* 13–25.

Sackett, G. The lag sequential analysis of contingency and cyclicity in behavioral interaction research. In J. Osofsky (Ed.), *Handbook of infant development.* New York: Wiley, 1979.

Schacter, S., & Singer, J. Cognitive, social and physiological determinants of emotional state. *Psychological Review,* 1962, *69,* 379–399.

Solomon, R. The opponent-process theory of acquired motivation: The costs of pleasure and the benefits of pain. *American Psychologist,* 1980, *35,* 691–712.

Solomon, R., & Corbit, J. An opponent-process theory of motivation: I. Temporal dynamics of affect. *Psychological Review,* 1974, *81,* 119–145.

Spitz, R. *The first year of life.* New York: International University Press, 1965.

Sroufe, L. A. Socioemotional development. In J. Osofsky (Ed.), *Handbook of infant development.* New York: Wiley, 1979.

Sroufe, L. A., & Waters, E. The ontogenesis of smiling and laughter. *Psychological Review,* 1976, *83*(3), 173–189.

Stern, D. Mother and infant at play: The dyadic interaction involving facial, vocal and gaze behaviors. In M. Lewis, & L. Rosenblum (Eds.), *The effect of the infant on its caregiver.* New York: Wiley, 1974.

Tomkins, S. *Affect, imagery and consciousness* (Vol. 1). New York: Springer, 1962.

Tronick, E., Als, H., Adamson, L., Weise, S., & Brazelton, T. B. The infant's response to entrapment between contradictory messages in face-to-face interaction. *Journal of Child Psychiatry,* 1978, *17,* 1–13.

Wessman, A., & Ricks, D. *Mood and personality.* New York: Holt, Rinehart & Winston, 1966.

White, R. W. Ego and reality in psychoanalytic theory. *Psychological Issues,* 1963, *3*(3), Monograph II.

Winnicott, D. *Playing and reality.* New York: Basic Books, 1971.

Young, P. *Motivation and emotion.* New York: Wiley, 1961.

3 Alteration of Mother and Infant Behavior and Heart Rate during a Still-Face Perturbation of Face-to-Face Interaction

Sherilyn Adler Stoller
Tiffany Field
University of Miami Medical School

During face-to-face interactions with their mothers, infants as young as 2 months old discriminate and respond to subtle changes in maternal facial expressions (Brazelton, Koslowski, & Main, 1974; Field, 1979a; Fogel, Diamond, Langhorst, & Demos, 1981; Stern, 1974; Trevarthen, 1977; Tronick, Als, Adamson, Wise, & Brazelton, 1978). During spontaneous face-to-face interactions, both the mother and her infant appear to modify their responses and actions according to the feedback each receives from the other. To better understand these processes, mother–infant interactions have been manipulated by modifying the mother's behavior and observing the effects of these modifications on the infant and on the mother–infant interaction. These manipulations have included asking the mother to imitate, to remain still faced, and to keep her infant's attention (Brazelton, Tronick, Adamson, Als, & Wise, 1975; Field, 1977, 1979a; Fogel et al., 1981; Trevarthen, 1977; Tronick et al., 1978). During interactions in which mothers were instructed to imitate their infants, normal and high-risk infants spent more time gazing at their mothers (Field, 1977). Field (1977) suggested that increased infant attentiveness may relate to mothers being less active and more attentive to their infants' gaze signals and behaviors during the imitation manipulation. In another manipulation, in which the mothers were asked to keep their infants' attention, the mothers became more active and the infants less attentive. The high levels of stimulation and the infants' inability to "get a word in edgewise" in this manipulation may have contributed to the infants' gaze-averting behaviors (Field, 1977).

One of the most frequent manipulations of mother behavior during early interactions is the "still-face" paradigm (Brazelton et al., 1975; Field,

1981b; Fogel et al., 1981; Trevarthen, 1977; Tronick et al., 1978). During this procedure, the mother is asked to remain silent while looking at her infant with a "still" face expression. The silent, still face of the mother appears to have an immediate and predictable effect upon the infant from a very early age (Tronick et al., 1978). The infant repeatedly looks "inquisitively" at the mother as if recognizing that the mother is not behaving "naturally." In addition, the infant vocalizes and reaches out to her as if attempting to elicit a response from her. However, after numerous unsuccessful attempts to obtain a reaction from the mother, the infant gaze averts and shows signs of wariness and withdrawal (Fogel et al., 1981). The intensity of the infant's distress may be related to the duration of the period of still-face behavior such that as the time spent in the still-face posture increases, the distress of the infant also increases (Field, 1981b). In addition, the infant continues to behave differently with the mother even after the still-face situation has ceased and the mother has returned to behaving "naturally" (Fogel et al., 1981).

Some investigators have suggested that the still-face posture is upsetting to infants because it is a violation of expectancy (Aronson & Rosenbloom, 1971; Sroufe, 1979). This view assumes that the infant has learned that looking at the mother will result in the mother's reacting in a certain fashion. When the infant receives a distorted response from the mother, this violates the infant's expectations and may lead to a state of disequilibrium. Within a Piagetian framework, the infant is unable to assimilate the discrepant event.

Even though the experimental manipulations of face-to-face interactions usually result in increased attentiveness and apparent positive affect of the infant (e.g., during imitation) or decreased attentiveness and apparent negative affect (e.g., during attention getting or still face), the effect of these depends very much on the mother's baseline behavior. For this reason, it is imperative to code the mother's behaviors as well. For example, Field (1981c) found that the typically distressing attention-getting manipulation was effective in enhancing infant attentiveness in the case of interactions involving mothers who were normally very inactive (Field, 1981c) Similarly, Brazelton (1980) has noted that the still-face manipulation is effective in enhancing infant attentiveness to a mother who is normally overactive.

Because infant attentiveness is only part of the dyadic relationship, many researchers have recently investigated the infant's affective responses occurring during the still-face situation. Although very little is known about the infant's affective experience because the infant cannot verbalize feelings, some have posited the existence of a "basic feeling experience" (Fogel, 1980). Tomkins (1962) refers to this experience as "fluctuations of stimulation" whereas Mandler (1975) speaks of "arousal," Sroufe (1979) talks about "tension release," and Field (1981a) labels the experience "activation." Tomkins (1962), Mandler (1975), Sroufe (1979), and Field (1981a) associate the emotions displayed by the infant as reflective of changes in the infant's level of arousal and/or stimulation.

A comprehensive theoretical model of infant emotion was developed by Sroufe and his colleagues (Sroufe, 1979; Sroufe & Waters, 1976). They postulate a tension-release experience involving psychophysiological processes and infant affect. This model has been schematically illustrated in several papers as an excitation–relaxation cycle, showing a hypothetical threshold and relationship to overt behaviors. (See Fig. 3.1.) They associate increasing tension with an infant's increasing attention to a stimulus in an

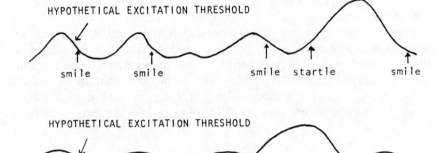

FIG. 3.1 Schematic illustration of the excitation–relaxation cycle, showing hypothetical threshold and relationship to overt behaviors. (Adapted from Sroufe & Waters, 1976.)

effort to process stimulus content. Orienting behaviors occur because they are an integral component of the attending process. Orienting responses are accompanied by heart-rate deceleration (Graham & Clifton, 1966). Kagan (1978) postulates that this behavioral quieting of the infant reflects an increase in cognitive activity with associated feelings of increased tension.

At this point, the infant can do one of two things. The first possibility is that the infant will assimilate the event and experience a pleasurable decrease in tension characterized by smiling and laughter (Sroufe, Waters, & Matas, 1974; Tomkins, 1962). Although the theory postulates tension decrease during smiling, there have been conflicting reports of associated heart-rate activity. Emde, Campos, Reich, and Gaensbauer (1978) report heart-rate acceleration during smiling whereas Sroufe and Waters (1976) found that smiling is accompanied by heart-rate deceleration. These discrepancies may relate to the measurement of heart rate at different points in the tension curve (i.e., at the onset or at the peak of smiling activity).

An alternative possibility is that the infant is unable to assimilate the new event. In this case, the tension continues to increase until it reaches an intolerable state at which point the infant becomes distressed as manifested by gaze aversion, fussiness, and crying. Distress behaviors seem to be accompanied by heart-rate acceleration (Emde et al., 1978; Field, 1981b; Vaughan & Sroufe, 1979; Waters, Matas, & Sroufe, 1975).

Brazelton et al. (1974) provide clinical descriptions of the emotional state of the infant during distress-free face-to-face interaction. These descriptions concur with the Sroufe and Waters model of tension fluctuations (1976). Brazelton et al. (1974) observed that the infant's level of excitement gradually increases after initially orienting to the mother. The peak of excitement culminates with a smile, after which the infant looks away from the mother. The cycle is presumed to be repetitive in the course of distress-free interaction.

Fogel and his colleagues (1981) assessed Sroufe's tension-release model utilizing the still-face paradigm. They fit a hypothetical tension function to the behavioral changes observed during naturally occurring face-to-face interaction (Fogel et al., 1981). (See Fig. 3.2.) They state that on the tension curve, points A and E are equivalent, both representing disengagement from the mother or low tension. Point C represents the peak of tension

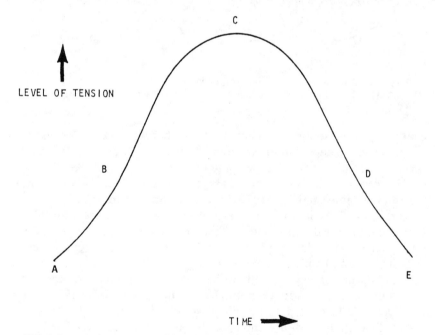

FIG. 3.2   Function corresponding to hypothesized changes in tension during face-to-face interaction. (From Fogel et al., 1981.)

when the infant appears the most active or involved. *B* corresponds to increasing tension during initial orienting and *D* reflects the decrease in tension due to smiling. Each of the points *A* through *D* is hypothesized to represent a different emotional experience for the infant (Fogel et al., 1981). Fogel et al. hypothesized that infants would respond to the still face differently if they were at point *B* rather than at point *D* on the tension curve. Infants who were just beginning to look at their mothers were thought to be attempting to assimilate the event: Their excitement at the expectations aroused by seeing this familiar person would be increasing. The authors suggested that if the mothers turned silent at this point, the infants would become disoriented and distressed. On the other hand, infants at point *D* who had just smiled at their mothers should have already assimilated the event and, therefore, the tension would be declining. A silent face at this time may not be as distressing to the infant who may be more prepared to terminate the interaction (Fogel et al., 1981).

Fogel and his colleagues (1981) recorded mother–infant face-to-face interactions using the following procedure: The mother and her infant participate in a natural face-to-face interaction. The mother then leaves the infant alone. When she returns, the mother assumes the still-face posture following either the infant's first look or the infant's first smile. After the still-face condition, there is another natural face-to-face interaction.

Each infant was randomly assigned to one of two groups prior to the session. In the first group, the experimenter signaled the mother to begin the still face as soon as the infant first looked at her and in the second group, after the infant's first smile. Fogel and his associates (1981) postulated that the infant's first look at the mother would be accompanied by increasing tension whereas the infant's first smile would represent decreasing tension. Fogel et al. (1981) confirmed that when the still face was presented following the infant's first look, there was significantly more gaze averting and distress behaviors than when the still face followed the first smile.

An alternative interpretation of the same data raised by Field's (1981a) model of activation and varying thresholds is that smiling occurs at high levels of activation (arousal) as manifested by physical movement and frequently ensuing laughter, and looking is characterized by low arousal levels (e.g., quiescence and cardiac deceleration) (Field, 1981a; Graham & Clifton, 1966). If the mother assumes the still-face posture at a point when the infant is at a low level of arousal (i.e., looking), she may contribute to nonoptimally low levels of activation, which lead to distress. However, if the mother ceases her stimulation at a point when the infant is already aroused (smiling), the infant might be more receptive to a "break in the interaction" and not be distressed (Field, 1981a).

Within mother–infant face-to-face interactions, the infant's behaviors of smiling and gaze averting may well play a key role in the modulation of arousal (Brazelton et al., 1974; Field, 1981a; Waters et al., 1975). Smiling has been proposed as the product of an "arousal jag" in which cortically mediated tension increases and recovers rapidly (Berlyne, 1969; Sroufe & Waters, 1976). Field (1979b) found that infants fixated the inanimate face of a Raggedy Ann doll for longer periods of time than they did the animated faces of their mothers. These results were interpreted as follows: The rapidly changing facial expressions of the mothers might place greater demands on the infants' information-processing and arousal-modulation abilities, causing the infants to gaze avert more often (Field, 1978). Although direct evidence is lacking for high arousal levels leading to gaze aversion, several investigators have reported a relationship between elevated heart rate and the looking-away associated with arousing face-to-face situations (Ellsworth & Ludwig, 1972; Field, 1981b; Vaughn & Sroufe, 1979).

Heart-rate activity provides an index of internal changes associated with gaze aversion (Field, 1981b; Waters et al., 1975), crying (Vaughn & Sroufe, 1979), smiling (Sroufe et al., 1974; Sroufe & Waters, 1977), and some facial expressions such as joy and interest (accompanied by deceleration) and anger and distress (accompanied by acceleration) (Provost & Govin-Decarie, 1979). Although we do not yet understand the functional relationships between affective behaviors and heart-rate changes, there appear to be temporal relationships between these.

The purpose of the present study was to investigate the functional relationships between infant affective behavior and heart rate during spontaneous and still-face interaction situations. The study was designed as an attempted replication of the study by Fogel et al., (1981). In addition, the study was to provide information about the internal physiological changes (indexed by heart rate) that accompany affective behavior and to identify possible relationships between these.

METHOD

Subjects

The subjects were 46 full-term, white, middle SES infants and their mothers. At the time of testing, 23 of the infants were 8 weeks of age and 23 were 12 weeks of age. Each mother–infant dyad was randomly assigned to one of the three experimental groups, and each group was balanced for the sex of the infant. The mean maternal age was 31 years. Both maternal age and parity were evenly distributed.

Procedure

Recording of behaviors.   The laboratory was set up to videotape face-to-face interaction between a mother and her infant. The infant was positioned in an upright infant seat placed on a table at eye level with the mother who was seated approximately 18 inches (46 cm) away facing the infant. The room was equipped with two Sony video cameras, one positioned to film the mother's face and torso and the other to film the entire body of the infant. The cameras were positioned 6 feet (1.8 meters) from the mother and infant at an angle such that they were in the periphery of the subjects' visual fields as well as partially obscured by surrounding curtains. The pictures from the two cameras were split-screen recorded on one tape using a special-effects generator. A digital time clock was used to generate a time (seconds) signal on the videotape.

Heart rate was recorded simultaneously for both the mother and her infant via Narco telemetry. The two electrodes required for each subject were attached, one to the sternum and one to the left lateral costal margin, with the necessary transmitters pocketed in a small cloth bag and worn like a necklace. Heart rate was recorded for 10 seconds prior to the first interaction sequence to provide a baseline measure and continued throughout the duration of the other four conditions. Heart rate was averaged separately for each of the manipulated situations for comparison with presituation (resting) heart rate. A signal spike was registered on the heart-rate tape at second zero of the videotape in order to synchronize the behavioral and heart-rate records for second-by-second analyses.

Interaction situations.   Each of the 46 infants was exposed to four experimental conditions: (1) *spontaneous I:* face-to-face interaction for 1.5 minutes; (2) *separation:* the mother goes behind interaction curtain leaving the infant alone for 1 minute; (3) *still face:* mother reenters and assumes still-face posture for 45 seconds; and (4) *spontaneous II:* mother resumes normal face-to-face interaction for 1.5 minutes. In condition (3), the mother was instructed to perform the still face upon reentering the interaction area when she heard a knocking sound made on the one-way mirror by the experimenter who was monitoring the videorecorder.

Prior to the taping session, each infant was assigned to one of two groups. In the first group (hypothesized to represent increasing tension), the experimenter knocked just after the infant first *looked* at the mother. The second group was comprised of infants for whom the experimenter knocked just after the first *smile.* Decreasing tension was assumed to be manifested in infant smiling.

If an infant was assigned to the smile group but failed to smile within 20 seconds of the mother's returning to the interaction area, the experimenter knocked the next time the infant looked at the mother. These infants comprised a third group.

Although this group was not included in the study conducted by Fogel et al. (1981), it was introduced as a control for the presumed differences between the "first-look" and "first-smile" groups on interaction time accrued prior to the still face. We anticipated that the first-smile group may experience a longer interaction prior to their first smile than the first-look group would experience prior to their first look. If time lapse until the infant's first smile is not comparable to time lapse until the infant's first look, one is not able to compare the two groups without some concern that it may be the time lapse per se and not the smile–look distinction that is causing differences in the infants' reactions to the still-face condition.

Behaviors coded. The infant behaviors that were coded from the videotapes are similar to those behaviors coded by Fogel et al. (1981). Our behavioral categories included gaze away from mother, distress brow, smile, cry, yawn, and motor movement. In addition to the six preceding categories, infant vocalization was also examined. (For operational definitions of categories, refer to Table 3.1.)

TABLE 3.1
Infant Behaviors

1. Gaze away	Turning of eyes and/or head to one side or the other at an angle of at least 30°
2. Smile	Corners of mouth upturned
3. Distress brow	Furrowed brow and inner corners of eyebrows upturned
4. Cry	Wailing sounds
5. Vocalization	Any sound excluding crying
6. Motor movement	Any movement of the arms and/or legs (including flexing, waving, shaking, kicking, bouncing, etc.)
7. Yawn	An intake of breath through the wide open mouth (not associated with crying).

Fogel et al. (1981) found a "carry-over effect" from the still-face procedure that appeared to alter the infant's behavior towards the mother even after she had resumed contingent responding (spontaneous II). They assumed that after the still-face condition, the mothers exhibited the same amount and types of behavior as they had during the first spontaneous interaction. However, it is quite conceivable (and perhaps probable) that the mothers would change their behavior during the final interaction situation (spontaneous II) after having observed the distress of their infants during the still-face condition (Fogel et al., 1981). For this reason, in the present study, maternal behaviors were also recorded. These included smile, tactile stimulation, kinesthetic stimulation, vocalization, and exaggerated facial expression. Several of these categories have been coded in mother–infant interaction studies (Field, 1977; Tronick et al., 1978). (Operational definitions can be found in Table 3.2.)

The videotapes were coded using a Texas Instrument Datachron 1790 for

TABLE 3.2
Mother Behaviors

1. Smile	Corners of mouth upturned
2. Facial expression	Exaggerated facial movements including: widening of the eyes, opening of the mouth, tongue protrusion, raising the eyebrows, and so on
3. Tactile stimulation	Physical contact including: patting, stroking, kissing, rubbing noses, holding hands, or adjusting position of the infant
4. Kinesthetic stimulation	Active "in and out" manipulation of infants' extremities including activities such as pat-a-cake
5. Vocalization	Talking, singing, or other sounds

duration of behaviors exhibited by the mothers and their infants. For the 15 seconds of behavioral analysis that corresponded to the period of heart rate studied, an event recorder was used to provide second × second output that preserved frequencies, duration, and sequences of infant behavior. Coders naive to the hypotheses were trained to greater than 80% reliability. Interobserver reliabilities were calculated by the number of agreements divided by the number of agreements plus disagreements, and are reported in Table 3.3.

All heart-rate data recorded using Narco telemetry were transmitted to disk storage on a MODCOMP II 32K minicomputer for data reduction and statistical analyses.

Analyses. A 2 (age group) × 3 (condition: first look, first smile, or late look) × 3 (interaction situation: spontaneous, still face, resumption) repeated measures MANOVA was performed on the behavioral measures with the interaction situation as the repeated measure. Following the MANOVA on multivariate dependent measures, univariate analyses were performed on each of these measures. A number of analyses were performed on heart rate including:

1. Tonic heart rate or the heart rate averaged over the interaction situations as compared to the average baseline heart rate (Field, 1981b). Analysis of tonic heart rate provides an index of the average physiological state of the infant during the conditions, with elevated situation heart rate (as compared to baseline heart rate) suggesting an aroused state and diminished, average levels of heart rate reflecting an attentive state.

2. Heart rate was retrieved for 5 seconds prior to and 10 seconds post the onset of the still-face situation. Trend analyses were conducted on these periods of heart rate (Field, 1981b) to determine phasic or directional heart-rate changes accompanying a sudden perturbation of the mother's behavior (still face) and the attentive and affective behaviors (smiling) of the infant.

TABLE 3.3

Mean Proportion of Interaction Time Infant and Mother Behaviors Exhibited during Spontaneous, Still-Face and Resumed Interaction Conditions (Interobserver Reliabilities)

BEHAVIORS	Spontaneous Baseline GROUPS			Still Face GROUPS			Spontaneous Resumption GROUPS		
	First Look	Late Look	First Smile	First Look	Late Look	First Smile	First Look	Late Look	First Smile
Infant gaze away (.93)	38.6	39.2	34.9	50.6	53.0	59.0	39.6	38.5	36.9
Infant smile (.99)	7.5	7.3	9.4	4.5	.3	4.3	3.8	3.7	8.1
Infant cry (.99)	1.4	.3	2.3	3.2	9.1	.3	6.3	13.1	5.8
Infant vocalization (.99)	3.8	3.8	7.5	7.3	12.4	6.1	8.9	6.7	6.4
Infant motor movements (.95)	18.8	10.6	14.3	25.1	32.6	29.4	14.9	22.7	22.1
Infant yawn (.99)	.2	.7	.8	.3	1.1	.0	.7	.5	.4
Infant distress brow (.96)	12.1	2.3	7.6	14.8	15.7	10.9	15.4	4.7	9.1
Mother smile (.92)	21.8	31.3	34.1	—	—	—	23.1	26.6	33.1
Mother face expression (.89)	10.8	8.6	7.9	—	—	—	13.1	8.3	9.1
Mother tactile (.92)	66.5	66.7	50.6	—	—	—	65.4	62.8	56.1
Mother kinesthetic (.99)	4.6	11.3	13.2	—	—	—	3.9	9.8	13.3
Mother vocalizations (.95)	52.3	54.1	57.1	—	—	—	53.9	54.5	55.7

RESULTS

For each of the seven infant behaviors and five mother behaviors, the proportion of interaction time the behavior occurred was derived by dividing the total duration of the behavior by the duration of the interaction condition. These proportions were then entered into multivariate analyses of variance and univariate analyses of variance, and post-hoc comparisons were made by Bonferroni t tests (Myers, 1972).

Prior to these analyses the data were examined for sex and age differences. A Hotelling's T^2 test on the multivariate data, using sex as an independent measure, failed to yield a significant T^2 value. Univariate t tests revealed only two significant sex differences. Girls showed more distress-brow behavior, $t(1,45) = 2.23$, $p < .05$, and more crying, $t(1,45) = 2.39$, $p < .05$, than boys during the still-face condition. Analyses of the data for age differences also yielded a nonsignificant Hotelling's T^2 and only a few significant differences on univariate t tests. During the spontaneous condition, the younger infants (8-week-old infants) exhibited more frequent motor movement, $t(1,45) = 2.69$, $p < .01$, and more distress-brow behavior, $t(1,45) = 2.80$, $p < .01$, than did the older infants (12-week-old infants). In addition, the mothers rated their younger infants as having more negative "mood" (one of the nine dimensions on the Carey Infant Temperament Scale) than the older infants, $t(1,45) = 2.79$, $p < .01$.

Because the multivariate t tests failed to yield significant sex and age differences and only a few significant differences emerged in the univariate tests, and in order to maximize the degrees of freedom available for group comparisons, the data for the different sex and age groups were combined for the remaining analyses.

Comparisons of First-Look and First-Smile Group

Comparisons were made between the first-look and first-smile groups in accordance with our attempt to replicate the Fogel et al. (1981) study. The comparisons were made by multivariate and univariate analyses of variance, and post hoc comparisons were made by Bonferroni t tests. Analyses of the demographic data (parity, mother's age, and educational level) and the Carey Infant Temperament Scale (Carey, 1970) scores failed to reveal any differences between these groups.

A 2 (group) × 3 (interaction condition) repeated-measures analysis of variance with interaction condition as the repeated measure yielded a number of significant differences. Although there were no differences between the behaviors of the infants during the baseline interaction condition (spontaneous interaction), the mothers of first-look infants differed from the mothers of first-smile infants (see Table 3.3 for means.) First-smile mothers smiled significantly more frequently than first-look mothers during the spontaneous interaction, $F(1,30) = 4.52$, $p < .05$, and they provided more frequent kinesthetic stimulation than first-look mothers during the spontaneous, baseline interaction, $F(1,30) = 5.17$, $p < .05$. These were the only main effects for the group variable.

Main effects for the repeated measure, interaction condition, suggested that during the still face as opposed to the initial and resumption spontaneous conditions, infants of both groups gaze averted a greater proportion of the time, $F(2,30) = 6.29$, $p < .05$, engaged in more frequent motor movements, $F(2,30) = 20.71$, $p < .001$, and exhibited less frequent smiling, $F(2,30) = 4.49$, $p < .05$.

Although group × condition interaction effects failed to reach the .05 level of significance, they are indicative of trends that lend support to the hypothesized variability of behavior of the first-look and first-smile infants during the still-face condition. First-look infants showed less frequent motor movements, $F(2,30 = 3.40$, $p = .08$, but vocalized more frequently, $F(2,30) = 2.72$, $p = .11$, and cried more frequently, $F(2,30) = 2.77$, $p = .11$, than first-smile infants during the still-face condition. First-look infants continued to show less frequent motor movements, $F(2,30) = 8.84$, $p < .01$, and to vocalize more frequently, $F(2,30) = 3.50$, $p = .07$, than first-smile infants during the subsequent resumption condition (the second spontaneous interaction).

The more frequent vocalizations of the first-look infants may represent their attempts to reinstate a normal interaction with the mother, and the more frequent crying may reflect their distress at the mother's remaining still faced despite those attempts. The infant who is looking at the mother when she adopts a still face may make more attempts (vocalizations) to reengage the mother or reinstate an interaction and may be more distressed by her still-face behavior than the infant who is smiling at her when she becomes still faced. The smile of that infant may signify closure to a round of interaction and an associated decrease in the arousal level of the infant, whereas the infant who is looking at the mother may be anticipating a response and when it is not forthcoming may experience an associated increase in arousal.

Comparisons of Late-Look and First-Smile Group

A third group of infants, the late-look group, was originally included to control for the presumed variability in interaction time preceding the first look and the first smile for the infants of those groups. The infants of those groups in the Fogel et al. (1981) study may have differed because the first-smile infants experienced more interaction time prior to their first smile and their mothers' assuming a still face. Surprisingly, the first-look and first-smile groups of this study experienced similar amounts of interaction time (9 seconds and 8 seconds, respectively), whereas the late-look and first-smile infants experienced very different durations of interaction time prior to the onset of their mothers' still face (33 seconds and 8 seconds, respectively). Nonetheless, comparisons were made between the late-look group and the first-smile group. Although the rationale for these comparisons was no longer that of providing a control for interaction time differences, we were concerned now about a different confound, that of the behavior differences between mothers of the first-look and first-smile groups as previously described.

Fortunately, a 2 (group) × 3 (interaction condition) repeated-measures analysis of variance with the interaction condition as the repeated measure yielded no significant differences between the behaviors of the mothers of the late-look and first-smile infants. However, the first-smile infants exhibited more distress-brow behavior than the late-look infants during the baseline spontaneous interaction, $t(1,21) = 2.21$, $p < .05$. Because more distress-brow behavior was predicted for late-look infants during the still-face condition, we considered that this baseline difference, showing more distress brow in the infants of the first-smile group, provided a more conservative test of our hypothesis. If first-smile infants showed more distress brow initially, but late-look infants showed more distress-brow behavior during the still-face condition, that condition would appear to be considerably more distressing for the late-look infants in order to exceed the greater frequency of distress brow observed initially in the first-smile infants.

The main effects noted for conditions included less frequent smiling, $F(2,29) = 9.06$, $p < .005$, more frequent gaze aversion, $F(2,29) = 7.43$, $p < .01$, more frequent motor movements $F(2,29) = 27.79$, $p < .001$, and more frequent distress brow, $F(2,29) = 7.58$, $p < .01$, for both groups during the still-face condition as compared to the initial spontaneous interaction. During the resumption interaction, there was more frequent motor movement, $F(2,29) = 11.55$, $p < .005$, and more frequent crying, $F(2,29) = 4.24$, $p < .05$, than during the initial spontaneous interaction.

Group × condition interaction effects suggested that the late-look infants vocalized more frequently, $F(1,29) = 6.87$, $p < .01$, and cried more frequently, $F(1,29) = 6.83$, $p < .01$, than the first-smile infants during the still-face condition. In addition, an interaction effect for the distress-brow behavior, although failing to reach the .05 significance level, $F(1,29) = 2.76$, $p = .11$, suggested a trend, with the late-look infants showing more frequent distress brow than the first-smile infants during the still-face condition despite the first-smile infants having shown more distress brow in the initial spontaneous condition.

Again, as in the earlier comparisons between first-look and first-smile infants, those infants who were looking at their mothers (in this case, the late-look group) appeared to make more frequent attempts to reengage their mothers (vocalizations) and were more distressed (more frequent crying) than those infants who were smiling at their mothers when they assumed still faces.

Heart-Rate Analyses

Heart-rate analyses were conducted on the 15-second period that corresponded to the 5 seconds prior to the initiation of still face and the subsequent 10 seconds of still-face interaction. The 5 seconds of baseline heart rate preceding the still face were also compared to the heart rate averaged over the entire still-face condition in order to obtain a measure of tonic heart-rate change (Field, 1981b).

An analysis of the change in beats per minute from the 5 seconds of heart rate prior to the onset of the still face and the 45 seconds postonset revealed no significant change in tonic heart-rate level from baseline to the still-face situation for any group. The mean baseline heart rate for first-look, late-look, and first-smile infants did not differ (153, 158, and 151, respectively) and mean tonic heart rate for the three groups during the still face did not differ (151, 160, 152, respectively).

The mean heart rates for the three groups during the 5 seconds prior to still face and the 10 seconds following the onset of still face are shown in Fig. 3.3. The data points corresponding to -5 through -1 represent 5 seconds of baseline heart rate averaged over subjects within groups prior to the onset of the still face. The data points corresponding to 1 through 10 on the X axis represent the 10 seconds of mean heart rate after the still face was initiated.

As can be seen in Fig. 3.3, the heart rate curves for the three groups are roughly parallel. A 3 (group) $\times$ 15 (seconds) repeated-measures analysis of variance with seconds as the repeated measure, however, yielded a significant group $\times$ seconds interaction effect, $F(28,252) = 1.74$, $p < .05$, suggesting that first-look and first-smile infants exhibited a greater heart-rate deceleration followed by a greater heart-rate acceleration than the late-look group during the first 10 seconds of the still-face situation.

To describe the second-by-second relationships between behaviors and heart-rate changes, we plotted the 15-second heart-rate curve for each group and mapped the corresponding percentage of infants showing the behaviors that were noted as directional changes in heart rate occurred. (See Table 3.4 for percentages and Fig. 3.4, 3.5, and 3.6 for heart-rate curves.) As can be seen in Fig. 3.4, 86% of the first-look infants were looking at their mothers during the first 2 seconds of baseline and heart rate was correspondingly decreasing. In the 2 seconds preceding the onset of the still face, 43% of the

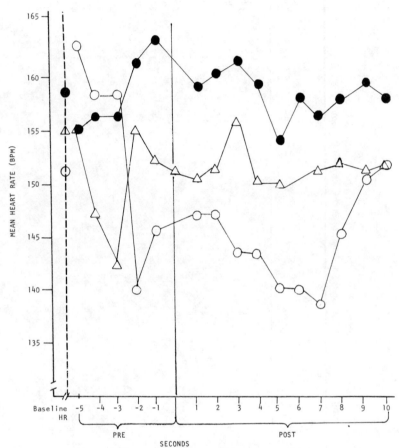

FIG. 3.3 Group comparison of mean heart rate during 5 seconds of pre-still-face interaction and 10 seconds of post onset of still-face interaction.

infants were gazing away with a large deceleration followed by an elevation in heart rate. One second prior to the still face, 86% of the infants looked at their mothers and by 2 seconds following the onset of the still face all infants were looking at their mothers. Also at second 2, 43% of the infants showed a distress brow, and at second 3, 29% smiled, and 43% gazed away as heart rate continued to decelerate for a total of 9 BPM. At second 7 of the still face, 57% of the infants gazed away and 50% were motorically active, which was paralleled by heart-rate acceleration of 11 BPM (seconds 7 to 10).

TABLE 3.4

Percentage of Subjects Exhibiting Target Behaviors during the 5 Seconds Prior to Onset of Still Face and the 10 Seconds Postonset of Still Face (— = 0 Frequency)[a]

Group	Cry			Vocalization			Distress Brow			Smile			Gaze Away			Motor Movement		
	1	2	3	1	2	3	1	2	3	1	2	3	1	2	3	1	2	3
Seconds																		
-5	—	.13	—	—	—	—	—	.13	—	—	—	—	.14	.25	.17	.14	.13	—
-4	—	.25	—	.29	—	—	.29	.25	.33	—	—	—	.14	.38	.33	.29	.38	—
-3	.14	.25	—	—	.25	.17	.14	.25	.17	—	—	.17	.43	.50	.17	.14	.25	—
-2	.14	.25	—	.14	.25	—	.33	.25	.17	—	—	.33	.43	.50	.17	.29	.25	.33
-1	—	—	—	—	—	.17	—	.25	—	—	—	.67	.14	.25	—	.14	.63	—
1	.14	—	—	—	.13	.17	.43	.63	.17	—	—	—	.14	.38	.17	.29	.38	.33
2	.14	.13	—	—	—	—	.43	.13	.17	—	—	.33	—	.63	.33	.14	.50	.50
3	—	.38	—	—	.25	—	.29	.50	.17	.29	—	—	.29	.63	.17	.29	.38	.17
4	.14	.13	—	—	.13	.17	—	.38	.50	.29	—	—	.43	.50	.33	.29	.25	.33
5	—	.38	—	.14	—	.33	—	.63	.50	.29	—	—	.29	.38	.33	.14	.38	.17
6	—	.25	—	—	.25	—	—	.50	.33	.14	—	.33	.43	.38	.17	.29	.50	.33
7	.14	.25	—	.14	.25	.17	—	.38	.17	—	—	—	.57	.50	.33	.43	.50	.50
8	—	.13	—	.14	.38	.33	.14	.25	.50	.29	—	—	.43	.38	.33	.43	.50	.33
9	.14	.13	—	—	.25	.17	.14	.25	.17	.14	—	—	.43	.25	.17	.43	.50	.50
10	—	.13	—	.29	.13	—	—	.25	—	.14	—	—	.43	.50	.17	.14	.38	.17

[a] Group 1 = first look, 2 = late look, 3 = first smile.

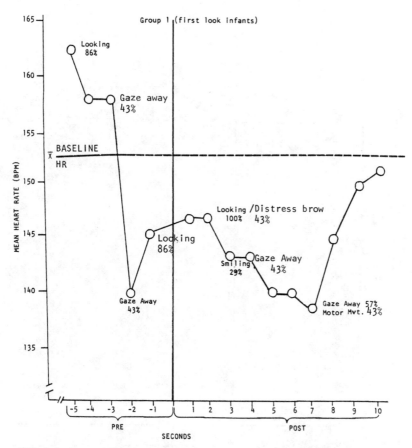

FIG. 3.4   Group 1 (first-look infants) heart-rate curve and corresponding behavioral changes.

For the late-look infants, Fig. 3.5 suggests that heart rate accelerated during baseline as 50% of the late-look infants gazed away from their mothers. Brief looking behavior by 75% of the infants at 1 second before still face paralleled a deceleration of heart rate. Heart rate accelerated, and 63% of the infants showed distress brow at second 1. At second 3, 50% of the infants showed distress brow (accompanied by a 7 BPM deceleration). At second 5 of still face, the behaviors of distress brow, crying, and motor activity occurred and paralleled a heart-rate acceleration of 5 BPM.

As depicted in Fig. 3.6, 83% of first-smile infants looked at their mothers and heart rate decelerated 12 BPM. Motor activity was preceded by a 12-BPM heart-rate acceleration until 1 second before still face when 67% of the first-smile infants smiled. Smiling was accompanied by a gradual car-

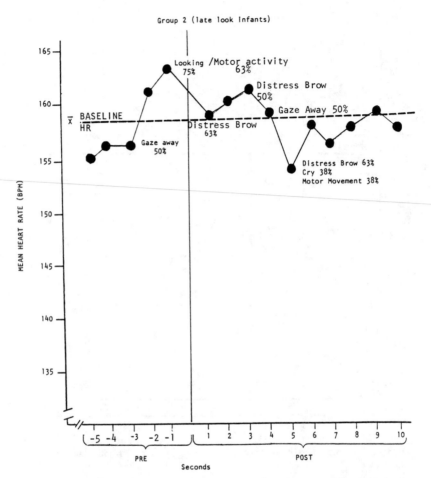

FIG. 3.5   Group 2 (late-look infants) heart-rate curve and corresponding behavioral changes.

diac deceleration. At 3 seconds, motor activity occurred for 50% of the infants; also at second 3, 67% of the infants looked at their mothers, and 50% showed distress brow, which was accompanied by a steep deceleration in heart rate (12 BPM). At second 6, heart rate accelerated and at second 7, 50% of the infants increased their motor activity (total acceleration 7 BPM).

Thus, although the group curves suggest a parallel heart-rate deceleration followed by an acceleration (of greater magnitude for the first-look and first-smile groups), plotting the behaviors on the heart-rate curves yielded very little consistency in the second-by-second correspondence between heart rate and behavior. The only behavior that was usually accompanied by a consistent heart-rate change (acceleration) was motor activity. Heart-

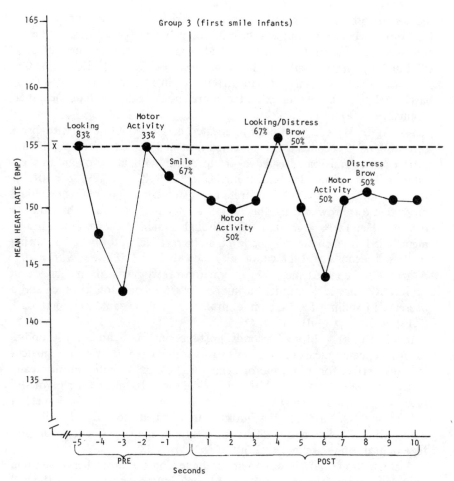

FIG. 3.6   Group 3 (first-smile infants) heart-rate curve and corresponding behavioral changes.

rate activity may be slower than behavioral change and is continuous, unlike the on/off characteristic of these behaviors. In addition, the occurrence of multiple behaviors that may have antagonistic effects (e.g., looking and motor movement) could have attenuated any consistent directional changes in heart rate.

In the next analysis, we examined larger sequences: the three 5-second segments, the 5 seconds prior to still face, the first 5 seconds postonset of still face, and the subsequent 5 seconds (seconds 6 to 10 postonset of still face). This division was selected because the second-by-second heart-rate output indicated trends during these segments. The proportions of time each behavior occurred during each 5-second segment were entered into analyses of variance. An ANOVA by group was conducted. During the 5 seconds of prestill-face baseline, group differences occurred for only two behaviors. Because smiling was the criterion behavior for an infant to be included in the first-smile group, it is understandable that smiling was only exhibited by the first-smile infants during baseline, $F (2,18) = 63.00$, $p < .001$. There were also group differences in motor movement during baseline; late-look infants exhibited more motor activity than the other infants, $F (2,18) = 3.52, p < .05$.

A 3 (group) $\times$ 2 (condition) repeated-measures ANOVA with pre-5 seconds/post-5 seconds as the repeated measure yielded several significant differences. Analyses revealed a group effect with late-look infants exhibiting less smiling (a zero incidence), $F (2,18) = 6.89, p < .01$. A repeated-measures effect for distress brow suggested that infants exhibited more distress brow during the first 5 seconds of still face than during baseline, $F (1,18) = 4.42, p < .05$. Although a main effect for motor movement failed to reach our $p < .05$ level, an increase in motor behavior during the first 5 seconds of still face was also indicated, $F (1,18) = 3.29, p = .09$. A group $\times$ repeated measures interaction effect revealed an increase in smiling for first-look infants during the first 5 seconds of still face and a decrease in smiling for first-smile infants during the same time period, $F (2,18) = 7.13, p < .01$.

In a 3 (group) $\times$ 3 (pre-5 seconds, post seconds 1 to 5, and post seconds 6 to 10) repeated-measures analysis of variance, there was a repeated-measures effect for infant motor behavior. Infants were more motorically active, $F (2,36) = 5.52, p < .01$, during the second 5-second period of still face than they were during baseline. Finally, there was an interaction effect for smiling behavior; the first-look infants smiled more during still face than during baseline and the first-smile infants smiled less during the still face than during baseline, $F (1,30) = 5.74, p < .001$.

A correlation analysis was then conducted on the mean heart rate and behavior proportions for the 5 seconds pre and post the onset of the still face. Several significant relationships emerged. Crying and mean heart rate during both of the 5-second periods were positively correlated ($r = .47, .48$, and $r = .45, .41$, respectively). Infant gaze aversion during the 5 seconds prestill face was correlated with mean heart rate during both the 5 seconds of prestill-face interaction ($r = .39$) and the 5 seconds postonset of the still face interaction ($r = .42$). Distress-brow behavior during the prestill face 5-second period was correlated with heart rate during both the 5 seconds prior to still face ($r = .59$) and the 5 seconds postonset of still face ($r = .66$). Likewise, the distress brow of infants during the post-5 seconds was correlated with mean heart rate during this same time period ($r = .51$). Infant smiling during the 5 seconds of poststill-face interaction was negatively correlated with heart rate during that same time period ($r = -.40$).

The just described variables were entered into a stepwise regression as independent measures with heart rate as the dependent measure to determine the amount of variance in heart rate accounted for by these behaviors. The only variables that entered the regression equation at F values > 4.0 were distress-brow behavior during the 5 seconds preceding the still face ($R = .66$) and distress brow during the 5 seconds following the onset of still face ($R = .79$). Together, these variables accounted for 62% of the variance.

DISCUSSION

The results of this study in part support the findings of Fogel et al. (1981). We found, as did Fogel et al. (1981), that during the still-face condition, infants smiled less frequently and gazed away from their mothers more frequently than they did during the spontaneous-play or resumption conditions. Fogel and his colleagues (1981) found group × condition interaction effects for distress-brow and crying behavior. First-look infants showed more distress brow and crying than first-smile infants during the resumption condition as compared to the spontaneous and still-face conditions. Our results differ slightly from theirs inasmuch as the first-look infants were observed to vocalize and cry more frequently than the first-smile infants during the still-face condition. In addition, they were motorically less active than first-smile infants during the still-face interaction. Differences in motor movement and vocalization continued during the resumption condition.

The decrease in motor activity, coupled with the increase in vocalization may represent an attempt by the first-look infants to reengage their mothers in normal interaction. The increase in crying behavior at this time may be associated with the distress that the infants experience when they are unable to reengage their mothers. The first-smile infants may have been less inclined to reengage their mothers in interaction after having just terminated a round of interaction. Assuming that the smile of the infant indicates closure of a completed interaction cycle and an associated decrease in arousal, as suggested by the tension-release model, the first-look infants who had not yet smiled may have been anticipating a response from the mother and when it was not forthcoming experienced an associated increase in arousal level. The vocalizing behavior may represent an appeal to the mother to return to her "natural" interaction behavior and the crying may represent the infant's distressful response to failing and an attempt to modulate a high level of arousal.

In general, although our results support those reported by Fogel et al. (1981), they are somewhat attenuated. Although infant behaviors did not differ during baseline interaction, differences in the behaviors of the mothers of our first-look and first-smile infants (those group conditions assessed by Fogel et al., 1981) were noted. The mothers of the first-smile infants smiled at their infants and kinesthetically stimulated their infants more frequently than the mothers of the first-look infants. The criterion for group assignment was the behavior of the infant. However, the group assignment may have been inadvertently affected by the mother, because a mother who smiles and kinesthetically stimulates her infant more frequently is more likely to elicit the criterion smile in the infant. Comparisons between the late-look and first-smile group suggested no differences between the mothers. Thus, comparisons between these two groups were less likely to reflect differential mother behavior. Again, the results suggest that infants who are looking at their mothers at the initiation of still-face behavior may be more disturbed by the perturbation and may more actively attempt to reinstate normal interaction with their mothers than infants who appear to have completed an interaction sequence by smiling. The infants who were looking at their mothers upon initiation of still-face behavior (late-look) were more vocal and cried more than infants who had smiled prior to initiation of the still-face condition. Although the distress-brow differences were not statistically significant, the late-look infants did show more distress brow during still face than did the first-smile infants even though the latter infants had shown more distress-brow behavior during the initial baseline spontaneous condition.

Another possible reason that the effects in this study were attenuated relative to the Fogel et al. (1981) study relates to our finding of significant sex differences. Sex differences in infant behavior during the still-face situation revealed that girls cried more and showed distress brow more frequently than did boys during the still-face condition. Although Fogel et al.'s smile group contained seven males and seven females, their first-look group contained four males and 10 females. Because we noted more frequent distress brow and crying among girls, it is possible that greater group differences noted by Fogel et al. (1981) were partially due to the preponderance of girls in their look group. The use of more girls in the look group may have increased their chances of finding more distress-brow behavior and crying in that group.

Fogel and his colleagues (1981) assessed Sroufe's tension-release model by using the still-face paradigm. Their findings suggest that the first-look group may have been experiencing increasing tension and their first-smile group decreasing tension, because the mother's still face appeared to be more distressing to the former group of infants (first-look) than to the latter (first-smile). Although there are trends in our behavioral data that partially replicate the findings of Fogel et al. (1981) and lend support to theirs and the Sroufe et al. (1974) models, the heart-rate data do not suggest that the first- or late-look groups were more aroused physiologically than the first-smile group either at the onset of the mother's still face or during the first 10 seconds of the still face. Although the heart-rate curves of Figs. 3.4, 3.5, and 3.6 suggest that heart rate is slowly accelerating for the first-look group at the onset of the still face and decelerating for the first-smile group at the onset of the still face (in accord with the Fogel et al. [1981] and Sroufe et al. [1974] models), heart rate is also decelerating for the late-look group. The cardiac change in this group is contrary to the prediction of the model, and none of these shifts in heart rate at the onset of still face were significant either within groups or between groups.

There are several possible interpretations of these data. First, the literature suggests that both looking (Graham & Clifton, 1967) and smiling (Provost & Govin-DeCarie, 1979) behaviors are accompanied by cardiac decelerations. Thus, cardiac deceleration in the late-look and the first-smile groups are not necessarily inconsistent. Further cardiac acceleration in the first-look group may represent increasing arousal or may be the effect of antagonistic action on the heart of both looking and movement with the motor activity disproportionately contributing to an acceleration.

Secondly, the cardiac change may lag behind the behavior. However, by 2 seconds postonset of the still face, the two groups who were showing a deceleration just prior to the onset (the first-smile and late-look infants) evidenced an acceleration, and the first-look infants, who were experiencing a cardiac acceleration at the onset were, by 2 seconds postonset, showing a deceleration. Thus, shifts in the direction of heart rate were parallel for the first-smile and late-look groups (contrary to the prediction of the model). By second 4, all three groups showed a deceleration and by second 7, an acceleration. A behavioral interpretation of these parallel, directional changes in heart rate may be that all three groups experienced a "what's happening?" orienting response, followed by an aversive response to the still-face mother even though the behaviors occurring at the time of the acceleration were somewhat different across groups. The first-smile group showed distress brow and motor activity, the first-look group motor activity and gazing away, and the late-look group distress brow, motor activity, and crying. However, despite the presumably more arousing distress brow and crying behavior of the late-look group, the magnitude of their deceleration/acceleration directional change was less than that that occurred for the behaviorally less aroused first-smile and first-look infants. The heart rate of the late-look group showed no significant change. Thus, the late-look group infants appear to be expressing distress primarily in their behavior with only minimal change in heart rate. This is surprising inasmuch as distress brow contributed a significant amount to the variance on heart rate, suggesting that distress-brow behavior is typically associated with cardiac acceleration, as can be noted in Table 3.4. The late-look group infants showed distress brow during every second of the still face, and distress brow was observed among several of the infants in that group. Although the first-smile group also showed distress brow for almost all of this period, fewer infants showed distress brow than in the late-look group. Fewer infants of the first-look group also showed distress brow and for fewer seconds. Just as the late-look infants were showing distress primarily in their behavior, the first-look infants seemed to manifest their distress primarily in cardiac activity. The first-smile group, on the contrary, appeared to evidence their distress in both distress-brow behavior and cardiac activity. Because a significant amount of the heart-rate variance was explained by distress brow, the absence of significant cardiac change in the group that was showing the greatest incidence of distress brow (late look) is surprising. It could be that different types of infants were preassigned to groups by using the behavior criterion of first look, first smile, and late look, netting a self-selection confound.

Jones (1950) has described three types of infants who correspond to the three types of adults described by Eysenck (1967). These are internalizers, externalizers, and generalizers. Internalizers are noted to be physiologically reactive but minimally expressive behaviorally. Externalizers, on the contrary, show behavioral expressivity with minimal cardiac reactivity, and generalizers are noted to be responsive both behaviorally and physiologically. A possible interpretation of the distress brow/cardiac activity relationship in these data is that our first-look infants are internalizer types (lesser incidence distress brow but significant cardiac change), our late-look infants are externalizers (greater incidence of distress brow but minimal cardiac reactivity), and our first-smile infants are generalizers (moderate incidence of distress brow and significant cardiac reactivity). Thus, the late-look group may not have shown the physiological change predicted by the Sroufe et al. (1974) and Fogel et al. (1981) models simply because they are less physiologically reactive.

Even though these data, then, do not provide strong support for the models of Sroufe et al. (1974) and Fogel et al. (1981), they do not refute them either. They simply suggest that there may be individual differences in the degree to which distress responses are evidenced behaviorally and/or physiologically. The procedure used here for assignment of infants to conditions based on their behaviors may have inadvertently confounded the assessment of the behavioral/cardiac relationships in response to stress. Nonetheless, the complexity of the relationships noted highlights the importance of investigating individual differences in the behavioral and physiological components of infants' affective responses to changes in their mothers' behaviors.

ACKNOWLEDGMENTS

We would like to thank the infants and mothers who participated in this research and Reena Greenberg and Jackie Zagursky for their assistance.

This research was submitted in partial fulfillment of the master's degree for the first author. The research was supported by grants from the Administration of Children, Youth and Families and the National Foundation—March of Dimes and a Research Scientist Development Award from NIMH to TF.

REFERENCES

Aronson, E., & Rosenbloom, S. Space perception in early infancy: Perception within a common auditory-visual space. *Science,* 1971, *172,* 1161–1163.

Berlyne, D. E. Laughter, humor and play. In G. Lindzey, & E. Aronson (Eds.), *Handbook of social psychology.* Boston: Addison-Wesley, 1969.

Brazelton, T. B. Personal communication, 1980.

Brazelton, T. B., Koslowski, B., & Main, M. The origins of reciprocity: The early mother–infant interaction. In M. Lewis, & L. Rosenblum (Eds.), *The effect of the infant on its caregiver.* New York: Wiley, 1974.

Brazelton, T. B., Tronick, E., Adamson, L., Als, H., & Wise, S. Early mother–infant reciprocity. In *Parent-infant interaction* (Ciba Foundation Symposium, 33). New York: Elsevier, 1975.

Carey, W. B. A simplified method of measuring infant temperament. *Journal of Pediatrics,* 1970, *77,* 188–194.

Ellsworth, P., & Ludwig, L. M. Visual behavior in social interaction. *Journal of Communication,* 1972, *22,* 375–403.

Emde, R., Campos, J., Reich, J., & Gaensbauer, T. I. Infant smiling at five and nine months: Analysis of heart rate and movement. *Infant Behavior and Development,* 1978, *1,* 26–35.

Eysenck, H. J. *The biological basis of personality.* Springfield, Ill.: Charles C. Thomas, 1967.

Field, T. Effects of early separation, interactive deficits and experimental manipulations on infant-mother face-to-face interaction. *Child Development,* 1977, *48,* 763–771.

Field, T. Interaction patterns of high-risk and normal infants. In T. Field, A. Sostek, S. Goldberg, & H. Shuman (Eds.), *Infants born at risk.* New York: Spectrum, 1979. (a)

Field, T. Visual and cardiac responses to animate and inanimate faces by young term and preterm infants. *Child Development,* 1979, *50,* 188–195. (b)

Field, T. Infant arousal, attention, and affect during early interactions. In L. Lipsitt (Ed.), *Advances in infant development* (Vol. 1). Hillsdale, N.J.: Lawrence Erlbaum Associates, 1981. (a)

Field, T. Infant gaze aversion and heart rate during face-to-face interactions. *Infant Behavior and Development,* 1981, *4,* 307–316. (b)

Field, T. Interaction coaching for high risk infants. *Prevention in Human Services,* 1982. (c)

Fogel, A., Diamond, G., Langhorst, B., & Demos, V. Affective and cognitive aspects of the two-month-old's participation in face-to-face interaction with its mother. In E. Tronick (Ed.), *Joint regulation of behavior.* New York: Cambridge University Press, 1981.

Graham, F. K. & Clifton, R. K. Heart rate change as a component of the orienting response. *Psychological Bulletin,* 1966, *65,* 305–320.

Jones, H. E. The study of patterns of emotional expression. In M. Reyment (Ed.), *Feelings and emotions.* New York: McGraw Hill, 1950.

Kagan, J. On emotion and its development: A working paper. In M. Lewis, & L. Rosenblum (Eds.), *The development of affect.* New York: Plenum Press, 1978.

Mandler, G. *Mind and emotion.* New York: Wiley, 1975.

Myers, J. L. *Fundamentals of experimental design.* Boston: Allyn & Bacon, Inc., 1972.

Provost, A. M., & Govin-Decarie, J. Heart rate reactivity of 9- and 12-month-old infants showing specific emotions in natural setting. *International Journal of Behavioral Development,* 1979, *2,* 109–120.

Sroufe, L.A. Ontogenesis of the emotions. In J. Osofsky (Ed.), *Handbook of infant development.* New York: Wiley, 1979.

Sroufe, L. A., & Waters, E. The ontogenesis of smiling and laughter. *Psychological Review,* 1976, *83,* 173–189.

Sroufe, L., Waters, E., & Matas, L. Contextual determinants of infant affective response. In M. Lewis, & L. Rosenblum (Eds.), *The origins of behavior. Vol. 2: Fear.* New York: Wiley, 1974.

Sroufe, L. A., & Waters, E. Heart rate as a convergent measure in clinical and developmental research. *Merrill-Palmer Quarterly,* 1977, *23,* 3–25.

Stern, D. N. Mother and infant at play. In M. Lewis, & L. Rosenblum (Eds.), *The effect of the infant on its caregiver.* New York: Wiley, 1974.

Tomkins, S. *Affect, imagery and consciousness* (Vol. 1). New York: Springer, 1962.

Trevarthen, C. Descriptive analysis of infant communicative behavior. In H. R. Schaffer (Ed.), *Studies in mother–infant interaction.* London: Academic Press, 1977.

Tronick, E., Als, H., Adamson, L., Wise, S., & Brazelton, T. B. The infant's response to entrapment between contradictory messages in face-to-face interaction. *Journal of Child Psychiatry,* 1978, *17,* 1–13.

Vaughn, B., & Sroufe, L. A. The temporal relationship between infant heart rate acceleration and crying in an aversive situation. *Child Development,* 1979, *50,* 565–567.

Waters, E., Matas, L., & Sroufe, L. Infant's reactions to an approaching stranger: Description, validation, and functional significance of wariness. *Child Development,* 1975, *46,* 348–356.

4 Maternal and Infant Affective Exchange: Patterns of Adaptation

Edward Z. Tronick
Margaret Ricks
Jeffrey F. Cohn
University of Massachusetts, Amherst

We have characterized early infant–caregiver social interchanges as a dyadic system in which affective messages are exchanged between the partners for the purpose of one partner's achieving his or her own goals in coordination with those of the other partner (Tronick, 1980). The infant's behavior in this context meets the criteria usually advanced for goal directedness: persistence, use of multiple means to the same end state, observance of a "stop rule" upon achievement of the goal, and appropriateness of actions as judged by an outside observer (Bruner, 1971). Such criteria have also been used to evaluate whether or not the infant is "intentional." (For a review of this issue, see Tronick, 1981). For present purposes it is sufficient to state that by 3 months the infant is goal directed in the context of social exchange (Sander, 1975). In this context the infant's task can be viewed as that of achieving a shared positive emotional state, that of mutual delight (Stern, 1974). The infant's affective displays coordinate social exchanges. The displays convey an emotional evaluation of the partner's action, the state of the interaction, and also signal the infant's direction of action. For example, smiles typically indicate a positive emotional evaluation and signal that the infant will continue his or her direction of action, whereas grimaces and frowns express a negative emotive state and a change in the infant's direction of action.

Our view is that from the emotions generated during interactions, a background emotional state or mood becomes stabilized in the child. This mood is not a particular affective response to a specific stimulus, but rather it is the accumulated distillate of the repeated positive or negative emotions the child has experienced in his or her interactions. Once established this mood is brought by the child to new situations. It functions to bias the infant's evaluation of the situation and behavioral tendencies even before the child has fully processed the information arising from the situation. For example, the infant whose background state is one of anxiety is biased to evaluate a new situation fearfully and to have a tendency to disengage from it even before confronting it. Thus, this mood acts as the infant's initial adaptive system in that it structures the "meaning" of a situation for the infant and so regulates behavior. It is primarily a social–emotional system of adaptation rather than one that is cognitive. The infant can usefully be thought of as a sensoriaffective being rather than as a sensorimotor being (Stechler & Carpenter, 1967). With development, the quality of this social-emotional system becomes a stable individual characteristic that is also increasingly influenced but not replaced by the cognitive adaptive system.

In order to study the structure of this adaptive system, we have engaged in a set of studies on individual differences in the quality of infant adaptation. Our strategy has been to challenge infants' interactive capabilities with an age-appropriate stress. The studies discussed here concern description of infant response, continuity of infant adaptation, and maternal correlates of individual differences observed in infants (Tronick, Krafchuk, Ricks, Cohn, & Winn, 1980).

Underlying this concern with adaptation is a focus on the child's feeling of effectance: the sense of what can and cannot be accomplished. We think the quality of this feeling is primarily structured during the infant's social exchanges. When the child's social interactions result in a shared, positive emotional state, the infant develops a sense of effectance out of their cumulative repetition, but when such interactions do not accomplish this goal the infant develops a sense of ineffectance or helplessness. Effectance can be thought of as stylizing the observable aspects of goal directedness: the amount of persistence in following a direction of action and the extent to which a varied repertoire of means are mustered by the child. And although it is during social interaction, during actual interchanges, that the child's sense of effectance is structured, any factor such as maternal personality or stress that affects the structure of the interaction will affect the infant's sense of effectance. Thus we have engaged in studies of maternal personality and maternal interactive style and have directly manipulated the structure of the interaction.

To study maternal personality correlates of the quality of infant adaptation, we examined the relationship between maternal self-concept and infant quality of attachment, as assessed in the Ainsworth Strange Situation (Ricks, Noyes, & Tronick, 1981). We hypothesized that maternal self-concept, as reflected in self-esteem and recollection of childhood relationships, should be related to the quality of the infant's attachment. To examine the continuity of infant adaptation we observed the relationship between the infant's reaction at 3, 6, or 9 months to a stressful interaction, the mother's remaining still faced, and the quality of the infant's attachment to the mother in the Ainsworth Strange Situation at 1 year (Ricks, 1981). Our work utilized Waters and Sroufe's (1981) view on assessing continuities in competence. If there is continuity in individual adaptation, they argue that it will be found by using broad-band age-appropriate assessment procedures that tap the coordination of affect, cognition, and behavior.

We also examined the relationship between particular patterns of maternal behavior—overcontrolling, undercontrolling, and elaboration—in normal interactions at 6 months and the infant's reaction to the still face (Ricks, 1981). Based on previous work on face-to-face interaction (Brazelton, Koslowski, & Main, 1974; Ricks, Krafchuk, & Tronick, 1979; Stern, 1974, 1977), we believed that the quality of maternal behavior during interaction should be related to the infant's response to stress.

To more directly demonstrate the impact of maternal behavior on the quality of the infant's behavior, we asked the mother to interact in a manner simulating clinical descriptions of maternal depression (Cohn, 1981). From our model we hypothesized that this display would produce negative affect in the infant and a modification of the sequencing of the infant's behavior as he or she attempted to, but nevertheless failed to, achieve the goal of a shared, positive affective state. Moreover, we expected that the effect of this experience would establish a mood in the infant, albeit brief, that would carry over to subsequent interactions, making the infant appear more affectively negative and more limited in his or her means.

MATERNAL PERSONALITY AND THE QUALITY OF INFANT ADAPTATION AT ONE YEAR

The assessment of maternal self-esteem was made using the O'Brien/Epstein Self Report Inventory (Epstein, 1976, 1979, 1980; Losco, 1981; O'Brien, 1980). This questionnaire is a measure of maternal self-esteem and eight evaluative realms of the self-concept (self-control, power over others, likeability/love worthiness, competence, morality, body health, body functioning, and body appearance). An additional defensiveness scale measures the degree to which respondents are likely to bias their answers towards gaining social approval. Maternal recollections of childhood relationships with each parent and with peers were assessed with the Mother–Father–Peer scale designed by Trussell (1963). The scale includes the dimensions of acceptance/rejection (by mother, father, and peers) and encouragement of independence/overprotection (by mother and father). Within 1 to 2 weeks of the Ainsworth Strange Situation (Ainsworth, Blehar, Waters, & Wall, 1978), mothers were given these two questionnaires to complete at home and return by mail. The infants were classified as secure or anxious in their attachment relationship with the mother on the basis of their pattern of behavior in the Strange Situation. The infant assessment provides information on how well infants coped with the developmental task of the 1 year old, that of forming an effective attachment relationship. The classifications are based on the extent to which the infant can use the mother as a secure base to engage in exploration of the environment, and to initiate contact when stressed (Ainsworth et al., 1978).

The important results of this paper as shown in Tables 4.1 and 4.2 were quite striking. Mothers of securely attached infants rated themselves

TABLE 4.1
Infant Attachment and Its Relationship to Maternal Self-Esteem

	Infant Attachment Classification	
Mothers' Self-Concept	Secure (N = 15)	Anxious (N = 13)
General self-esteem[a]	4.20	3.87
Likability/Love worthiness[b]	4.14	3.82
Competence[b]	4.09	3.69
Defensiveness	3.14	3.11

[a] $p < .05$.
[b] $p < .01$.

TABLE 4.2
Infant Attachment and Maternal Evaluation of Previous Relationships

	Infant Attachment Classification	
Mothers' Own Childhood Relationships	Secure (N = 12) M	Anxious (N = 12) M
Mother		
Encouragement of independence/ overprotection[b]	9.17	-3.58
Acceptance/Rejection[b]	23.25	3.42
Father		
Encouragement of independence[b]	7.58	-3.25
Acceptance/Rejection[b]	16.25	3.09
Peers		
Acceptance/Rejection[a]	15.75	1.83

[a] $p < .05$.
[b] $p < .01$.

significantly higher on self-esteem, likability/love worthiness, and competence than did mothers of anxiously attached infants. That there was no difference on the defensiveness scale indicates that these results were not simply a response bias. A similar but even more striking pattern was found in the data on recollection of past relationships. Mothers of securely attached infants evaluated their relationships with peers and parents as more accepting and their parents as more encouraging of independence than did mothers of anxiously attached infants. The relationship between maternal acceptance and quality of infant attachment is particularly strong: There was virtually no overlap between mothers of securely attached and mothers of anxiously attached infants on this scale. The importance of these results does not rest on whether or not mothers are giving us an accurate evaluation of their own early relationships. What is important is that those mothers who feel positively about themselves and their early relationships have infants who feel secure in their primary relationship and, inferentially, in their own capabilities. This conclusion is consistent with hypotheses from a variety of theoretical perspectives. Although the data do not establish conclusively that infant–mother relationships are related to the mother's early childhood experience, they provide a basis upon which prospective studies of individual differences in infants and mothers can be designed.

THE STABILITY OF THE INFANT'S QUALITY OF ADAPTATION OVER THE FIRST YEAR

To assess the stability of the infant's adaptation over the first year, we examined the performance of three groups of infants aged 3, 6, and 9 months in a stressful face-to-face interactive setting, the still-faced mother, as related to the quality of attachment to the mother, assessed at one year. To characterize the quality of the infant's performance at 3, 6, and 9 months of age, we specified three patterns of infant reaction to the still face. The first was *positive elicits:* While oriented towards the mother the infant positively vocalizes, smiles, initiates a game, or performs action that in normal circumstances would produce a response by the mother. For example, the infant might sober, then smile, sober again, and turn away but return with another smile. Eventually the infant might cry but only after initially engaging in positive elicits. The second pattern was labeled *negative elicits:* The infant becomes fussy or cries and makes no positive elicits. The third pattern was *no elicits:* The infant looks at and away from the mother but does nothing that could be characterized as eliciting. This pattern is actually quite disturbing to observe because the infant appears to be stressed by the display but unable to act. For example, as one mother assumed the still face, her infant was looking away but he soon looked up at her and sobered, staring at her for almost 15 seconds. While looking, his breathing became labored and his hands clenched and unclenched repeatedly until he finally looked off for several seconds but again looked back towards her with his chin tucked, his face tensed, and his eyes narrowed. At no time did he vocalize or even brighten; nor did he cry or fuss. He appeared overwhelmed and stressed as he repeated the tense looking towards and away cycle.

Table 4.3 presents the results of his analysis and its relationship to the infants' classifications at 1 year in the Ainsworth Strange Situation. Focusing

TABLE 4.3
Predicting Attachment from Responses to Still-Faced Mother

	3-Month Response		
	Pattern 1 Positive Elicits	Pattern 2 Negative Elicits	Pattern 3 No Elicits
Secure	6	1	3
Anxious	1	0	1
			$L_B = .17$

Attachment Classification (At 1 Year)	6-Month Response		
	Pattern 1 Positive Elicits	Pattern 2 Negative Elicits	Pattern 3 No Elicits
Secure	10	2	0
Anxious	1	0	4
			$L_B = .80$ [a]

	9-Month Response		
	Pattern 1 Positive Elicits	Pattern 2 Negative Elicits	Pattern 3 No Elicits
Secure	10	3	1
Anxious	2	3	0
			$L_B = 0$ [a]

[a] L_B = Goodman-Kruskel Index of Predictive Association.

first on the 6-month data, the results are clear and striking. Infants who elicit at 6 months are quite likely to be securely attached at 1 year, in contrast to infants who fail to elicit. The Goodman-Kruskel Index of Predictive Association, Lambda B (Castellan, 1979; Hays, 1973) was used to evaluate this Table. Lambda B indicates the proportional reduction in the probability of error in predicting outcome by knowing the antecedent variable. Values of Lambda B above .30 indicate a clear relationship between antecedent and consequent classification. At 6 months Lambda B was .80. This was not the finding at 3 months, when Lambda B was .17, or at 9 months, when Lambda B was .0.

At this point, our interpretation is as follows: At 3 months infants are establishing their patterns of engagement with their mothers, but these patterns are not yet stabilized. That is, the structure of the interaction is still being negotiated and the infant's interactive competence is being formed in this on-going context. By 6 months the infant has cumulated sufficient experience in the interaction such that his or her competence is stabilized, as is his or her feeling of effectance. The infant can now bring that competence and feeling to a new situation. When the 6 month old confronts the nonresponsive mother his or her coping reflects this stabilization and it is probably maintained over the next 6 months because the infant's interactional experience is also stable.

The finding at 9 months is particularly interesting because predictions over shorter periods of time are expected to be more efficient than predictions over longer periods. We think there are two possible but related explanations. First, at 9 months the task may no longer be age appropriate. Second, a finer-grained scoring system might discriminate better among the older infants.

It is important to emphasize a point made in the preceding discussion. We do not thing that infant competence at 6 months is a trait that results in infant competence at 1 year. Infant competence is generated and maintained by the quality of the infant's interactions with its environment. It is this interactive process that is stable from 6 months to 1 year and its stability is responsible for the stability of the infant's competence. The assessments used reflect that underlying process, not a trait or a particular behavior. To examine the process itself it is necessary to characterize what the mother does with the infant and how it affects the infant.

MATERNAL PATTERNS OF INTERACTIVE BEHAVIOR AND INFANT COPING

Maternal pattern of interactive behavior was characterized along three dimensions—elaboration, overcontrol, and undercontrol—during 2 minutes of face-to-face interaction that preceded the still-face interaction at 6 months. The relationship of the maternal behavior to infant reaction to the still face was then evaluated. *Elaboration,* a modification of Ainsworth's sensitivity scales (Ainsworth, Bell, & Stayton, 1974), scaled the extent to which the mother is responsive to the infant's actions, the extent to which she imitates or exaggerates infant social actions, and "backs off" briefly during infant averts. *Overcontrolling,* following the ideas of Brazelton (Brazelton et al., 1974) and Stern (1977) reflects the extent to which the mother intrudes on the infant's activities or is persistently engaging the infant even when the infant is looking away from her. *Undercontrolling,* the opposite of overcontrolling (Stern, 1977), reflects hesitancy and withdrawal during the interaction; mothers who scored high on undercontrolling appeared reluctant to organize the infant's attention or behavior. Note that undercontrolling and overcontrolling were two different scales although one might think of them as end points on a single scale. What we found was that some mothers had periods of both; giving them a middle-scale score would not have been descriptive of their actual behavior.

Our expectation was that mothers who elaborated their infants' behavior during the interaction and were neither extremely overcontrolling nor extremely undercontrolling would have infants who engaged in positive elicits during the still face. No elicits were expected for the infants whose mothers were low on elaboration and at the extremes of undercontrolling or overcontrolling. We made the latter prediction because the undercontrolling mother, while allowing the infant initiative, does not reciprocally respond, and the overcontrolling mother does not allow the infant to take the initiative.

We found that infants who engaged in positive elicits at 6 months had mothers who were scored significantly higher on elaboration than did mothers of infants who made no elicits. Mothers of infants who made negative elicits were intermediate on the elaboration scale. Compared to the mothers of infants who made positive elicits, mothers of infants who made no elicits were more likely to be extremely over- or undercontrolling. Thus, as indexed by the 2 minutes of normal interaction, the mother's sensitivity and style or control with her infant is related to the infant's reaction in a subsequent stressful situation. To examine this impact more directly we experimentally manipulated the mother's behavior and examined its immediate and short-term impact on the infant.

Simulated Maternal Depression and the Infant's Reaction

Mothers were instructed to flatten or depress their affect during face-to-face interchange with their infants. This was accomplished through verbal instructions and by showing them a videotape of a woman simulating a depressed interaction. This was a most useful demonstration along with the particular instruction "get as you do on those days that you feel tired and blue." Few women had trouble following these instructions! The effect was to slow them down, eliminate all smiles or bright faces, limit their to and fro movements, and restrict their touching of the infant. For example, as one mother turned towards her infant, she said his name in a long, low drawl and although she looked at him there was no brightness in her face or eyes. She then began a narrative about their ride over with a flat voice lacking all animation and with no accompanying movements of body or hand. She maintained this behavior for the full 3 minutes except for one brief instant when she almost smiled (because of an infant elicit).

Twenty-four 3-month-old infants were seen in a procedure in which mothers interacted normally and in a depressed fashion. We coded six infant affective states: *look away, protest, wary, social monitor, brief positive,* and *play. Look away* describes periods in which the infant is predominantly averting his or her gaze (very fast glances towards the mother with durations of 1 1/4 seconds or less were allowed) and affect is not distressed. *Protest* describes infant fussing, thrashing about in the seat, or crying, with gaze either towards or away from the mother. *Wary* describes gaze towards the mother with head partly averted and with a sad or sober face. *Monitor* also describes gaze towards the mother, but with a neutral facial expression. *Brief positive* (positive elicits) refers to attenuated positive displays. *Play* refers to longer-duration positive displays with or without accompanying vocalizations.

We predicted that if the mother's behaviors were distorted so that she conveyed primarily negative affect and did not facilitate the normal interactive goal, then the infant would pick up on this distortion and engage in activities aimed at eliciting her normal response. We also expected that if the infant continued to try and continued to fail, then he or she too would become negative. These effects would be indicated by a change both in the proportion of time the infant was affectively negative and in the pattern of infant response during the interaction. Additionally, if the infant were capable of having a mood, then even when the stimulus situation changed, his or her behavior would reflect that underlying mood.

Figs. 4.1 and 4.2 provide schematic representation of the organization of infant behavior in each condition. The proportion of time spent in each state is indicated by the area of the circles representing that state.

Looking at Fig. 4.1, we see that while oriented towards their mothers infants in the normal condition spent the major proportion of their time in *monitor, brief positive* (positive elicits), and *play.* Over the 3 minutes of interaction, normal-condition infants spent 12% of their time in *monitor* and 25% in *brief positive* (2%) or *play* (23%). The proportion of *look away* was 50%. Only 6% of their time is spent in *protest,* only 7% in *wary.*

Looking now at Fig. 4.2, notice that the infants in the depressed condition apportion their time very differently. They are far less positive and more negative than the infants in the normal condition. Depressed-condition infants spend a scant 2% of their time in *play* and only 6% of their time in *monitor.* The proportion of time spent positively eliciting the mother is increased to 6%. The vast majority of their time is spent in three states—*look away* (34%), *wary* (28%), and *protest* (22%). The depressed interaction proved extremely stressful. One-fourth of the infants cried steadily for over 30 seconds. There was no comparable upset in the normal condition.

Looking at the transition data (arrows between states), we see that there are pronounced differences in the organization of behavior within each condition. In the normal condition we find smooth cycling among the neutral to positive states, which is indicated by the thick striped arrows among them. The infants cycle between *monitor* and *brief positive* (positive elicits) and between *monitor* and *play,* both with greater-than-chance probability. This positive cycling among *brief positive, monitor,* and *play* is part of a larger on–off cycle on engagement–disengagement similar to that described by Brazelton et al. (1974). About 40% of the transitions from *play* and

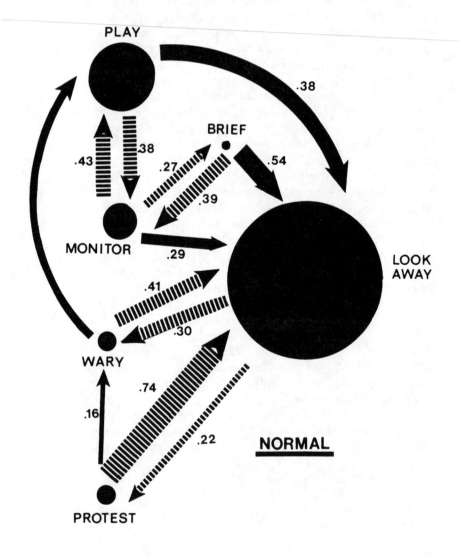

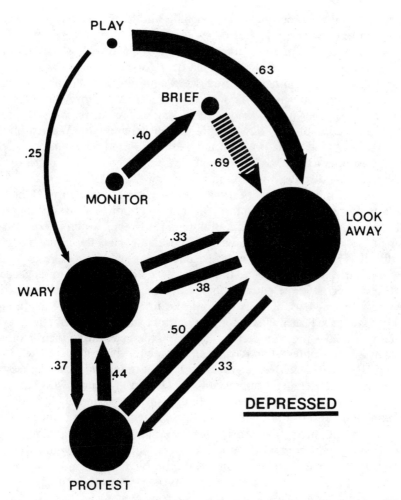

FIG. 4.1 and 4.2   State transition diagrams from the normal and depressed conditions. The relative proportion of infant time spent in each state is indicated by the size of the circle representing that state. The thickness of the arrows represents the relative size of the conditional probabilities of event-sequence transitions. Striped arrows indicate those transitions for which the conditional probability is significantly greater than that expected, $p < .05$. Solid arrows indicate those transitions for which conditional and unconditional probabilities do not significantly differ, $p < .05$. Only the highest conditional probabilities from each state are shown. The numbers next to the arrows indicate the exact size of conditional probabilities.

about one-half the transitions from *brief positive* lead to *look away* and a state of disengagement from the interaction. From *look away*, the infant then returns to the positive cycle primarily through transitions to one of the three states in this positive cycle. Notice that although normal-condition infants are unlikely to become wary, when they do, they are likely to return to the positive cycle (see Fig. 4.1).

The organization of communicative displays is markedly different in the depressed condition (Fig. 4.2). Instead of the smooth cycling among *brief positive, monitor,* and *play,* we find that the infants predominantly cycle in a loosely organized way among *wary, protest,* and *look away,* as indicated by the thick solid arrows among these states. Also different is the contrasting function of *brief positive* (positive elicits) and *play.* Whereas in the normal condition *brief positive* and *play* each lead to *monitor,* in the depressed interaction *brief positive* and *play* each result in a return to the negative cycle through a transition to *look away.*

The transition from *brief positive* (positive elicits) to *look away* is the one well-organized pattern within the depressed condition. This transition gives the appearance of being an elicitation pattern. In the normal interaction in which mothers respond to these brief positive elicits, the infant remains positively engaged. In the depressed interaction in which the mother remains relatively unresponsive, the infant averts and becomes disengaged.

We wanted to know whether these differences would persist even after mothers resumed normal interaction. We had hypothesized that infants who experienced such distortions of normal maternal interaction, even briefly, would show some effect of that experience after their mothers resumed normal interaction (cf. Fogel, Chapter 3, this volume; Fogel, Diamond, Langhorst, & Demos, 1982). What we found was that depressed-condition infants remain appreciably more wary. Mothers who had previously simulated depressed interactions experienced initial difficulty in eliciting their infants to resume the normal interaction and become positive.

These results strongly supported our hypotheses that simulated maternal depression produced not only infant distress, but more importantly that it results in a different organization of infant behavior. The most impressive example of this is the two cycles we observed. Depressed-condition infants cycle among *protest, wary,* and *look away,* and they also positively elicit (*brief positive*) more often than infants in the normal condition. Normal-condition infants cycle among *brief positive, monitor,* and *play.* Second, we found that even brief experience with simulated maternal depression results in an organization of behavior that is likely to continue after mothers resume more appropriate interaction. More generally, we feel that we have demonstrated a clear relationship between the quality of maternal affective displays and the infant's behavior. In this specific case, when maternal affect is experimentally depressed, infants become clearly upset and organize their behavior very differently. Babies adapt to depressed affect on the part of the mother, and this adaptation persists into the next period of time in which the mother acts normally.

DISCUSSION

Our model of the regulation of infant–mother interaction and its effects on development has two aspects that are addressed by these data: the infant's capacity for affective regulation and the stabilization of affect or mood within the infants. Whether or not young infants have the capacity to regulate exchanges is controversial. In a recent article, Tronick (1981) has argued that this ability is present by 3 months of age. Others argue that it is not (Schaffer, 1977). These data support the former position.

In the simulated depressed condition, the infants change the pattern of their affective displays from that found in the normal interaction. They do not simply get "unhappy" or "look away" but rather they change the sequencing of affective states. In the depressed condition they cycle among the negative states and even when they move into positive states they are most likely to go to *look away* and then get "reabsorbed" into a cycle of negative affective states. This absorption is a clear demonstration of a change in the syntax of affective states and is indicative of the regulatory capabilities of the infant. Changes in the infant's behavior not only act as self-regulation, but also would have the effect, under normal circumstances, of regulating with adult's behavior. It is not necessary to invoke intentionality to account for the infant's behavioral change, but note that the behavior has all the characteristics of goal-directed activity.

By 3 months the infant is not only under immediate stimulus control. The change in behavior that occurred in the 3 minutes of depressed interactions is carried forward into the following normal interaction. There is also the evidence relating maternal behavioral style—control and elaboration—to the infant's response to the still face. These findings suggest that the infant's social interactive experience affects the child's mood, which then modifies the child's subsequent performance in other interactions. Further, these regulatory reactions at 6 months are predictive of the infant's attachment classification at 1 year. Clearly, by this time the infant's affective adaptive system has begun to stabilize.

These data also argue strongly against a set of alternatives based on some version or other of the discrepancy hypothesis (Kagan, 1974; McCall & McGhee, 1977). Briefly, these hypotheses would not predict the finding of positive and negative affect being sequentially interwoven in the still-face elicit pattern nor would they predict the simulated depressed cycle and carry-over effects found in the depressed condition. The discrepancy hypothesis would predict, in the case of moderate amounts of subjective uncertainty/discrepancy, some displays of negative affect and maximum attention and sustained positive affect; or if the simulated depressed condition is defined as an extreme amount of discrepancy, it would predict displays of maximum negative affect and then, if the infant is successful in resolving the discrepancy, prolonged attention and positive affect. Note, as do Hinde (1974) and McCall and McGhee (1977), that the discrepancy hypothesis is actually unable to make either prediction a priori, but even when it is done these data do not conform. There is simply no discrepancy-related prediction that can account for these findings.

From these data we think the infant must be said to be reacting to the quality of what the mother is doing. Most infants' behavior is initially well organized and goal directed in response to the still face and simulated depressed interactions. That goal is to change what the mother is doing. It is only after repeated failure to regulate her behavior that the infant's affective displays become less well organized and no longer directed towards that goal.

There is another related issue—specificity or nature of the stimuli to which the infant responds. In the discrepancy model, the infant responds to an internal variable, discrepancy, which particularly in early development is affected by the quantitative characteristics of the stimulus. Our regulatory model argues that the infant must perceive the qualitative or message value of the partner's display regardless of its quantitative aspect by 3 months. The infant's reaction to the manipulated displays reported here supports this position. Regardless of whether or not the mother is more or less discrepant, she is clearly doing less in the manipulated interactions—that is, she is a less variable stimulus. Additionally there is evidence presented by Kozak and Tronick (1981) that even the 2 month olds vocalize or smile in response to specific combinations of maternal turn-taking signals and not others.

These results indicate that 1-year competence can be predicted from earlier behavior. The infant's pattern of response to the still face at 6 months is strongly related to the quality of attachment at 1 year. Moreover, the infant's pattern of response is coherently related to maternal interactive styles of control and elaboration. Mothers who elaborate and are neither too overcontrolling nor too undercontrolling have infants who have a positive and varied repertoire for coping with an interactive stress, whereas mothers who do not behave in such a manner have infants who fail to effectively cope with the stress. Indeed, we have demonstrated that the dramatically undercontrolling style in the simulated depressed condition has a negative effect on the infant. These findings are similar to Ainsworth's and her colleagues' findings (cf. Ainsworth et al., 1978) that secure infants have sensitive mothers. Ainsworth's work was based on extensive home observations. Here we have shown that brief episodes of interaction in the laboratory again find a clear relationship between sensitive maternal behavior and quality of infant attachment. This suggests the robustness of this phenomenon and the utility of the still-face procedure as an assessment of mother–infant interaction at 6 months.

Consistent with our own and others' observations on maternal behavior related to quality of attachment (Ainsworth et al., 1978; Main, 1977) is the finding that maternal self-concept is clearly related to the quality of infant attachment. Mothers of infants classified as securely attached reported more positive feelings regarding themselves and their childhood relationships than did mothers of infants classified as anxious in the attachment relationship. These results help clarify research showing that mothers of infants classified as anxious are less available psychologically, less responsive, and less sensitive to these infants than are mothers of infants seen as secure (Ainsworth, Bell, & Stayton, 1972; Ainsworth et al., 1978; Matas, Ahrend, & Sroufe, 1978). Further work has shown that mothers of anxious-avoidant infants are less affectively expressive (Main, Tomasini, & Tolan, 1979) and seem to have an aversion to close bodily contact with their babies (Blehar, Ainsworth, & Main, in preparation, cited in Ainsworth et al., 1978). Although other investigations have attempted to link such caretaking characteristics to maternal personality variables, a sole focus on relatively narrow personality variables has not proved fruitful. The Ricks et al. (1981) data presented here suggest that self-concept measures with empirically demonstrated global implications for an individual's behavior would be useful in work on the origins of individual differences in infant adaptation.

We also think that these data address the issue of infant effectance and the transmission of affect between mother and infant. Effectance, in White's (1959) definition, is the infant's sense of what can and cannot be accomplished. It is an emotional mood that modifies or stylizes the infant's interactive behavior. An infant with a clear sense of his or her effectance will be persistent in the face of obstacles to goal achievement, will muster and deploy various means, and will generally show a positive mood. An infant who feels ineffective or helpless will be easily stressed, negative, and withdrawn. This feeling, we think, develops in the context of interactive experience. When infants are able to accomplish their interactive goals, when their displays are responded to appropriately, a feeling of effectance cumulates; when interactive goals are thwarted, a sense of helplessness develops. Such thwarting of goals occurs in the still face and depressed affect manipulations and we also think that it occurs in normal interactions when mothers are overcontrolling or undercontrolling or fail to elaborate. Mothers who fail to respond to infant signals or intrude on infant-initiated activities distort the interactive structure. The infant may initially attempt to redirect the interaction, but with repeated failure the infant gives up and withdraws.

From this perspective the transmission of affect between mother and infant is no longer a somewhat magical unobservable process of interchange (Kohut, 1971). Rather, it is behavior that can be seen and described. For example, one can hypothesize that an anxious mother is likely to misperceive and fail to respond to infant signals. This lack of maternal responsivity or insensitivity makes the infant insecure about his or her ability to affect the environment. The infant becomes anxious, not because the mother in some mysterious way gives her feeling to the infant but because the failure in their interactive regulation generates feelings of ineffectance in the infant. With repeated experience in such interaction, the anxiety may become a stable characteristic of the infant.

ACKNOWLEDGMENTS

The authors would like to express their sincere thanks to Janet Droge and Donna Noyes for their untiring assistance on this project. The research was in part supported by a Faculty Research Grant from the University of Massachusetts.

REFERENCES

Ainsworth, D. M. S., Bell, S. M., & Stayton, D. J. Individual differences in the development of some attachment behaviors. *Merrill-Palmer Quarterly,* 1972, *18,* 123–143.

Ainsworth, M., Bell, S., & Stayton, D. Infant–mother attachment and social development: "Socialization" as a product of reciprocal responsiveness to signals. In M. P. M. Richards (Ed.), *The integration of a child into a social world.* London: Cambridge University Press, 1974.

Ainsworth, M., Blehar, M., Waters, E., & Wall, S. *Patterns of attachment: A psychological study of the strange situation.* Hillsdale, N.J.: Lawrence Erlbaum Associates, 1978.

Blehar, M., Ainsworth, M., & Main, M. Mother–infant interaction relevant to close bodily contact: A longitudinal study. Monograph in preparation. Cited in M. Ainsworth, M. Blehar, E. Waters, & S. Wall. *Patterns of attachment: A psychological study of the strange situation.* Hillsdale, N.J.: Lawrence Erlbaum Associates, 1978.

Brazelton, T. B., Koslowski, B., & Main, M. The origins of reciprocity: The early mother–infant interaction. In M. Lewis, & L. Rosenblum (Eds.), *The effect of the infant on its caregiver.* Ne York: Wiley, 1974.

Bruner, J. The growth and structure of skills. In K. Connelly (Ed.), *Motor skills.* New York: Academic Press, 1971.

Castellan, N. J., Jr. The analysis of behavior sequences. In R. Cairns (Ed.), *The analysis of social interactions: Methods, issues, and illustrations.* Hillsdale, N.J.: Lawrence Erlbaum Associates, 1979.

Cohn, J. *Three month old infant's response to simulated maternal depression in the context of face-to-face interaction.* Paper presented at the Biennial Meeting of the Society for Research in Child Development, Boston, 1981.

Epstein, S. Anxiety, arousal and the self-concept. In I. G. Sarason, & C. D. Spielberger (Eds.), *Stress and anxiety* (Vol. 3). Washington, D.C.: Hemisphere Publishing, 1976.

Epstein, S. The ecological study of emotions in humans. In K. Blankstein (Ed.), *Advances in the study of communication and affect.* New York: Plenum, 1979.

Epstein, S. The self-concept: A review and proposal of an integrated theory. In E. Staub

(Ed.), *Personality: Basic issues and current research*. Englewood Cliffs, N.J.: Prentice-Hall, 1980.

Fogel, A., Diamond, G., Langhorst, B., & Demos, V. Affective and cognitive aspects of the 2-month-olds' participation in face-to-face interaction with its mother. In E. Tronick (Ed.), *Social interaction in infancy: Affect, cognition, and communication*. Baltimore: University Park Press, 1982.

Hays, W. *Statistics for the social sciences* (2nd ed.). New York: Holt, Rinehart & Winston, 1973.

Hinde, R. *Biological bases of human social behavior*. London: McGraw-Hill, 1974.

Kagan, J. Discrepancy, temperament, and infant distress. In M. G. Lewis, & L. A. Rosenblum (Eds.), *Origins of fear*. New York: Wiley, 1974.

Kohut, H. *The analysis of the self*. New York: International Universities Press, 1971.

Kozak, M., & Tronick, E. *Infants take their turn in response to maternal turn yielding sigals*. Paper presented at the Biennial Meeting of the Society for Research in Child Development, Boston, 1981.

Losco, J. Reactions to positive and negative evaluations as a function of level of self-esteem, level of defensiveness, and psychological centrality. Unpublished doctoral dissertation, University of Massachusetts, 1981.

Main, M. Analysis of a peculiar form of reunion behavior seen in some day-care children: Its history and sequence in children who are home-reared. In R. Webb (Ed.), *Social development in childhood*. Baltimore: Johns Hopkins University Press, 1977.

Main, M., Tomasini, L., & Tolan, W. Differences among mothers of infants judged to differ in security. *Developmental Psychology*, 1979, *15*, 472–473.

Matas, L., Ahrend, R., & Sroufe, L. A. Continuity of adaptation in the second year: The relationship between quality of attachment and later competence. *Child Development*, 1978, *49*, 547–556.

McCall, R. B., & McGhee, P. E. The discrepancy hypothesis of attention and affect in infants. In E. C. Uzgiris, & F. Weizmann (Eds.), *The structuring of experience*. New York: Plenum, 1977.

O'Brien, J. The sources of self-esteem scale: A multidimensional personality inventory. Unpublished doctoral dissertation, University of Massachusetts, 1980.

Ricks, M. *Predicting one-year competence from earlier infant behavior: A methodological inquiry*. Unpublished manuscript, University of Massachusetts, 1981.

Ricks, M., Krafchuk, E., & Tronick, E. *A descriptive story of mother–infant face-to-face interaction at 3, 6, and 9 months of age*. Paper presented at the Biennial Meeting of the Society for Research in Child Development, San Francisco, 1979.

Ricks, M., Noyes, D., & Tronick, E. Z. *Secure babies have secure mothers*. Unpublished manuscript, University of Massachusetts, Amherst, 1981.

Sander, L. Infant and caretaking environment: Investigation and conceptualization of adaptive behavior in a system of increasing complexity. In E. G. Anthony (Ed.), *Explorations in child psychology*. New York: Plenum, 1975.

Schaffer, R. *Studies in mother–infant interaction*. London: Academic Press, 1977.

Stechler, G. S., & Carpenter, G. A viewpoint on early affective development. In J. Hellmuth (Ed.), *The exceptional infant* (Vol. 1). New York: Brunner/Mazel, 1967.

Stern, D. The goal and structure of mother–infant play. *Journal of the American Academy of Child Psychiatry*, 1974, *13*, 402–421.

Stern, D. *The first relationship*. Cambridge, Mass.: Harvard University Press, 1977.

Tronick, E. On the primacy of social skills. In D. Sawin, R. Hawkins, L. Walker, & J. Penticuff (Eds.), *Exceptional infant* (Vol. 4). New York: Brunner/Mazel, 1980.

Tronick, E. Infant's communicative intent. In B. Stark (Ed.), *Language behavior in infancy*. Amsterdam: Elsevier, 1981.

Tronick, E., Krafchuk, E., Ricks, M., Cohn, J., & Winn, S. *Social interaction, "normal and abnormal" maternal characteristics and the organization of infant social behavior.* Seminar in the Development of Infants and Parents, Boston, 1980.

Trussell, W. D. Unpublished doctoral dissertation, University of Massachusetts, Amherst, 1963.

Waters, E., & Sroufe, L. A. *Competence as a developmental construct.* Manuscript in preparation, 1981. Available from E. Waters, Psychology Department, State University of New York at Stony Brook, Stony Brook, L.I., New York, 11794.

White, R. W. Motivation reconsidered: The concept of competence. *Psychological Review.*

5 Affective Displays of High-Risk Infants During Early Interactions

Tiffany Field
University of Miami Medical School

"Brian looked at his mother's face, found her smiling, and smiled in return. Encouraged by this, she made a funny face, tickled him on the tummy, and he laughed and looked away from her. She sighed and waited, knowing he would come back for more." Although this same sequence occurs with some regularity on videotapes of early interactions (as is illustrated in Fig. 5.1), this description of Brian at 3 months was taken from his father's diary. A father's diary on a high-risk infant might read very differently—probably it would describe fewer smiles and less laughter.

In this chapter data are presented on the affective displays—the smiles, laughs, frowns, and cries—of high-risk infants as observed during early interactions with their mothers. Other important ingredients of the young infant's interactions, such as gaze behavior and physiological responses, the background against which affective displays occur, are also discussed. Finally, a model is proposed that includes hypotheses about relationships between these behaviors, and a possible explanation for the frequent observation that high-risk infants and their parents seem to have "less fun" during early interactions.

AFFECTIVE DISPLAYS, GAZE BEHAVIOR, AND HEART RATE

Affective displays or emotional expressions such as smiling, laughing, frowning, and crying are frequently coded by early-interaction researchers. However, the specific affective displays are often grouped together under

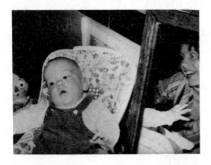

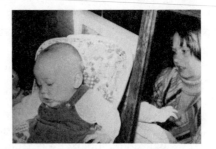

FIG. 5.1   A typical sequence observed during early interactions of normal infants and their mothers: (a) the infant looks at the mother and the mother shows an exaggerated facial expression (mock surprise here); (b) the infant and mother smile; (c) the infant laughs, the mother "relaxes" her smile; and (d) the infant looks away, the mother ceases smiling and watches her infant.

categories such as playful/distressful or positive/negative affect to map the cycles of affective changes that occur during early interactions (Brazelton, Koslowski, & Main, 1974; Tronick, Als, & Brazelton, 1980). Others have described affective changes, but have focused their reports instead on gaze behaviors (Field, 1977a; Stern, 1974). Thus, for both normal and high-risk infants, there is less information in the literature on the frequency of different affective displays than there are data on gazing/gazing away or the rhythmic cycles of attentive/involved and inattentive/disengaged behaviors. Although we have argued elsewhere that attentive and affective behaviors should be analyzed together as they occur in time (Field, 1981), some simple descriptive data are first provided on the frequency with which affective displays occurred during the early interactions of high-risk and normal infants.

Method

For these descriptive purposes the videotapes of 20 normal and 40 high-risk infants were coded. The infants called "normal" had experienced an uncomplicated delivery at term age. The high-risk group included 20 postterm, postmaturity-syndrome infants and 20 preterm, respiratory-distress syndrome (RDS) infants. These infants were considered at-risk for disturbed interactions because they presented atypical interactive behaviors at birth. For example, the preterm RDS infants were less alert, less attentive to stimulation, and less active than term, normal infants on the interaction items of the Brazelton Scale (Brazelton, 1973). The postterm, postmaturity-syndrome babies were conversely hyperactive, very easily aroused, and irritable during the same assessment (Field, Hallock, Ting, Dempsey, Dabiri, & Shuman, 1978). Even though these infants appeared to be on opposite ends of an activity and irritability continuum, they presented similarly difficult behavior to their parents during early interactions (Field, 1977a, 1977b).

When these infants were approximately 4 months old (corrected age), 3 minutes of spontaneous face-to-face interactions with their mothers were videotaped, and heart-rate activity of both infants and mothers were recorded via telemetry. The videotapes were coded for infant gaze and gaze aversion (or looking at and looking away from mother), vocalizing, laughing, crying, and the basic eight facial expressions—happy, sad, interested, surprised, afraid, angry, disgusted, and ashamed (Ekman & Friesen, 1975). Because all of these expressions except happy, sad, and interested occurred at very low frequencies, only these three were included in analyses of group differences. Similar behaviors were coded for the mothers along with the incidence with which they tactilely stimulated their infants and the frequency with which they played "infant games" such as "peek-a-boo," "pat-a-cake," "I'm gonna get you," "itsy bitsy spider," and "tell me a story." The infants' contingent responses to their mothers' smiles, vocalizations, and smiles plus vocalizations were also coded using the criterion that the infants' responses (smiles, vocalizations, or smiles plus vocalizations) occur within 3 seconds of the mothers' behaviors. Finally, the coders, who were unaware of the type of infant, rated the overall expressivity of the infants and their mothers on a 5-point Likert-type scale with a 5 representing a positive expression and 1 a negative expression.

Results

The data were analyzed by multivariate analysis of variance. Because this analysis yielded a significant value, univariate analyses of variance were performed on each of the dependent measures. Post hoc comparisons were made by Bonferroni t tests (Myers, 1972).

Affective displays.   As can be seen in Fig. 5.2, the following results emerged for the affective displays data: The normal-term infants exhibited significantly more happy faces than the postterm and preterm infants. The preterm infants exhibited significantly more sad faces than the postterm infants who, in turn, looked sad more frequently than the term infants. Interested faces occurred equally often among all infants. Analyses of the data on vocalizations suggested that cooing occurred more often among the normal than the high-risk infants, whereas crying occurred more frequently among the high-risk infants than the normal infants (see Fig. 5.3). Analyses of contingent behaviors by the infants suggested that contingent vocalizations occurred with approximately equal frequency for all three groups. Contingent smiling responses occurred more frequently among the normal than the high-risk infants. Contingent smiling and vocalizing responses also occurred more frequently in the group of normal infants (see Fig. 5.4). Analyses of the 5-point Likert-type ratings of expressivity suggested that the group of term, normal infants received more positive expressivity ratings, as did their mothers (see Fig. 5.5).

Infant gaze behavior and maternal activity. Fig. 5.6 depicts the proportion of interaction time that the mothers talked to their infants and the pro-

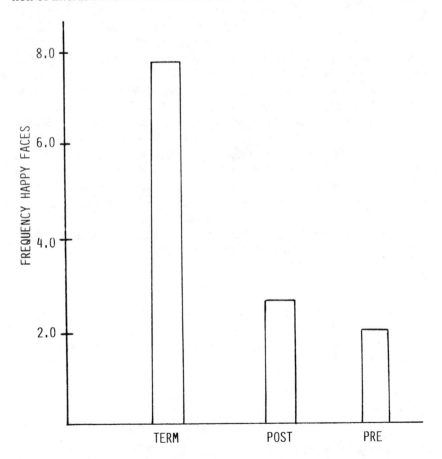

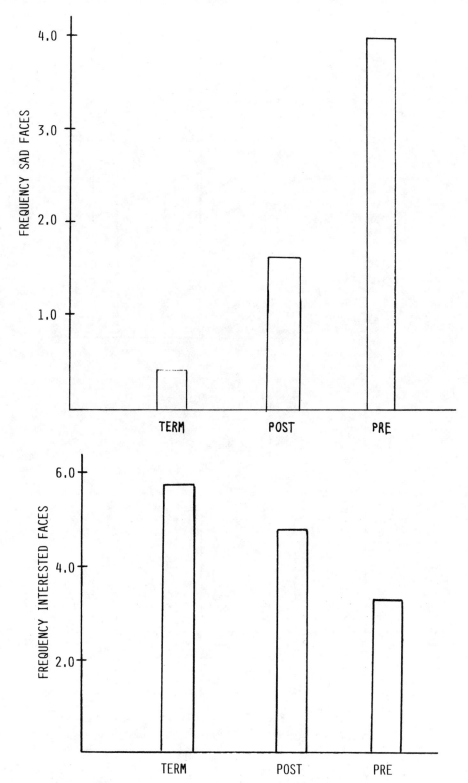

FIG. 5.2 Frequency of happy, sad, and interested facial expressions emitted by normal, postterm, and preterm infants during 3-minute spontaneous face-to-face interactions with their mothers.

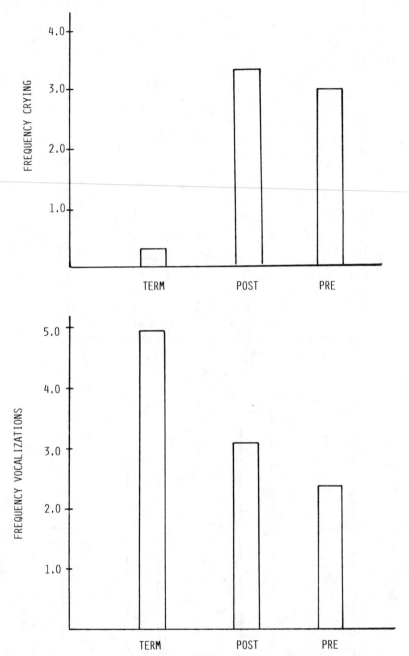

FIG. 5.3 Frequency of contented vocalizations and cries by normal, postterm, and preterm infants during 3-minute spontaneous face-to-face interactions with their mothers.

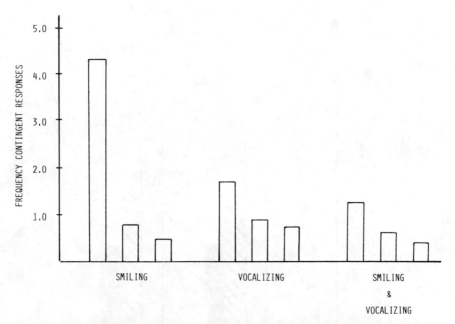

FIG. 5.4   Frequency of smiling, vocalizing, and smiling and vocalizing contingent responses of term (left bars), postterm (middle bars), and preterm (right bars) infants during 3-minute spontaneous face-to-face interactions with their mothers.

portion of interaction time that the infants gazed or looked at their mothers. The mothers of preterm RDS infants talked more than mothers of postterm, postmaturity-syndrome infants who, in turn, talked more than mothers of term, normal infants. The term, normal infants looked at their mothers for more of the interaction time than the postterm, postmaturity-syndrome infants who, in turn, gazed at their mothers more than the preterm, RDS infants. Thus, there appeared to be an inverse relationship between the amount of mother talking and infant gazing at mother. A similar relationship has been reported for interactions in which the mothers' activity level was manipulated and changes in infant gaze behavior were observed (Field, 1977a, 1979b).

Heart-rate activity.   For the analysis of interaction heart-rate activity, 10 seconds of baseline heart rate were averaged and compared to the mean heart rate for the 3-minute interactions. A 2 (baseline and interaction) × 3 (group) repeated-measures analysis of variance was conducted with baseline and interaction heart rate as the repeated measure. Fig. 5.7 illustrates the change in beats per minute from baseline heart rate to interaction heart rate. The heart rate of both preterm and postterm infants was significantly elevated during the spontaneous interaction as compared to baseline.

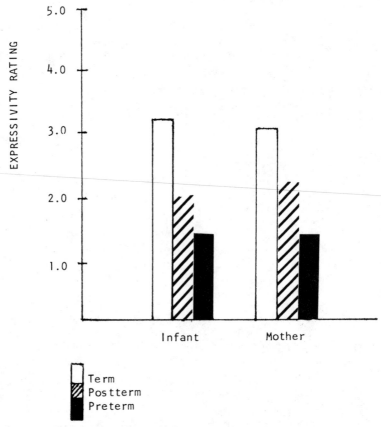

FIG. 5.5   Expressivity rating (1 = negative expressivity, 5 = positive expressivity) of term, postterm, and preterm infants and their mothers during spontaneous face-to-face interaction.

Discussion

These data suggest that the high-risk infants, both preterm RDS and post-term, postmature infants, spent less time looking at their mothers and appeared to "enjoy" their interactions less than normal-term infants. Their smiles and contented vocalizations were less frequent and their frowns and cries were more frequent than those of term infants. The greater incidence of negative affective displays among these infants together with their elevated heart rate suggest that these interactions may have been more stressful for the high-risk infants. Although the direction of effects for the amount of maternal talking and infant gazing away cannot be determined in this study, these data suggest that maternal stimulation and infant gaze

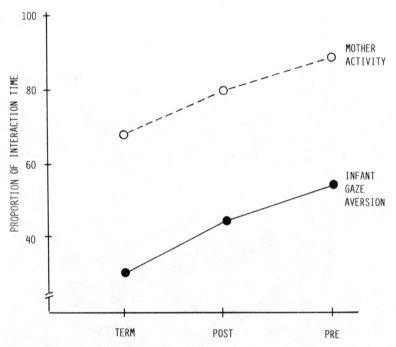

FIG. 5.6   Proportion of interaction time mothers spent talking and infants spent gazing at their mothers during spontaneous face-to-face interaction.

behaviors may be related. Elevated heart rate, gazing away, and negative affective behaviors of the infants may relate to an information overload and elevated arousal levels deriving from excessive stimulation. In their natural attempts to elicit positive affective responses, the mothers appeared to provide a level of stimulation that seemed to be counterproductive.

The attentiveness and positive affect of these infants can be enhanced by modifying the mothers' behaviors. In a previous study we asked mothers to imitate the behaviors of their infants (Field, 1977a, 1979b). The effect of this manipulation was that mothers became less active and their infants became more attentive than they had been during spontaneous interactions. Corresponding decreases were noted in tonic heart rate (see Fig. 5.8). Conversely, during an attention-getting manipulation in which we asked mothers to keep their infants' attention, mother activity increased, as did infant gaze aversion and heart rate. The interpretation of these data was that these infants may have limited information-processing and/or arousal-modulation abilities, thus requiring more frequent "breaks" from the conversation to process information and modulate arousal.

Although these studies combined might suggest that infant gaze aversion, negative affect, and elevated heart rate may be related to excessive maternal

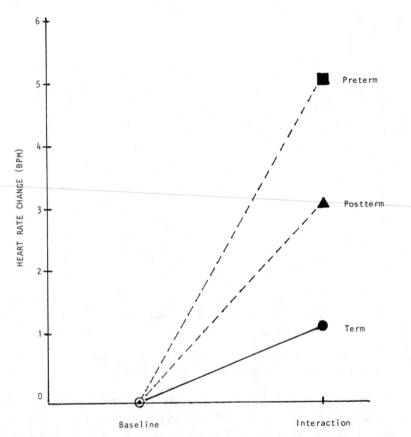

FIG. 5.7 Mean tonic heart-rate changes in beats per minute from baseline to spontaneous interaction for term, postterm, and preterm infants.

stimulation, other studies suggest that these infants show even more frequent gaze aversion during interactions with their fathers (Field, 1981a) and during interactions with less-active infant peers and preschool siblings (Field, 1981b), as can be seen in Fig. 5.9.

In all of these interaction situations, the high-risk infants appear to gaze avert more frequently than the normal infants. The only situation in which we have observed equivalent amounts of visual attentiveness by high-risk and normal infants was an interaction with an inanimate Raggedy Ann doll. Face-to-face with an inanimate doll, normal and high-risk infants showed equivalent amounts of looking at the doll and very similar tonic heart rate. When the doll was animated—that is, when we mechanically nodded its head and it emitted taperecorded sounds, "Hi there baby. How are you?"—the high-risk infants showed more gaze aversion and higher levels of tonic heart rate (Field, 1979c). These data appear in Fig. 5.10.

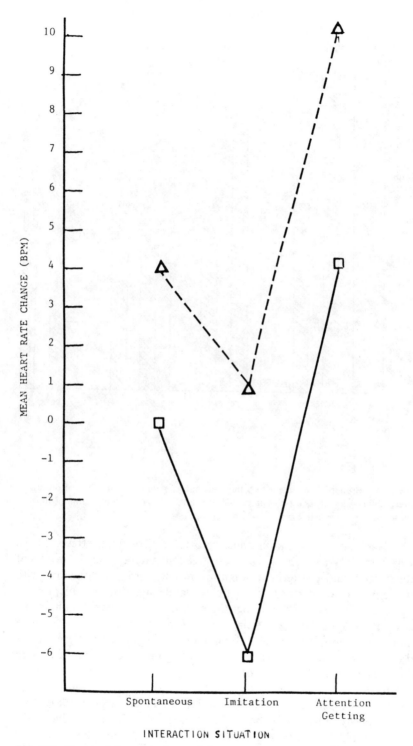

FIG. 5.8 Mean tonic heart-rate changes in beats per minute from baseline situation to spontaneous, imitation, and attention-getting manipulated interactions for normal infants (-) and for high-risk infants (---).

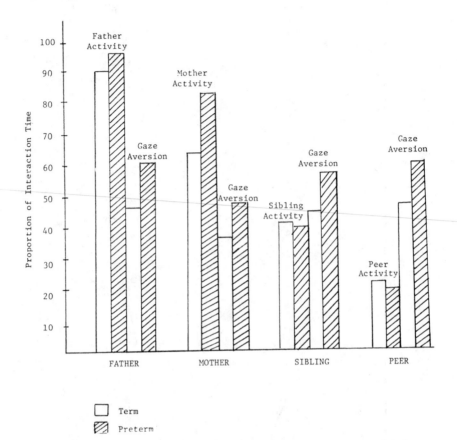

FIG. 5.9 Proportion of interaction time that infant gaze aversion occurred during peer, sibling, mother, and father interactions as a function of the proportion of time those partners were active (vocalizing and/or touching).

Thus, animated stimulation appears to have differential effects on the normal and high-risk infants. The more-frequent gaze-averting behaviors of preterm RDS and postterm, postmature infants during interactions with animate interaction partners from the neonatal stage, for example, during Brazelton assessments, suggest that these infants may have difficulty processing information or modulating arousal in the presence of animate stimulation. Appropriate levels of stimulation may differ for these infants and they may respond to a narrower range of stimulation, creating a more difficult task for their parents of fine tuning the intensity and amount of stimulation.

Elsewhere we have described an activation band model (Field, 1981c) that includes the hypothesis that normal and high-risk infants may have different thresholds and ranges of responsivity to stimulation. This model was presented as follows:

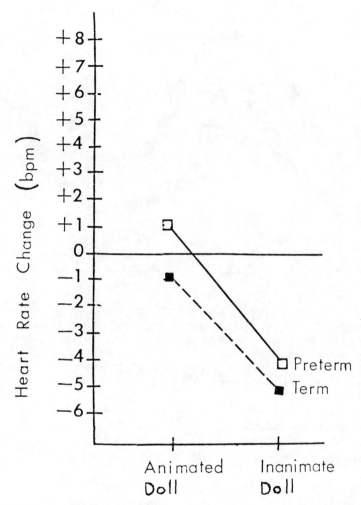

FIG. 5.10   Mean tonic heart-rate changes in beats per minute from baseline to situations of animated and inanimate doll.

1. Attentiveness and positive affect during early interactions may occur within a range or band of activation that has as its lower limit an attention threshold and as its upper limit an aversion threshold. An hypothetical activation band for normal infants is depicted by the dotted lines in Fig. 5.11. The lower limit reflects a threshold for accepting or attending to stimulation and the upper limit a threshold for rejecting or averting stimulation.

2. The upper and lower thresholds of this activation band may shift and the band width may vary as a function of the infant's rest–activity and arousal cycles.

3. An intrinsic curvilinear relationship between stimulation and arousal/

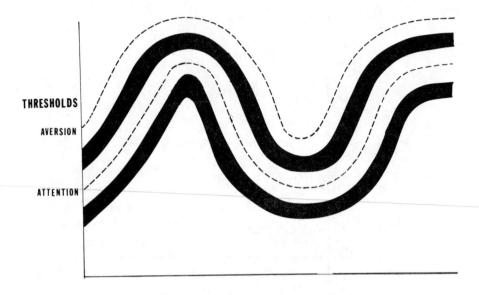

REST-ACTIVITY/AROUSAL CYCLES

FIG. 5.11   Posited activation band model. Upper solid line is posited activation band for preterm infants, broken-line band for term infants, and lower solid band for post-term infants. Lower and upper limits of band represent attention and aversion thresholds, respectively, and bands represent range of stimulation to which infant responds attentively and with positive affect.

attention/affect processes suggests that only moderate stimulation (be that quantitatively moderate or moderately discrepant stimulation) would fall within the activation band. As the thresholds of the band shift, the relative discrepancy or amount of stimulation perceived by the infant may also shift.

4. Within the activation band, positive affect may occur and vary in form and energy (e.g., from smiling to laughing) as a function of both the parameters of stimulation and the arousal level and attentive/affective response energy of the infant.

5. Moderate levels of positive affect such as smiling and laughing may serve to modulate arousal and sustain attention (Sroufe & Waters, 1976).

6. If and when stimulation and/or affective responsivity exceed moderate levels, the upper limit of the activation band is approached, at which point the infant will manifest an inattentive response (for example, gaze aversion). If that limit or threshold is exceeded, an aversive reaction or negative affect (e.g., fussing or crying) will occur.

7. As the infant develops, arousal cycles may lengthen and the proposed activation band may widen as manifested by longer periods of attentiveness and more modulated affective responses.

8. The activation band width and thresholds vary as a function of in-

dividual differences; for example, thresholds may differ, the activation band may be narrower, and the arousal cycles may be shorter in infants experiencing developmental delays or deficits (be they perceptual, motor, cognitive, or physiological delays or deficits). More specifically, as depicted in the upper solid curve of Fig. 5.11, there may be a narrower band for hyporesponsive infants such as preterm, Downs syndrome, and autistic infants, which may feature a higher-than-normal attention threshold and a lower-than-normal aversion threshold. Similarly, there may be a narrower band for hyperreactive infants (e.g., postterm, hyperactive, and autistic infants). In contrast to the posited activation band of hyporesponsive infants, the band of hyperreactive infants may be delimited by both lower attention and lower aversion thresholds.

This model could be tested by shifting stimulus parameters in the range of the hypothesized thresholds and monitoring operationally defined, observable behaviors (e.g., gaze, facial expressions, vocal expressions, and body movements) and physiological behaviors (e.g., heart rate, respiration, and muscle tension.)

Based on Brazelton neonatal data of these infants (Field et al., 1978), on neonatal responsivity and habituation to tactile and auditory stimulation (Field, Dempsey, Ting, Hatch, & Clifton, 1979), on data from interaction studies on these infants (Field, 1977a, 1979b, 1981b), and on data from this study, we would hypothesize that the preterm RDS infants have higher thresholds to stimulation, that the postterm, postmature infants have lower thresholds to stimulation, and that both groups may have more delimited activation bands within which they show attentive and positive affective behaviors. The mother of the preterm RDS infant would need to provide more intense or variable stimulation to elicit her infant's attention whereas the mother of the postterm, postmature infant would need to provide less intense or variable stimulation to elicit her infant's attention. But both groups may have narrower activation bands or a narrower range of stimulation to which they would respond with attentiveness and positive affect. The mothers of these infants would, thus, be "walking a narrow line" in gauging their stimulation so as not to exceed the upper or aversion thresholds and elicit gaze-averting or fussy behavior. The following study on game playing between these infants and their mothers was an attempt to more directly study that question.

GAME PLAYING BETWEEN HIGH-RISK INFANTS AND THEIR MOTHERS

Game playing is a high-frequency event during early interactions. Among the most popularly played games for this age group are "peek-a-boo," "pat-a-cake," "I'm gonna get you," "itsy bitsy spider," "so-big," and "tell me a story" (Field 1979a). Infant games of this kind have been noted to occur approximately 39% of the interaction time for normal infants and their mothers and fathers, but significantly less frequently (28% of the time) among high-risk infants and their parents (Field 1979a). Games of this kind appear to be directed towards eliciting positive affect such as smiling and laughing, and have been used by some researchers to assess the developmental course of smiling and laughter during infancy (Sroufe & Wunsch, 1972). Occasionally the repetition of games or the intensification of stimulation during a game that is eliciting positive affect will suddenly elicit averting and crying behaviors, as "the child who laughed so hard his laughter turned to crying." As suggested in our description of the activation band model, an important rule of game playing may be to modify, reduce, or cease stimulation when the infant becomes aroused, or when the infant is attempting to modulate arousal, as manifested by behaviors such as smiling or laughing.

The purpose of this study was to determine the frequency of game playing among these groups, as a replication of our earlier study (Field, 1979a) and to observe the frequency with which the infant's mother would decrease or cease stimulation at high points of arousal as indicated by smiles and laughter. In addition, a game-playing manipulation was introduced in which the mother was given an instruction to play a game repeatedly until the infant laughed to determine the infant's threshold to laughter and the probability with which gaze aversion and crying would closely follow laughter. This, then, was an exploratory study on the attention and aversion thresholds of these infants in the context of natural interaction activity such as game playing.

Method

The sample was the same as was described in the previous study. The game-playing manipulation followed the spontaneous 3-minute interactions described in the previous study. The mothers were given a demonstration of the game "I'm gonna get you." That game was selected because it was frequently observed during the spontaneous interactions of an earlier study (Field, 1979a). The game consists of the mother's eyes widening and her head looming forward and making contact with the infant's stomach. As the mother looms forward, she repeatedly says, "I'm gonna get you," "I'm gonna get you" with increasing frequency and intensity. She then shakes her head in the infant's stomach as if tickling the infant with her head. The mothers were instructed to pause a few seconds between trials of the game and to cease playing the game at the point at which the infant began to laugh.

We considered having the experimenter play this game with all infants to standardize the procedure or limit the amount of individual variability in the playing of the game. However, we were concerned that the experimenter, by virtue of being a "stranger," might alter the infant's arousal and affective behaviors inasmuch as infants even this young have been noted to respond differently to strangers (Field, 1977b; Fogel, 1981b).

Results

Analyses of the coded videotapes of spontaneous interactions indicated that the normal-term infants and their mothers played "infant" games such as those already listed a greater percentage of the interaction time (39%) than the postterm, postmature infants and their mothers (22% of the interaction time) or the preterm RDS infants and their mothers (21% of the interaction time). In addition, the term infants and their mothers played a greater number of different games ($M = 4.2$) or a greater variety of games than the postterm infants and their mothers (2.3) or the preterm RDS infants and their mothers (1.9).

To determine the percentage of the time mothers of term, postterm, and preterm infants decreased or ceased stimulation at the point of infant laughter, gaze aversion, and crying, the videotapes were scanned for each instance of these infant behaviors by one coder. The behaviors of the mothers preceding and following infant laughing, gaze aversion, and crying were recorded by another coder. If the mother decreased the amount of stimulation, for example by ceasing stimulation in the auditory or tactile modalities, or ceased stimulating the infant in all modalities, that instance was scored as a decrease or cessation of stimulation. The percentage of time a decrease or cessation of stimulation occurred was then determined by the ratio of decreases/cessations to the frequency with which those infant behaviors occurred.

As can be seen in Table 5.1, the mothers of term infants decreased or ceased stimulation a greater percentage of the times that infants laughed, averted gaze, or cried than the mothers of preterm or postterm infants.

Analyses of the data on the "I'm gonna get you" game included the following measures: (1) the number of trials or episodes of the game prior to the onset of infant laughter; (2) the probability with which infant gaze aversion followed laughter; and (3) the probability with which infant crying occurred following gaze aversion.

The results of analyses of variance for group differences suggested the following: (1) postterm infants laughed after the least number of trials, and more trials were required by the preterm infants than by the term infants; (2) following laughter, the probability of gaze aversion was significantly greater for the postterm and preterm infants than for the term infants; and (3) following gaze aversion, the probability of crying was significantly greater for the high-risk infants than for the normal infants.

TABLE 5.1
Means for Game Playing Measures

	Term	Groups Postterm	Preterm
Game playing time (%)	39	22	21
Different games (#)	4.2	2.3	1.9
"I'm gonna get you" game			
Infant			
Trials to laughter (#)	4.6	2.1	7.3
Probability gaze aversion (%)	18	47	57
Probability crying (%)	07	43	41
Mother: Probability ↓ or cease stimulation			
Postlaughter (%)	62	38	41
Postgaze aversion (%)	71	57	53
Postcrying (%)	84	64	67

Discussion

The mothers of preterm and postterm infants engaged in significantly less game playing and a lesser variety of games during spontaneous interactions with their infants. Judging from the data on the game-playing manipulation, the instruction to "play the 'I'm gonna get you game' repeatedly until the infant laughs," the mothers may have played games less often because they were less effective in eliciting and sustaining positive affect in their infants.

The preterm infants required a greater number of game trials before laughing, which may relate to their hypothesized higher thresholds, and the postterm infants required very few trials, which may relate to lower thresholds. However, both preterm and postterm infants were more likely than term infants to gaze avert subsequent to their laughter and cry subsequent to gaze aversion. Thus, once the preterm and postterm infants began to laugh, they were also more likely to gaze avert and cry. Understandably, then, if gaze aversion and crying in the infant are aversive to the mother, as they appear to be given that mothers often look distressed and show elevated heart rate during those behaviors (Field, 1979b), she will less frequently play games. However, because smiling and laughing by the infant are pleasant behaviors, the mother may occasionally play games, presumably to elicit those behaviors.

These infants may laugh less frequently, just as they smile less frequently, and when they do, as in the "I'm gonna get you" game, the mother may wish to prolong the laughter. When the high-risk infant laughed during spontaneous interactions, the mother was less likely to decrease or cease her stimulation; perhaps because laughter was a rare event, she wanted to sustain it. She appeared to continue her stimulation, perhaps thinking that the same stimulation that elicited laughter would sustain laughter. Unfortunately, her sustained stimulation appeared to have the opposite effect. That is, instead of prolonging laughter, her continued stimulation may have contributed to the ensuing gaze aversion and in some cases crying by the infant. If these high-risk infants, who appear to have atypical thresholds and more delimited ranges of positive affective responses, will laugh, then gaze avert, and ultimately cry with greater probability than normal infants, and if behaviors such as laughter, gaze aversion, and crying serve the function of modulating arousal as has been suggested by some investigators (Sroufe, Waters, & Matas, 1974), then the mothers' persistence in stimulating the infants may drive the infants towards and beyond aversive thresholds.

The mothers of these high-risk infants seem to be faced with the task of providing only the necessary amount of stimulation, not too much nor too little, to elicit a response, but then having a narrower range within which they can behave without "driving" the infant to aversive behaviors. Upon eliciting a positive affective behavior, the mother may have to realize that "more of the same stimulation" may not sustain that positive affective behavior. The infants' "high arousal" behaviors such as laughter, gaze aversion, and crying must be read as signals that the infant may need a break to process information and modulate arousal. Unfortunately, it appears that once a mother elicits positive responses, which may be rare for these infants, she may persist to elicit more of those responses instead of modulating her behavior. In the last analysis, it may be easier not to engage in infant games than to play them not so well and experience the discomfort of infant gaze aversion and crying.

What appeared to be happening during mother–infant games was that the mother added on behaviors and intensified them as the game proceeded. The infant's affective responses increased in intensity, as, for example, he or she moved from smiling to laughing. In the "I'm gonna get you" game, the mother first used only her voice, which gradually increased in frequency and intensity. She added to this her widened eyes as in a mock surprise face, gradually loomed her head forward, and then shook her head in the infant's tummy as in tickling. The infant first looked attentive, then smiled, and ultimately laughed. Typically as the infant smiles, there is a diminution of activity on the part of the mother; for example, her face relaxes from mock surprise to smile and then she looms and tickles, frequently eliciting laughter in her infant. The mother then often decreases or ceases a number of her behaviors (as was noted in our probability analysis). If she persisted in stimulating her infant, as was noted for the majority of the mothers of preterm and postterm infants, the infant then gaze averted and/or cried.

Analyses of heart rate during interactions suggest that the infant may be aroused autonomically during smiles, laughter, gaze aversion, and crying.

Although heart-rate increases surrounding these behaviors have been typically attributed to movement artifacts, a number of studies have reported that the heart-rate accelerations occur prior to these motoric, affective behaviors. For example, in the study by Stoller and Field (Chapter 4, this volume), heart-rate acceleration frequently occurred prior to smiling. In another study in our lab, heart-rate acceleration occurred prior to gaze aversion with heart rate returning to baseline during the gaze-aversion period (Field, 1981d). A similar heart-rate acceleration preceded crying behavior in a study of Vaughn and Sroufe (1979).

Thus, smiles, laughter, gaze aversion, and crying may be the affective components of autonomic arousal. They may serve as signals to the mother that the infant is aroused and thereby may function as effective "cut-off" behaviors or behaviors that serve to minimize incoming stimulation. During laughter, for example, the eyes are often closed and the ears may also be unreceptive to external stimulation as the peals of one's own laughter predominate. Gaze aversion and crying may even more effectively block external stimulation. It is interesting, in this vein, that two of the most effective types of stimulation for overriding an infant's crying is a vestibular bouncing motion (stimulation in a competing modality), or a louder, higher-pitched, "ah" sound gradually decelerating in pitch (an auditory stimulus with competing frequencies that could be perceived during infant crying).

Smiling and laughing may reflect a positive state during which arousal levels may be within a tolerable range as we have suggested in our activation band model. Others have suggested that smiles and laughter are tension-release behaviors that enable the infant to modulate arousal while still maintaining attention to the stimulation (Fogel, Diamond, Langhorst, & Demos, 1981; Sroufe et al., 1974). Mothers, at least, treat these behaviors as signals to modulate their own behavior. For example, most of the mothers of normal infants reduced stimulation at the point at which infants laughed, and fewer mothers waited until the infants gaze averted or cried. There appears to be a relationship between the infant's ability to modulate arousal with smiles and laughter without reverting to gaze aversion and crying and the mother's immediate reduction in stimulation following the smiling and laughing behaviors.

A schematic illustration of the progression of behaviors during game playing can be seen in Fig. 5.12. The X axes depict sustained attention of the infant and variation or modulation of stimulation by the mother. The Y axis depicts heart rate. Within the Figure, the solid ascending curve represents increasing heart rate and the dotted descending curves represent decreasing heart rate. The hatched bars represent variation in the mothers' use of stimulus modalities or varying intensity of stimulation (the "adding on" and "dropping out" of behaviors by mothers). Heart rate is depicted

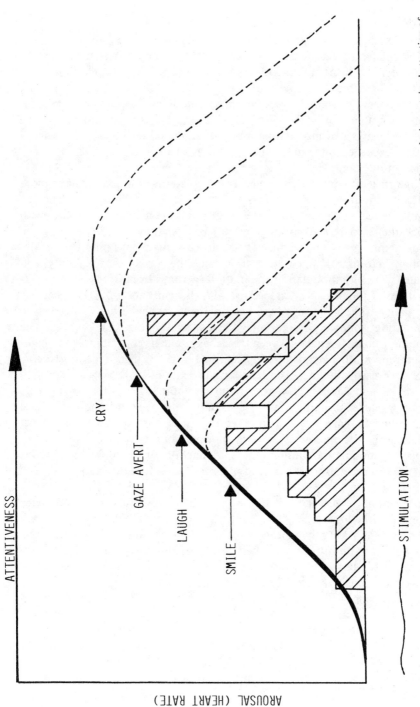

FIG. 5.12 A schematic illustration of the progression of infant and mother behaviors during game playing. The X axes depict sustained attention of the infant and variation or modulation of stimulation by the mother. The Y axis depicts heart rate. Within the Figure, the solid ascending curve respresents increasing heart rate and the dotted descending curves represent decreasing heart rate. The hatched bars represent variation in the mothers' use of stimulus modalities or varying intensity of stimulation.

121

as progressively increasing prior to smiling, laughing, gaze-averting, and crying behaviors. As the behaviors occur, the level of maternal stimulation decreases, and heart rate peaks and gradually returns to baseline.

Thus, the affective displays may enable the infant to modulate arousal and may serve as signals to the mother to modulate stimulation. If the infant is less able to modulate arousal or the mother is not responsive to the affective displays by modulating stimulation, the infant's aversive threshold may be exceeded, and the infant may gaze avert and cry, essentially terminating the game.

High-risk infants such as preterm and postterm infants may have more difficulty modulating arousal, as is suggested by the lesser incidence of positive affective displays in these infants and the greater probability with which they progress from laughter to gaze aversion to crying during the "I'm gonna get you" game. Their mothers may have more difficulty reading their infants' signals (in part because they occur less frequently) and greater difficulty modulating stimulation (perhaps because they are "seeking more of the pleasure" associated with their infants' infrequent smiling and laughter). This is suggested by their lesser probabilities of decreasing stimulation following infant laughter, gaze averting, and crying. The hypothesized differences between the behavioral curves of normal and high-risk infant–mother dyads are depicted in Fig. 5.13. The uppermost curve might represent the high-risk dyad with the mother's starting her stimulation at a high enough level to attract her infant's attention, as appears necessary with a preterm infant, for example, but then sustaining that level despite infant gaze aversion and crying. In contrast, the lower curve, representing the interaction of the normal infant–mother dyad, shows varied or modulated stimulation as a function of the infant's affective signals and a cessation of behavior at gaze avert before the infant reaches a crying state.

Determining the origins of the problem in complex streams of behavior such as interactions is difficult at best. However, manipulations of interactions, such as asking the mothers to imitate their infants, to be silent during gaze aversion, and to simplify their behaviors by repetition (Field, 1981e), appear to diminish gaze aversion and crying and effect increases in attentiveness and positive affective displays such as smiling and laughing. More complex forms of analyses may be required to determine the temporal relationships between the infants' affective displays and the mothers' responses to these and how the parents of the high-risk infants such as these might modify their behavior to effect more positive affect in their infants (Field, 1981; Fogel, 1981a). In the interim, we may continually observe that high-risk infants and their parents appear to have "less fun" during early interactions.

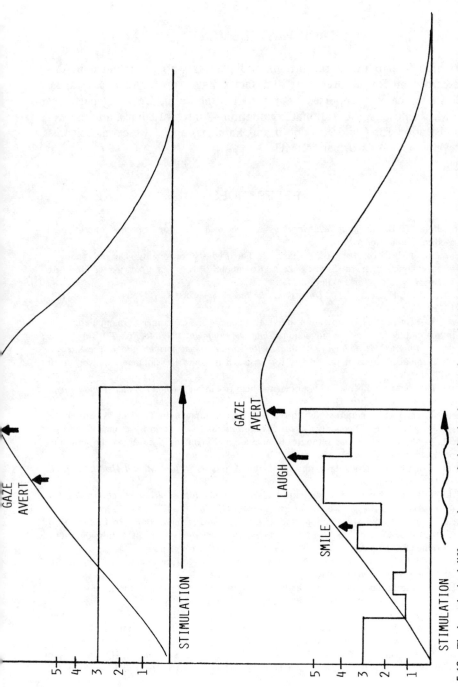

FIG. 5.13   The hypothesized differences between the behavioral curves of normal and high-risk infant–mother dyads. The upper curve represents the hypothetical high-risk dyad with the mother stimulating her infant at a level sufficient to attain her infant's attention but then sustaining that level rather than modulating stimulation during infant gaze aversion and crying. The lower curve depicts the normal infant–mother dyad, showing varied or modulated stimulation by the mother as a function of the infant's affective signals and a cessation of behavior at infant gaze aversion with the infant never reaching a crying state.

ACKNOWLEDGMENTS

I would like to thank the infants and parents who participated in this research and Reena Greenberg and Jackie Zagursky for their assistance. This research was supported by grants from the Public Health Department of Massachusetts, the National Foundation—March of Dimes, and the Administration for Children, Youth and Families, and a Research Scientist Development Award from NIMH.

REFERENCES

Brazelton, T. B. *Neonatal behavioral assessment scale.* London: Spastics International Medical Publications, 1973.

Brazelton, T. B., Koslowski, B., & Main, M. The origins of reciprocity: The early mother–infant interaction. In M. Lewis, & L. A. Rosenblum (Eds.), *The effects of the infant on its caregiver.* New York: Wiley, 1974.

Ekman, P., & Friesen, W. V. *Unmasking the face.* Englewood Cliffs, N.J.: Prentice-Hall, 1975.

Field, T. Effects of early separation, interactive deficits and experimental manipulations on infant–mother face-to-face interaction. *Child Development,* 1977, *48,* 763–771. (a)

Field, T. *Interactions of high-risk infants with various social partners.* Paper presented at the Biennial Meeting of the Society for Research in Child Development, Denver, April 1977. (b)

Field, T. Games parents play with normal and high-risk infants. *Child Psychiatry and Human Development,* 1979, *10,* 41–48. (a)

Field, T. Interaction patterns of high-risk and normal infants. In T. Field, A. Sostek, S. Goldberg, & H. H. Shuman (Ed.), *Infants born at risk.* New York: Spectrum, 1979. (b)

Field, T. Visual and cardiac responses to animate and inanimate faces by young term and preterm infants. *Child Development,* 1979, *50,* 188–194. (c)

Field, T. Fathers' interactions with their high-risk infants. *Infant Mental Health Journal,* 1981, *2,* 249–256. (a)

Field, T. Gaze behavior of normal and high-risk infants during early interactions. *Journal of the American Academy of Child Psychiatry,* 1981, *20,* 308–317. (b)

Field, T. Infant arousal, attention, and affect during early interactions. In L. Lipsitt, & C. K. Rovee-Collier (Eds.), *Advances in infant development* (Vol. 1). Hillsdale, N.J.: Lawrence Erlbaum Associates, 1981. (c)

Field, T. Infant gaze aversion and heart rate during face-to-face interactions. *Infant Behavior and Development,* 1981, *4,* 307–316. (d)

Field, T. Interaction coaching for high-risk infants and their parents. In H. Moss (Ed.), *Prevention and human sciences,* New York: Haworth Press, 1981. (e)

Field, T., Dempsey, J., Ting, G., Hatch, J., & Clifton, R. Cardiac and behavioral responses to repeated tactile and auditory stimulation by preterm and full-term infants during the neonatal period. *Developmental Psychology,* 1979, *15,* 406–416.

Field, T., Hallock, N., Ting, E., Dempsey, J., Dabiri, C., & Shuman, H. H. A first year follow-up of high-risk infants: Formulating a cumulative risk index. *Child Development,* 1978, *49,* 119–131.

Fogel, A. Early adult–infant interaction: Expectable sequences of behavior. *Journal of Pediatric Psychology,* 1981. (a)

Fogel, A. *Face-to-face interaction with 2-month-olds: Mother vs. stranger.* Paper presented at the Biennial Meeting of the Society for Research in Child Development, Boston, 1981. (b)

Fogel, A., Diamond, G. R., Langhorst, B. H., & Demos, V. Affective and cognitive aspects of the two-month-old's participation in face-to-face interaction with its mother. In E. Tronick (Ed.), *Social interchange in infancy.* Baltimore: University Park Press, 1982.

Myers, J. L. *Fundamentals of experimental design.* Boston: Allyn & Bacon, 1972.

Sroufe, L. A., & Waters, E. The ontogenesis of smiling and laughter: A perspective on the organization of development in infancy. *Psychological Review,* 1976, *83*(3), 173–189.

Sroufe, L. A., Waters, E., & Matas, L. Contextual determinants of infant affective response. In M. Lewis, & L. Rosenblum (Eds.), *The origins of behavior, Vol. 2: Fear.* New York: Wiley, 1974.

Sroufe, L. A., & Wunsch, J. P. The development of laughter in the first year of life. *Child Development,* 1972, *43,* 1326–1344.

Stern, D. N. Mother and infant at play. In M. Lewis, & L. Rosenblum (Eds.), *The effect of the infant on its caregiver.* New York: Wiley, 1974.

Tronick, E., Als, H., & Brazelton, T. B. Monadic phases: A structural descriptive analysis of infant–mother face-to-face interaction. *Merrill-Palmer Quarterly,* 1980, *26,* 3–24.

Vaughn, B., & Sroufe, L. A. The temporal relationship between infant heart rate acceleration and crying in an aversive situation. *Child Development,* 1979, *50,* 565–567.

II OLDER INFANTS AND TODDLERS: PLAY INTERACTION

6

Facial Expressions of Infants and Toddlers: A Descriptive Analysis

E. Virginia Demos
Boston University School of Medicine

This chapter represents a beginning effort to explore the form and variety of facial expressions in early childhood. At present, we have little information relating to the developmental history of these behaviors. There are, for instance, no continuous records of facial expressions from infancy through childhood (Charlesworth & Kreutzer, 1973). This represents an enormous gap in our knowledge of affect; issues relating to subtle changes in facial expression over time, the appearance of new expressions (e.g., surprise as distinct from startle, fear as distinct from distress, and anger as distinct from distress), and the process of learning to disguise or to "fake" affective expressions remain unexplored. Nor do we have continuous records of the total expressive repertoire from infancy through childhood.

Indeed, these goals may prove to be impossible. Paul Ekman, after spending many years analyzing adult faces, has now become interested in infant faces as a result of the recent birth of his daughter. He reported, in conversation, that he was seeing many changes within each week during the first month, changes as big as those between the first and second month, so that even filming an hour a day, as he did, was not sufficient to obtain a record of the developments. Now, of course Paul Ekman is a representative of the most stringent criteria for looking at faces. But using even the loosest of standards, records documenting the changes in expressive behaviors in the first two or three years of life do not exist. It is generally assumed that as children get older, they become less expressive (e.g., they cry and shriek less, temper tantrums diminish, etc.) but we know virtually nothing about the processes involved or the consequences for the children. How and when do children learn to express their affects in a socially acceptable and appropriate manner, intensity, and context? The process involves the learning of what Ekman (1972, 1977) calls cultural display rules. Children can articulate rules for expressing affect by the age of 9 (Demos, 1974), but behavioral mastery of these rules must occur considerably earlier.

Although this study cannot hope to supply all the data necessary to resolve even some of these issues, it does make an initial foray into the territory. The data I present were collected in the context of a larger study of the socialization of affect in early childhood that was begun in 1976. One of the goals of that study was to collect baseline data on expressive behaviors in young children in naturalistic settings. The design of the study was influenced by the theories and work of Charles Darwin (1872/1965), Silvan Tomkins (1962, 1963), and Paul Ekman (1972) concerning affects and affective expressions. All three have postulated the importance of the face in the experience and communication of affect. Thus there was an emphasis placed on obtaining a good record of facial expressions, as well as a record of the whole child and the context. Without going into an elaborate theoretical justification at this time (see Demos, 1975, 1982), I would like to make it clear from the outset that in adopting this particular theoretical framework (I refer here to the differential affect theory set forth by Silvan Tomkins [1962, 1963] and its subsequent elaboration by Paul Ekman and Carroll Izard), we are making the assumption that facial expressions in young children represent the primary, the most precise, and the clearest indicators of affective states. However, we have not assumed, and neither do Tomkins, Ekman, or Izard, that facial expressions are the only indicators. Thus we have utilized vocalizations, body movements, and context in an effort to understand the meaning of the facial behaviors, although our knowledge of these other indicators is less detailed and precise than our knowledge of facial behaviors.

Paul Ekman and Wally Friesen have produced the most exhaustive and precise analysis of facial behavior to date (1975, 1978).[1] What follows is a brief summary of some of the parameters they have discovered and a brief definition of terms that we use throughout our description of children's facial behavior. Ekman has described the face as a multisignal system. It possesses static features such as shape, color, size, and spacing of eyes, eyebrow, nose, and mouth that convey information about sex, race, and so on. The face goes through slow changes, such as the development of wrinkles, that convey information about age. It also produces rapid facial signals, produced by movements of the facial muscles, that change the appearance of the face for a matter of seconds or fractions of a second, and that convey information primarily about affect. Ekman has designated the specific signals in each part of the face (the upper face—brows and

---

[1]For brevity, these works are subsequently referred to under the name of the senior author only.

forehead; the eyes; and the lower face—cheeks, nose, mouth, and jaw) that convey messages of fear, surprise, sadness, happiness, anger, disgust, and combinations thereof. Table 6.1 contains a description of the specific movements in the three areas of the face for each discrete affect. Blends of two affects can occur in which one area of the face conveys one affect and another area of the face conveys the second affect—for example, a distressed brow with an angry mouth. Mixed blends can occur when affects are mixed in the same area of the face—for example, if the mouth is dropped open as in surprise, but the corners of the mouth are turned up in happiness. The reader is urged to practice producing on his or her own face (preferably with the aid of a mirror) each of the movements described in Table 6.1 in order to experience directly the movements we describe here.

Ekman has also described three major ways of managing and controlling these facial expressions of affect:

1. One can qualify an expression by adding a further expression as a comment on the expression one has just shown—for instance, smiling right after an angry expression. Such a qualification of anger usually conveys the message "I'm angry, but I've got it under control."

2. One can modulate the intensity of an expression to show either more or less than is actually felt. This can be done by varying (1) the number of facial areas involved; (2) the duration of the expression; or (3) the strength of the muscle action.

3. One can falsify an expression. This can be done by simulating an expression—for example, showing a feeling when none is felt; by neutralizing an expression—for example, showing nothing when feeling something; or by masking an expression by covering one expression with another expression. For example, microexpressions, with a duration of less than .2 of a second, represent interruptions and usually indicate an effort to mask or neutralize the microexpression. There are also macroexpressions, with durations of 5 to 10 seconds. These generally represent playful exaggerations or mock expressions.

In addition to the role of rapid facial signals in conveying the emotional messages just described, there are other messages conveyed using some of the same facial movements. Thus, rapid facial signals are also used as conversational punctuators, or to send what Ekman has called emblematic messages that have a culturally shared, specific meaning, such as an eyebrow raise when asking a question, or a wink in a flirtatious situation. There are also emotion emblems, which look like facial expressions of emotion but are different enough so that it is clear to the observer that the person is not feeling the emotion at the moment but is commenting on it. An example would be a quick wrinkling of the nose when discussing something disgusting.

This brief summary of Ekman's system for describing rapid facial signals

TABLE 6.1
Description of Facial Movements for Discrete Affects

Affect	Upper Face	Eyes	Lower Face
Surprise	Brows raised so they are curved and high. Skin below brow stretched. Horizontal wrinkles across forehead.	Eyelids opened. Upper lid raised, lower lid drawn down. White of the eye shows above the iris; often below as well.	Jaw drops open so that lips and teeth are parted. No tension or stretching of mouth.
Fear	Brows raised and drawn together. Wrinkles in center of forehead.	Upper eyelid raised, white of eye shows. Lower eyelid tensed and drawn up.	Mouth open. Lips either tensed slightly and drawn back, or stretched and drawn back.
Disgust	Brows lowered, lowering the upper lid.	Relaxed. Appear narrow because of brow action and cheek raise.	Upper lip raised. Lower lip also raised and pushed up to upper lip, or lowered and slightly protruding. Nose wrinkled. Cheeks raised. Lower lid pushed up, but not tense, with lines showing below it.
Anger	Brows lowered and drawn together. Vertical lines between the brows.	Lowered lid tensed, may or may not be raised. Upper lid tensed, may or may not be lowered by brow action. Eyes have a hard stare, may have a bulging appearance.	Lips either pressed firmly together, with the corners straight or down; or open, tensed, in squarish shape as if shouting.
	There is ambiguity unless anger is registered in all three facial areas.		
Happiness	Brows relaxed.	Crow's-feet wrinkles in outer corners of the eye. Lower lid may be raised but not tense.	Corners of lips drawn back and up. Mouth may or may not be parted. Teeth may or may not be exposed. A wrinkle (nasolabial fold) runs down from nose to outer edge beyond lip corners. Cheeks raised. Lower lid shows wrinkles below it.
Sadness	Inner corners of brows drawn up, may or may not be drawn together as well. Skin below the brow triangulated, with the inner corner up.	Inner corner of upper lid raised. Lower lid may or may not be raised.	Corners of lips down, or lips loose and trembling, or mouth open in vocal cry.

represents the culmination of years of study of adult faces. One of the goals of this study was to explore the question of how much of this complexity is visible on the face of the young child. Careful, systematic coding of infant faces has only recently begun, but the data thus far suggest that the specific facial movements designated by Ekman for each discrete affect are present on the infant's face, and convey the same emotional messages (Ekman, 1980; Izard & Buechler, 1980; Oster, 1978; Oster & Ekman, 1978). The resolution of developmental issues such as how many of these discrete expressions are present at birth, what is the nature of the changes in earliest infancy (e.g., changes in number of facial areas involved, or in duration, or in strength of muscle action, or in blends gradually separating out into two discrete expressions) awaits the results of future empirical work. But because we were beginning our study with children 6 months of age or older, we did not expect to find facial patterns of discrete affects that differed from those described by Ekman. However, we did not know if we would find examples of the various blends and mixed blends, and all the varieties of managing the face, such as qualifying, modulating, simulating, neutralizing, and masking, or if young children would produce emblematic messages and conversational punctuators. We also hoped to be able to relate the facial expressions to other expressive behaviors of the child, and to the interpersonal context, so that we could begin to articulate with more precision the expressive and communicative meanings of different kinds of smiles, frowns, and so on, and to note the beginnings of characteristic styles of expressive behaviors. And finally, we hoped to be able to provide some information on the relative prevalence of blends versus discrete affects in naturalistic settings.

SUBJECTS

The subject population consisted of two male and two female infants at each of three age levels—6 months, 12 months, and 18 months—and their parents. Subjects came from white, middle-class, intact families in which the mother performed the major share of child-care tasks. Ten of the infants were first-born, two were second-born.

PROCEDURES

Our goal was to obtain a representative record of naturally occurring expressive behaviors and transactions. Thus the data were collected in the homes, yards, and playgrounds of the subjects, with the only instruction to the mother being to proceed as she normally would during the course of the day. The physical movements of the subjects were not restricted in any way. Two video cameras were used (Sony Video Rover II portable systems); one was fitted with a wide-angle lens (VCL–08) and the other with the zoom capabilities of the standard lens. They were both fitted with long-life batteries, and with extension cables to increase their mobility, and the zoom camera had a unidirectional external microphone attached (F–98) in order to eliminate unwanted background noise.

The cameraman operating the zoom lens was instructed to try to keep the child's face and upper torso on camera; the second cameraman, operating the wide-angle lens, was instructed to keep the whole child in the center of his picture, and to include the surrounding environment within a 5 or 6 foot radius of the child. This perimeter usually included the mother, although even when not on the video record she is almost always on the audio record. An audio signal (a hand clap) occurred 5 seconds after each taping session began, so as to enable the two cameras to be synchronized later in playback. In this way we obtained a simultaneous record of the child's facial expressions and the on-going interpersonal transactions in sufficient detail to allow for a microlevel of data analysis.

Each family, or infant–mother pair, was seen once a month for 6 months. Each visit was scheduled to occur at a different time of day, in order to cover the full day's span of activities, mood, routines, and so on, over the 6-month period. Hence a taping session could occur any time from 7:30 A.M. to 8:00 P.M. At each visit, three 10-minute segments of behavior were taped. The timing of these segments was kept as random as possible so as not to fall into a pattern of taping set sequences—for example, feeding, baths, and so on—and to keep the atmosphere spontaneous and natural. The range of intervals between segments was from 0 to 48 minutes, with a mean of 10.7 minutes between segments. A typical visit lasted an hour and one-half, and included playing back one of the tapes on the family T.V. set for the mother. In the course of 6 months, we collected 3 hours of behavioral data on each family.

QUALITY OF DATA

Before describing our data analysis, I would like to discuss briefly the quality of the data we were able to collect. We did not observe the extreme poles of expressive behaviors—neither staring into space, thumb-in-mouth stupors, nor yelling, screaming, temper tantrums—or fearful expressions. The absence of the blank or bored end of the spectrum was probably because our presence increased the frequency of mother–child interaction and was often experienced as an exciting event. The absence of temper tantrums or fearful expressions was partly due to bad luck in sampling (e.g., tantrums occurring after the cameras had been turned off); and partly to the rarity of the phenomena. When mothers were asked directly whether we had obtained a representative picture of their child and themselves, all, with the exception of one, answered in the affirmative, and only a few mothers stated that they had altered their behavior because we were present by waiting until the end of a 10-minute segment to change locations (e.g., to go from outdoors to indoors) or before putting the baby down for a nap.

In summary, then, we were able to obtain a representative sample of a broad middle range of expressive behaviors of infants from 6 months to 2 years of age, and of their parents' interactive styles, as they occurred in natural settings. The 3 hours of behavioral data on each family are represented in two sets of tapes, one that contains a relatively good record of the infant's facial expressions, and another that contains the broader context. Longitudinally, each infant can be followed for a 6-month period, with a half hour of data per month, and 3 hours total per infant.

DATA ANALYSIS

Before we could begin coding, we had to select the segments of tape containing good facial expressions, and copy them in order to record a digital timer at the bottom of the picture. Good expressions were defined as being clearly visible, which meant that there was sufficient lighting and that the entire face was turned at least three-quarters towards the camera. We tried to be as inclusive as possible. Thus, whenever we could discern facial movement—defined as a deviation from the neutral or resting facial configuration—that complied with our visibility criteria, we copied the segment. Each segment consists of the sequence of facial movements, as well as a few seconds before and after the movement occurred.

The most comprehensive and detailed coding system for facial movement is FACS (Facial Action Coding System) developed by Paul Ekman and Wallace Friesen (1978). However, because we began working on this data before FACS became available, we used a modified version of the facial components that are described in Ekman and Friesen's earlier book *Unmasking the Face* (see Table 6.1 for movements related to emotional expressions). Coders were trained until they had mastered the 54 practice expressions at the end of Ekman's book. They then began to practice coding the expressions produced by the young children on our tapes. The training took roughly 6 to 8 weeks.

In determining an index of agreement, we utilized a method suggested by Ekman (1978) and derived from Wexler (1972). Because most expressions involve several facial actions, a determination of agreement is not simply a matter of determining the presence or absence of a particular facial action, but rather of determining the degree of agreement on the combination of facial actions that occur. Thus, a mean ratio was calculated for two coders, across a random sample of 40 "events" utilizing the following formula for each event:

(number of facial actions on which Coder 1 and Coder 2 agreed) × 2

divided by

the total number of facial actions scored by the two coders.

We obtained a mean ratio of .817. We also calculated the percentage of agreement for locating the onset and the offset time of an event within .1 of a second. We obtained an 85% agreement for onset and a 73% agreement for offset. It proved difficult to determine the end point when the expression faded slowly from the face.

In the actual coding of the data, all disagreements were resolved by discussion and a joint viewing of the expression. Coding was done while viewing the expression in slow motion, and each expression required several complete viewings of the entire sequence of facial movements, focusing first on the upper face and eyes, and then on the lower face. Before and after coding each expression in slow motion, it was viewed in real time. This enabled us to clearly distinguish mouth movements, for example, that were related to chewing or speaking, as opposed to changes in expression.

At this point in time, we have analyzed half of the facial expression data. Thus, here I present preliminary results on two children at each age level. We focus on the six expressions described in Table 6.1 and other facial signals such as emblems. We do not discuss the affect interest, which is not conveyed by facial movement but rather by focusing the eyes and orienting the body towards an object, event, person, and so on (Ekman, 1980; Demos, 1982).

RESULTS

Seven- to Twelve-Month-Old Infants

I begin with the two youngest children, a boy and a girl whom I call Dick and Jane, and I describe the expressions we taped from their seventh through their 12th months of life. Both children produced a preponderance of positive expressions (but Dick produced a third more positive expressions than Jane) and both produced roughly the same number of negative expressions. The ratios were four to one positive to negative expressions for Dick and three to one for Jane.

Positive Expressions

The positive expressions included expressions of the discrete affect of enjoyment, as well as blends of enjoyment with elements of excitement, surprise, and disgust. But the expressions of pure, or unblended, enjoyment were in the majority, comprising 75% of Dick's and 56% of Jane's smiles. These pure expressions of enjoyment were produced with a range of intensities, going from a minimum of the upturned corners of the mouth to a full smile with lips pulled back, teeth exposed, cheeks raised, lower eyelids pushed up, and accompanied by laughing or panting. Both children showed this full range of intensity in their smiles, which they directed in roughly equal measure to their mothers and to the cameramen, in relatively similar pleasant, friendly, and playful contexts. It was difficult to predict the intensity of the child's smile from the context alone, and thus it seems that the intensity of the child's enjoyment was determined more by the child's experience and interpretation of the situation at any given moment.

Aside from these similarities in the children's behaviors, there were also some characteristic differences in their smiling behaviors. We have already noted that Dick produced more smiles (128 compared to 79 for Jane), but he also produced a repertoire of playful, friendly behaviors such as nose wrinkles, jaw drops, blinks, blows, brow raises, waves, and vocal "hi's," which were embedded in sequences of full, open-mouth, cheek-rise smiles and which were substantially lacking in Jane's record. A typical sequence might include a full smile, a nose wrinkle lasting about .4 of a second, then a jaw drop also lasting about .4 of a second, or a blow lasting 1½ seconds, and then back to a full smile again. Dick's mother referred to these behaviors as flirting, and indeed they seemed to be directed exclusively to the cameramen. The association of nose wrinkling with flirting is made often, so much so that Paul Ekman assumed it was a culturally learned behavior, seen only in adolescent and adult women. Thus he was surprised to see it appear in his own daughter's repertoire somewhere in her second month, and in this sample by 6 months for both boys and girls (1980). These findings raise the possibility that this is not a learned behavior. However, the issue cannot be resolved without more complete data on the developmental history of both infant and parent expressions. In the present context, Dick's use of the nose wrinkle, as well as the blow, the blink, and the jaw drop, indicate that they are functioning as emblems (a nonverbal signal comparable to a head nod for "Yes") communicating flirtation or "I'm teasing you."

Jane, by contrast, seemed less exuberant and playful (this was the one child whose mother described her as more subdued on the tapes than in real life). And even though she did produce the full range of intensities of smiling, and even two or three playful nose wrinkles, she smiled less often than Dick and frequently tongued before and during her smiles, occasionally ending up sucking her lower lip. The prevalence of her tongue might well have been due to teething, at least initially; however, it was present throughout the 6 months of our observational records, which suggests that it might represent the beginnings of a characteristic idiosyncratic way of smiling.

The most common blend with the smile of enjoyment for both children was a smile combined with a jaw drop (see Fig. 6.1). This combination occurred in 23% of Jane's smiles, and 12.5% of Dick's. It occurred with smiles of all intensities and was characteristically held for several seconds at a time. The jaw drop could also occasionally begin before the smile occurred and stay on the face after the smile had faded. Because of its long duration on the face, the meaning of this mixture does not seem to be surprised enjoyment, since by definition surprise must be brief (Ekman & Friesen, 1975). Nor does it seem to be serving the emblematic function described earlier in relation to the manner in which Dick flashed (less than half a second) nose wrinkles, jaw drops, and blinks to the cameramen. If we examine the contexts in which this expression occurred, they all seem to have had in common the quality of anticipated pleasure—for instance, mother approaching to nuzzle the child's neck, or to put the blanket over the child's head; child approaching the cat; child watching mother or cameraman as they play or talk. These expressions were not accompanied by vocalizations; indeed, one gets the impression that the jaw opened as if to speak, but that the vocalization was suppressed. Thus the mouth hanging open combined with a smile created the impression of pleasurable suspense.

The next most frequent blend, comprising 11% of Dick's and 14% of Jane's positive expressions, involved a blending of enjoyment and excitement. For Dick this blend was manifested by intense smiling that often included a tightening around the mouth, plus excited vocalizations such as high-pitched squealing, vigorous bodily movements, bouncing up and down, or waving the arms up and down. These expressions occurred at the most intense moments of playful exchanges with his mother. For Jane this blend was also manifested by intense smiling, but the smiling was combined with an intense nose wrinkle, which was held on the face for at least 2 to 3½ seconds, and was often accompanied by a high-pitched squeal. Occasionally the nose wrinkle included a lowered brow or an upper-lip rise as well, and at such times the face had the appearance of intense pleasure mixed with disgust. This is a perplexing combination, and I report it without fully understanding its meaning.

Perhaps some clarification can be gained by looking at some closely related expressions. Jane also produced 14 instances of the standard facial pattern for expressing disgust (nose wrinkle, lowered brows, and an upper-

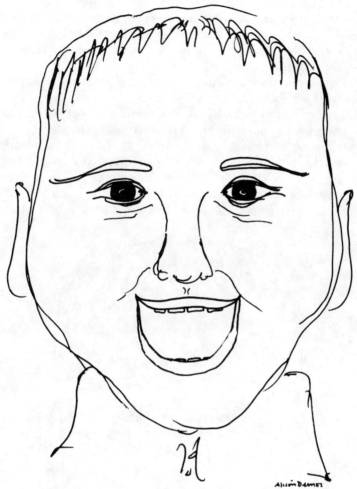

* These sketches were drawn free-hand from the video-screen. They are meant to illustrate a prototype of the expression, and do not represent any particular infant.

FIG. 6.1   Jaw-drop smile.

lip rise), held for a mean duration of 2.5 seconds, without any components of a smile. But most of these expressions occurred just before smiles or just after smiles, occasionally involving an intense squeal or yell, and they occurred in playful contexts (e.g., crawling, trying to pick up a pen, or looking at the cameramen while sitting near or interacting with her mother). These expressions certainly communicated intensity, and because they were often bounded by smiles, and held on the face for several seconds, perhaps they are best understood as playful "mock" expressions, representing this child's way of expressing a particular kind of excitement. Indeed, on one occasion Jane's mother referred to this expression as a "joke." If this interpretation is correct, then the blends previously described as well as these intense nose wrinkles alternating with smiles would represent an expression of mock or exaggerated excitement.

Jane also produced a mixed blend, not seen in Dick's record, but comprising 6% of her smiles, that combined a smile with an upper-lip rise (see Fig. 6.2). The upper-lip rise is usually considered a mild indicator of disgust, representing an effort to reject a foul-smelling or foul-tasting stimulus (Ekman & Friesen, 1975; Tomkins, 1962). In social situations it still carries the connotation of rejecting or distancing oneself from an undesirable person or situation. In Jane's case, combining a smile with an upper-lip rise created the impression of tentativeness or caution, as if anticipating something unpleasant. When this mixed blend is held on the face

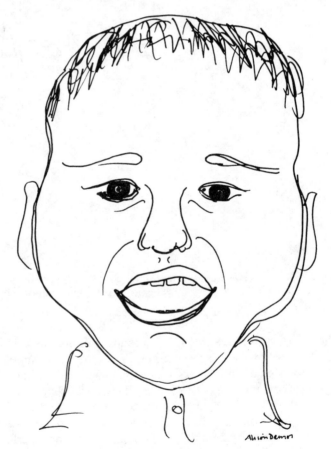

FIG. 6.2 Upper-lip–raise smile.

for several seconds, it gives the impression of apprehensive or uncertain enjoyment. It occurred most often in situations in which Jane was watching the cameramen, as if she were trying to appraise the situation.

We observed only one expression of surprise in the records of these two children; this occurred on Dick's face for half a second as he was walking towards his cat and he tripped slightly on the rug. It included the raised, curved eyebrows and the jaw's falling open, but did not seem to involve an opening of the eyelids as described in Table 6.1.

On two occasions Jane raised her eyebrows, signaling a question, while looking at the cameramen and vocalizing. This occurred in her eighth month, indicating her ability to use a facial signal as an emblem.

Negative Expressions

If we turn now to the distress expressions produced by these two children, we find once again that Dick produced more (27 versus 12) than Jane, and that the pure expressions occurred more frequently than the blends, comprising 93% of Dick's and 83% of Jane's expressions of distress. Nearly all such expressions included both the distress brow, with the inner corners of the brows raised, and sometimes pulled together, and a variant of the distress mouth, with the corners of the lips turned down, and/or loose trembling lips, as in a precry mouth, or an open cry mouth.[2] The type of mouth action was correlated with the type of vocalization, but not perfectly; thus an open cry mouth was often, but not always, associated with a cry vocalization, and loose trembling lips were often, but not always, associated with whimpering and whining. Not all expressions included a vocalization, and on two occasions there was a distress vocalization, but no sign of distress on the child's face. The eyelids, with the inner corners of the upper lid raised and the lower lid raised, seemed to be involved only in the more intense expressions—for example, when there was a strong muscle action in the brows, and the presence of the cry of distress somewhere in the sequence. But it is extremely difficult to detect the movement of the eyelids in less intense expressions, so it is possible that they may have been raised slightly at such times, and that either because of the quality of the picture or the degree of our skill, the movement escaped our notice.

We looked for regularities in the timing of the brow and the mouth movements, in terms of their onset and offset times and duration in relation to each other. By far the most typical pattern, observed in 71% of the cases, was to have the brow and mouth actions begin simultaneously, with the brow being held as the mouth went through variants of the distress expres-

---

[2]There were only four expressions that involved only one part of the face: two variants of the distress mouth only, and two distress brows only.

sion, and then to relax simultaneously. It should be noted that in the remaining 29% of the cases all the possible variations of the relative timing of these facial actions were observed, and they occurred with about equal frequency. However, there was a slight tendency for the mouth to relax first and thus for the distress brow to be held longer. Ekman & Friesen (1975) have argued that in trying to control their expressions of sadness and distress adults will concentrate on suppressing the vocalization by tightening the mouth—such as by keeping a stiff upper lip, or controlling the mouth in other ways. Thus the distress indicated in the brow becomes a more reliable indication of genuine sadness. The data on these two children show no evidence of such attempts to control or suppress their expressions of distress.

The contexts in which these expressions occurred represent the usual range of events that tend to distress young children, although there was almost no overlap for Dick and Jane in the kinds of situations that evoked distress. This difference could, of course, be due to sampling gaps as much as to any real differences between the children. The one kind of event in which they both produced expressions of distress involved being fed by their mothers.

The context for the majority of Jane's other distress expressions involved physical pain. In one long nursing sequence, Jane seemed to be experiencing teething pain in her gums, which caused her repeatedly to let go of the nipple and to produce the facial pattern of distress and the vocal cry. Each of these episodes lasted from 16 to 19 seconds, and ended with resumed nursing or thumb sucking. Izard (1981) has proposed a distinction between pain and distress, arguing that in pain the eyes are closed, and in distress they are open. In this sequence, three of the five crying episodes began with the eyes open, and throughout the crying the eyes closed and opened several times. The other two episodes began with the eyes closed. The eyes opened, and remained open in one case, and they opened and closed again, remaining closed until the end in the second case. There is no way of knowing if the pain was more intense at the moment the eyes closed each time, and less intense when they opened. It should be noted that the duration of the opening and closing of the eyes was usually between 1 to 3 seconds. In another painful event, Jane hit the back of her head on the edge of the table. She sat for 3.6 seconds without uttering a sound and looked around with a neutral expression on her face. Then she began to cry loudly, and her face took on the full-blown distress expression. Unfortunately, at the moment she began to cry, her face was turned away from the camera, so we were unable to determine whether her eyes were open or closed; however, throughout most of the 53 seconds that the cry lasted, her eyes were open.

Several of Dick's expressions of distress occurred in the context of fatigue, before he was put down for a nap or put to bed at night. In one sequence his expressions of distress alternated with a smile as he tried to prolong his play time. He also expressed distress on one occasion for 17.3 seconds when left by himself outside in the playpen. However, the majority of Dick's expressions of distress occurred in a long 4-minute sequence that also took place outside in the playpen and that involved a game with his mother in which he would throw his blanket over the side of the playpen, she would throw it back in or cover their heads with it, and he would try to pull it off or put it over his head. This game evoked moments of intense enjoyment and excitement that alternated with periods of neutral expression and with moments of distress when Dick became tangled in the blanket, or was unable to make it do what he wanted. Initially, during roughly the first minute and a half of this game, enjoyment and excitement predominated and only one brief vocal fuss and two nose wrinkles and lowered brows occurred at effortful moments. Near the end of this initial period, however, on two occasions the intense smiling included a clenched jaw indicating a growing tension, or mild anger and frustratin. For the next 2½ minutes, Dick alternated between expressions of distress and expressions of enjoyment–excitement at least seven times, with a gradual attenuation in the intensity and duration of the positive expressions and an increase in the distress. The peak of the distress occurred in the fourth minute, lasted for 24 seconds, and included, in addition to an intense expression of distress on the face, whimpers, screams, bouncing up and down, and bringing his hand to his ear. The screams and the bounces probably represented nonfacial components of anger combining with the distress, but there was no indication of anger on the face at such moments. During this intense phase, Dick's mother helped him with the blanket and offered verbal support. The episode ended with a 20-second period of recovery, at the end of which Dick smiled at his mother for nearly 8 seconds.

This child's capacity to sustain his enjoyment and excitement, and to keep bouncing back after repeated distressing and difficult moments, is impressive. Earlier we saw him smiling in between two expressions of distress related to fatigue, and here we see a more prolonged sequence of alternation with the enjoyment and excitement being reestablished after each distressing moment. Only at the peak of the distress does Dick seem unable to recapture the enjoyment and excitement of the game, although even during this 25-second period there were moments when he did combine the facial components of distress with a jaw drop, which may have represented the expectant, suspenseful aspects of the game. In both of these situations—the smiling in the midst of his fatigue, and the prolonged game—his mother was present, supportive, and actively contributed, both with words and with actions, to his capacity to persist. Tomkins (1978) has postulated that individuals acquire particular affective sequences as a consequence of their socialization experiences. Perhaps this present case is an example of such a sequence in that Dick is learning, through these interpersonal transactions, that distress and frustration do not signal the end of the game or the need to give up. They are tolerable and manageable, and with persistence, one can once again experience enjoyment and excitement.

We observed very few expressions of anger in these two children. Both children produced a vocal protest in the feeding situation described earlier. But the only facial components of anger we saw were produced by Dick, and each one included vocal components as well. Dick showed two blended expressions of anger (brows lowered and together and a square mouth) and disgust (a nose wrinkle) that lasted for .42 and 1.42 of a second, and one unblended expression of anger that lasted for .45 of a second, and was immediately followed by a facial and vocal expression of distress lasting 1.4 seconds. These expressins occurred during a sequence in which he was crawling on the floor, and he first bumped into and then became tangled in a toy.

Dick also produced several jaw clenches in the long game sequence described earlier, two combined with smiles and one long (3.5 seconds) jaw clench followed immediately by an expression of distress. It was suggested, because of their timing in the sequence, that these jaw clenches might represent either tension or anger. However, because they were never combined with other components of anger, such as lowered and pulled-together brows, or pressed lips, it seems appropriate to interpret them as signs of tension rather than as specific indicators of anger. In addition, both children on occasion lowered their brows when exerting effort (reaching, grunting, etc.), which seems best understood as signaling concentration in such contexts, rather than as an anger component (Ekman & Friesen, 1975; Oster, 1978).

To summarize briefly the findings for the two youngest children: Pure expressions of enjoyment and distress were more frequently observed than blends in both children. This was particularly true for expressions of distress, which showed few individual differences. The most common blend was the jaw-drop smile, which we suggested conveyed a suspenseful enjoyment. There were also blends of enjoyment–excitement, and enjoyment and mock excitement. We saw no fear, only one expression of surprise, and only three expressions of anger, two of which were anger–disgust blends. Jaw clenches were interpreted as indicating tension, and lowered brows as indicating concentration, rather than as anger components. We noted the beginning of what might become a characteristic affective sequence for Dick of enjoyment–distress–enjoyment. Both children produced emblems by the eighth month of age, which included the raised brow to signal a question and various flirtatious behaviors. We were unable to detect any attempts by the children to disguise or deintensify their expressions, but we did speculate that Jane was exaggerating her expressions of excitement.

Thirteen- to Eighteen-Month-Old Infants

The next two children we looked at in detail, a boy and a girl whom I call Tom and Mary, were taped from age 13 months through 18 months. They produced roughly the same number of expressions, but the ratio of positive to negative was strikingly different. Tom's expressions were predominantly positive in a ratio of 10 to one, whereas Mary produced an equal number of positive and negative expressions. Mary was also unusual in that she was the only child in the sample who produced more than an occasional asymmetrical facial movement. These movements occurred in the mouth area, where several kinds of muscle actions (e.g., jaw clenches, upper-lip rises, corners of the lips raised) were stronger on the left side of her face, thus often pulling her mouth up on that side.

The positive expressions were almost entirely expressions of enjoyment and the jaw-drop smile blend. We saw no expressions of surprise, and only two instances of enjoyment–excitement. Once again the pure expressions of enjoyment were in the majority, comprising 85% of Tom's and 56% of Mary's smiles. The jaw-drop smile made up the other 15% of Tom's smiles, and accounted for 38% of Mary's. The other 6% of Mary's smiles were combined with jaw clenches, most likely representing a mixed blend of enjoyment and tension. These two children differed also in the intensity of their smiling behavior. Tom's smiles were characteristically relaxed, full, open-mouth smiles with raised cheeks and raised lower lids. Mary's, by contrast, were often of mild intensity, involving only the corners of the mouth turned up, or the lips only partly pulled back. Also, nearly a quarter of her smiles were immediately preceded or followed by a mild indicator of tension or anger (in the form of a jaw clench or lip press), or by mild apprehension (in the form of a slight tightening of the lips in the pulled-back position). These behaviors occurred in all the same contexts in which smiling without any sign of tension occurred, such as when playing with toys, interacting with her mother or father, or looking at the cameramen. Because they often occurred immediately after or in between smiles, they seemed to be functioning as qualifiers of the smiles. Thus the full meaning of the sequence might be something like "I'm not really as happy about this situation as I look. I'm also a little annoyed or apprehensive about it."

The contrast between the expressive styles of the two children may be a reflection of a characteristic difference in the transactional styles of the two families. Mary's parents tended to be somewhat didactic in their transactions with her, instructing and urging her to perform much of the time, and devising games with her that had an egging-on or teasing quality to them. Tom's mother, by contrast, was remarkably relaxed, playful, and patient in her transactions with him. And although she did on occasion try to teach him the names or colors of objects, she tended on the whole to let him explore and use objects in his own way, rather than trying to teach him the "correct" way. Mary and Tom also evidenced distinctive styles of expressing negative feelings, which we discuss later, that were consonant with the parental styles just described. Thus it is possible that we are seeing in these children's records the beginnings of idiosyncratic expressive styles occurring in distinct transactional environments.

Both children produced smiles that included playful behaviors directed at the cameramen. Tom went through a series of tonguings that involved moving the tongue from side to side, and extending it way out and pulling it back, all in combination with full, open-mouth smiles. He also produced two upper-lip funnels. We have labeled these behaviors mugging. Mary produced a variety of nose wrinkles, similar to those described in the previous section in relation to Dick's flirting behavior, but Mary's nose wrinkles typically lasted .6 of a second, compared to .4 of a second for Dick's. Mary also nose wrinkled to her mother, and these, interestingly enough, were only .2 of a second in duration. These playful nose wrinkles were often combined with squinting eyes and/or lowered brows. Other nose wrinkles, not produced in conjunction with smiles, seemed to be part of a blend of disgust with intense effort. Mary produced one nose wrinkle and lowered brow (.7 of a second) while concentrating on walking across the grass, and a prolonged 3-second nose wrinkle with brows lowered and together in a frustrating attempt to place her doll in a swing.

Negative Expressions

If we focus now on the negative expressions these children produced, we find that Tom provided 11 examples whereas Mary provided 53. The majority of Tom's expressions (eight) were unblended or full-faced expressions of distress that included whimpers, cries, and fusses. Five of these occurred during a hair-washing sequence in which he alternated between expressions of enjoyment and distress as he became alternately more and less comfortable with having the soap rinsed out of his hair. The only expression of fear he produced occurred at the beginning of this sequence. As his mother lowered him onto his back towards the sink to begin rinsing his hair, his eyes and mouth widened and his lips pulled back briefly (.43 of a second) into a tense fear mouth. His face then took on a distress expression with the inner corners of the brows pulled up and together and with loose, trembling lips. Soon he began to whimper. Throughout the rinsing sequence, which lasted 1 minute and 40 seconds, his parents reassured him and provided distractions. Their active support undoubtedly helped Tom to modulate his distress and even experience moments of enjoyment. It is interesting to note that the brief moment of fear occurred as his body was being moved down and back. Although his mother did not make the move suddenly, nor fail to support him securely, he nevertheless, perhaps because of his inability to see what was behind him and the unusual backward motion, may have experienced a momentary loss of support and/or orientation, thereby evoking fear.

His other expressions of distress occurred on the changing table, at the end of a game with his mother, and while having his face washed. The latter situation also produced a blend of distress (shown in the eyebrows) and disgust (shown as an upper-lip rise). Tom produced one pure expression of disgust in response to having taken a bite of food that was too hot.

Mary's negative expressions were almost entirely expressions of anger, or distress, or a blend of the two, with the blends comprising 38% of the total. However, the most striking aspect of these data was how closely related distress and anger were for this child. Of the 32 instances in which distress was expressed, in only one did it occur alone (and then for only .34 of a second), without having been preceded by, blended with, or followed by anger. The same can be said of her angry expressions, with the exception of the mild expressions, involving only a lip press, which we described earlier in relation to her smiles. The unblended, pure angry expressions that occurred in alternation with distress expressions or with blends all involved the eyebrows pulled down and together, with a tense, bulging lip press or a square mouth. The most common blend of distress and anger for Mary involved the angry eyebrows, and sometimes closed eyes, combined with a variant of the distress mouth and/or distress vocalization (see Fig. 6.3). These expressions tended to occur in frustrating situations, such as trying to put her doll in a swing that would not hold still, or trying to turn over a plastic slide that was just a little too big for her to handle, or refusing to get off a living-room chair, so that her other could replace the cushion. The feelings of distress, anger, and stubborn persistence evoked in these situations were sometimes expressed simultaneously in a blend, and at other times in a series of alternations with each other (sometimes as rapidly as every .3 of a second). At such times Mary received verbal suggestions and instructions from her parents, but was offered no physical assistance (e.g., with the swing or the slide).

We observed seven instances of Mary's trying to deintensify her distress by controlling her mouth. All of these cases involved a variant of the distress mouth and a distress vocalization. Her efforts took the form of sucking her lips or producing a lip funnel, and they usually continued until the whimpering or crying ceased. She sucked her lip in the context of anger–distress blends, and used the lip funnel with full-faced expressions of distress.

One other noteworthy aspect of Mary's distress, and distress–angry expressions, was that several of them involved closed eyes. There could be no possibility of physical pain in the situations in which these expressions occurred. But, because distress and anger were so closely related for this child, the presence of the closed eyes in these expressions suggests a connection

FIG. 6.3   Anger brow/distress mouth.

between closed eyes and angry distress.

Mary also produced a mild fearful expression, which involved primarily the lower face, with the lips pulled way back and tensed. This expression occurred in an interaction sequence in which Mary's mother was squirting water into a little coffee pot that Mary was playing with. As the mother approached with the water, Mary's lips retracted, and her eyes closed, and then her hands came up to cover her face. The lip retraction and closed eyes were very brief, .15 of a second, and preceded the movements of her hands to her face by .1 of a second. The hands remained covering her face for nearly 3 seconds, while the eyes opened and closed several times, in order to "keep an eye" on what was happening.

Each child also produced nonemotional facial signals. We have already mentioned the mugging and nose wrinkles directed primarily at the cameramen. In addition to these facial actions, Mary produced some examples of facial emblems. She raised her brows briefly (for .27 of a second) and uttered a vocalization to signal a question as she listened to her mother tell her to "throw the ball." In the same sequence, she twice lowered and pulled her brows together in concentration as she watched another child and as the ball was being thrown to her. Tom lowered and pulled his brows together as a conversational punctuator when demanding that his mother continue a game.

In summarizing the expressions of these two children, we might say that in contrast to the younger children, individual differences were the dominant trend, present across the full range of expressions, and involved differences in frequency of positive and negative expressions, in intensity and in individual facial components and sequences. Pure expressions of enjoyment and distress were more frequently observed than blends in Tom, in whom the jaw-drop smile represented the most-common enjoyment blend. This statement holds for Mary's smiles as well, but hers were of lesser intensity and were sometimes qualified by expressions of mild annoyance or apprehension. Mary's expressions of distress and anger were closely related, either occurring in blends or in quick alternation with each other, and at times leading to efforts to deintensify the distress. It was noted that closed eyes in these expressions may have represented an indication of angry distress. We suggested that the observed differences between these two children in affective patterns and sequences looked like the beginnings of distinct, characteristic styles emerging from and related to the characteristic interpersonal transactional styles of their respective families. Each child produced one expression of fear and several playful antics directed to the cameramen. They also used their eyebrows as facial emblems or as conversational punctuators.

Nineteen- to Twenty-Four Month-Old Infants

The final two children for whom we have completed our data analysis are both boys. We call them Benjamin and Billy, and our records show them from ages 19 months to 24 months. They, too, are strikingly different in their styles of expression. After describing these differences, I try to relate them, in a more detailed way than in the previous section, to the contrasting transactional styles of their mothers. Billy produced slightly more expressions than Benjamin (84 versus 71) and had the only record in which blends were in the majority. He was also unusual in that he spent more time looking at the cameramen than any other child in the entire sample. Benjamin, by contrast, hardly seemed to notice our presence, and spent most of his time engaged with his toys or in playful interaction with his mother.

Positive Expressions

Billy produced 71 smiles, but only 29.5% of these were simple, unblended smiles. Forty-four and a half percent were combined with either a jaw clench or an upper-lip rise, or both. We have already discussed the jaw clench as a possible sign of tension when describing Mary's smiling behavior. But Billy always clenched his jaw *as* he smiled, rather than clenching between smiles or immediately after smiling, as typically occurred in Mary's case. Thus the expression represented a mixed blend of enjoyment and tension, which gave his smiles a forced or somewhat fake quality. This impression was enhanced on several occasions by the addition of a forced laugh. This kind of laugh was unique to Billy's record, and was in striking contrast to his own spontaneous laughter on other occasions. For the most part, the forced laughs occurred in the only session that Billy's father was present, and during which Billy seemed even more aware than usual of the cameras. Billy's smiles which contained an upper-lip rise conveyed the same distancing or cautious quality that we described in relation to similar smiles produced by Mary. When both a jaw clench and an upper-lip rise occurred with a smile, they conveyed the feeling of a tense cautiousness.

The other 55.5% of Billy's smiles were relaxed, and the majority of these were simple, unblended smiles. About a quarter of the relaxed smiles included a jaw drop, and about a fifth of them were blends of enjoyment and excitement, which we describe later. Eleven of Billy's smiles were combined with head tilts. These were just as likely to occur with tense smiles as with more relaxed smiles, and seemed to add a coy or shy quality to the expression. Billy's relaxed smiles occurred (1) while playing with a slighter older child; (2) with physical activity involving large muscle movements; (3) in a brief face-to-face playful exchange with his mother; and (4) in some exchanges with the cameramen. Billy's smiles were about equally distributed in terms of intensity: corners up; corners up plus lips pulled back; and corners up, lips pulled back, mouth open, and a cheek rise. His more intense smiles were more likely to occur in playful interactions with a peer or with his mother, and in these contexts they were relaxed smiles. However, a third of his full smiles occurred in other contexts and contained jaw clenches or upper-lip rises. Indeed, with the exception of the peer-play context, the smiles blended with mild tension or mild disgust occurred across all contexts.

Billy produced seven expressions indicating excitement. All but one of these occurred outdoors at a playground. The other one occurred indoors, while playing with another child. These expressions all involved smiling, but they have been classified separately as indicating excitement as well as enjoyment, because of their intensity and vigor. They might include any of the following components: jumping up and down; open-mouth smiles with a cheek rise and a jaw drop; a "play-face" (Van Hooff, 1972), which involves the same components just described, but with the lips covering the teeth; laughing and shouting; rapid opening and closing of the jaw; and widening of the eyes. When Billy shouted outdoors, he also closed his eyes and lowered and pulled his brows together. In this context the eye and brow action indicated concentration and effort. Several of these expressions of excitement also contained jaw clenches at various points—for example, while riding on a toy horse and trying to make it go back and forth faster, or in the midst of a series of intense smiles or shouts. In these contexts the jaw clench takes on the meaning of effort or sheer intensity of feeling. Finally, Billy sometimes sucked his lower lip in between smiles or after a series of intense smiles.

Billy produced an unusual mixture of an open-mouth smile combined with elements of anger (brows lowered and pulled together, eyes narrowed) and disgust (a nose wrinkle). This expression was repeated several times without the nose wrinkle, and occurred in a sequence of behavior that included full-faced expressions of anger, Billy's hitting the cameraman, and then emitting two loud screams. The context of this sequence is perplexing. Billy's mother was helping him do somersaults on the living-room floor, as his father sat across the room on the sofa. After several successful somersaults, which produced full, relaxed smiles, Billy looked at the cameraman, and produced the unusual expressive blend and sequence of behavior just described. Thus it is unclear what caused the shift in Billy's behavior.

Anger blends can ocur in several ways (Ekman & Friesen, 1975). Anger components can occur in one area of the face and not in another, or they can occur in a mild form in all three areas of the face, or they can occur in only one or two areas, and so on. The most common blend is the anger-disgust blend. In the sequence just described, Billy utilized most of these possibilities, and at times alternated the facial components of anger with physical action (hitting) or with intense vocalizations (screams). The anger components appeared first in the upper part of Billy's face, and involved an anger-disgust blend. The unusual feature was that Billy combined this with an open-mouth smile. Given the actual sequence of events, the brief unambiguous anger expression, and the subsequent hitting of the cameraman, I think we are correct in interpreting this expression as an anger-disgust-enjoyment blend. Billy repeated it without the disgust component after his first scream, followed it with a fake laugh and an unambiguous angry expression, and then repeated it again, in a less intense form combined with a fake laugh, after his second scream. Ekman and Friesen (1975) have referred to such expressions as "I've gotcha" expressions, indicating an enjoyment of the anger, or the triumph over another person (see Fig. 6.4).[3]

---

[3]This anger-enjoyment blend was also exemplified by two instances of what we have called "fake laughs." The laugh sounded forced or tense but is perhaps more accurately understood as an anger-enjoyment blend.

FIG. 6.4   "I've gotcha" expression.

Let us now look at the positive expressions produced by Benjamin, which consisted of 57 smiles. Forty-nine percent of these were unblended, simple smiles, and 39% were the most common mixed blend observed in the records of the younger children—namely, a smile with a jaw drop. All of Benjamin's expressions, in contrast to Billy's were relaxed and smooth, and two-thirds of them were full, intense smiles. Most of them occurred in playful exchanges with his mother, and the remainder occurred in exchanges with the cameramen. In contrast with the two pairs of younger children described thus far, Benjamin's exchanges with his mother were almost entirely verbal. He was fairly advanced linguistically, and seemed to enjoy repeating rhymes, answering his mother's verbal probes, and even teasing her by purposefully mispronouncing words.

Benjamin also produced a few instances of a variety of other blends. There were two occasions on which he showed an enjoyment–excitement blend, consisting of a very intense smile combined with laughter. One occurred while he was being chased around a tree by his mother, and the other while he was watching a top spin. He displayed two enjoyment–surprise blends that involved raised and curved brows combined with a jaw drop and a smile. The first of these expressions lasted only .15 of a second, and occurred in the middle of a longer smiling sequence, at the moment when his mother suddenly bent down and kissed him on the arm. The second of these occurred while he was sitting on his mother's outstretched legs, talking and smiling, and he suddenly lost his balance and began to fall over backwards. This expression differed from the first blend of enjoyment–surprise in two respects: First, as he began to fall backwards, Benjamin closed his eyes; and second, he held the expression on his face for .90 of a second. Thus, it may have begun as genuine surprise, but it then became a playful exaggeration as he realized the fall was under control. Benjamin produced two smiles that included a blend of relatively prolonged eyebrow raises (2.9 seconds and 1.78 seconds). The first example of this blend occurred several seconds after he had been mugging at the cameramen, and may have been either a continuation of the mugging, or a look of expectant pleasure as he waited for a response. The second expression occurred while he was splashing in the bathtub, and again conveyed the impression of expectant pleasure. And finally, he produced one "play-face" smile (an open-mouth smile with the lips covering the teeth) that occurred after a long (2.9-second) open-mouth smile, and as his mother was moving his hand along the page in the book they were looking at together.

Benjamin also produced three surprise faces, with the brows raised and a jaw drop, that were not blended with a smile. They all occurred in the context of his having heard the siren of a fire engine outside. Probably only one of them was brief enough (.33 of a second) to have represented genuine surprise, although even that expression occurred 2½ seconds after he first heard the noise and turned his head in the direction of the sound. The other two expressions, one held for .76 of a second, and the other for 3.0 seconds, were accompanied by pointing, orienting his body, and the words "Fire engine!" and seemed to represent an exaggerated surprise expression functioning as an emotional emblem, as if to say "How surprising!" Benjamin produced a variety of other brow raises as well. He greeted the cameramen with a brief brow flash. He raised his brows while saying "moo," thus using them to emphasize or punctuate the word in the rhyme he was reciting. And he raised them once as he was trying to look up and to his right. He also lowered his brows several times as he concentrated his attention on a book at which he and his mother were looking. Thus Benjamin's record shows a versatile use of the eyebrows and mouth as facial signals serving a variety of functions.

The differences between these two children in their expressions of enjoyment—the tension and uncertainty present in nearly half of Billy's smiles versus the relaxed, spontaneous, playful variety of Benjamin's expressions —seem to be part of different transactional patterns. Elsewhere (Demos, 1982) I have described in detail the transactional sequences occurring in a 10-minute play session with each of these boys and their mothers. In a summary, I characterized the transactional styles of the mothers in the following way:

Billy's mother was focused on maintaining a standard of behavior. This goal was manifested by the mother's predominant use of structuring comments (e.g., commands, declarative sentences, etc.) and actions (e.g., arranging paper and crayons, picking up toys, etc.), the relatively few instances of inviting the child's response, the absence of sharing the child's interest by using the toys herself, and the response to the child's playfulness with disapproval. This mother seemed most certain and decisive when expressing disapproval, and when structuring the child's interests with commands, and at such times she clearly emphasized the differences between them in authority. She seemed less certain and persistent when inviting a response from her child, and on two occasions produced ambiguous communications. There were no shared moments of enjoyment in this segment. The child's expressions of interest were sometimes only minimally responded to, were at other times ignored completely, and were twice responded to and then interrupted by the mother's insertion of a negative suggestion.

Benjamin's mother, by contrast, manifested a variety of behaviors directed towards maintaining mutuality and allowing the child scope to express and pursue his interests. This mother frequently invited the child's response by the use of questions; she responded to his inquiries and expressions of interest both verbally and behaviorally by participating in his activities; she enjoyed his playfulness and communicated her smiling approval; she deemphasized the power differential between them, thus enabling the child to stand his ground in a disagreement; and she took the lead in changing undesirable situations by redirecting the child's interests, without criticizing him for his silliness or his stubbornness. Only on the two occasions of redirecting the child's interest did the mother utilize structuring comments and actions.

It seems possible that the unusual characteristics of Billy's expressive style are related to the transactional style he participated in for at least the 6 months of his life that we studied. We are in no position to argue that his capacity to experience enjoyment has been seriously impaired, for he is capable of spontaneous relaxed expressions in certain contexts. But it must be remembered that all the children in the study were presented with the same stimulus of two cameramen and a researcher coming into their homes and videotaping. Yet Billy was the only child whose expressions of enjoyment were so frequently mixed with tension, uncertainty, and anger. Perhaps it is possible to say, merely, that many more situations for this child evoked mixed enjoyment than was true for the other children in the study.

Negative Expressions

The expressions of distress that these two boys displayed did not differ from each other nearly as much as their smiling behavior just described, and on the whole were relatively mild when compared to those produced by the younger children. Billy produced 12 expressions, nine of which involved unblended distress components, often displayed only in the lower face. He also produced two mixed blends of a distress face with an upper-lip rise, and one blend of distress eyebrows combined with an angry mouth. On three occasions his expressions involved a lip press, which seemed to indicate an effort to control the distress vocalization. Benjamin produced 17 expressions of distress, 11 of which involved unblended distress components, mostly showing on both the upper and lower face. He also produced four distress-anger blends, in which the anger was seen in the brows (lowered and pulled together) and the distress in the mouth, and two mixed blends, in which the corners of the lips were turned down, indicating distress blended with an upper-lip rise, indicating mild disgust. Thus the boys did not differ substantially in the frequency of distress, in the ratio of unblended to blended expressions, and in the types of blends they produced.

The following differences were observed, however. Billy's expressions of distress almost always included a distress vocalization—for example, fussing, whining, or crying; Benjamin's never did. Benjamin, as we have seen earlier in relation to his positive expressions, utilized his eyebrows more frequently than Billy, thereby displaying more full-faced expressions of distress. And finally, the contexts for the expressions were different for the two children. All of Billy's expressions of distress occurred in situations of struggle with his mother. Some issues involved food—for example, Billy's wanting to feed his mother, or to eat the coffee roll she was eating, and his mother's refusing; some involved discipline—for example, his mother's insisting that Billy put his toys away before he could eat dinner, or removing objects she did not want him to play with. Benjamin, by contrast, produced almost all of his expressions of distress in the context of being left alone briefly in the room with the cameramen. Nine of these occurred in the first visit, and included the four blends of distress and irritation. These seemed directed at his mother who was leaving the room to find a pencil, or to make a phone call, and so on, thus making it difficult for Benjamin to keep track of her. Five other expressions occurred during the final taping session, when his mother was out of the room for nearly a minute. His distress on this occasion was twice blended with mild disgust as the cameramen tried to urge him to remain in the room and to reassure him that his mother would return soon. He produced one distress expression on the playground, when his mother was pushing him up the steps of a ladder on a tall slide, which he did not want to go down. Only one expression of distress occurred in the context of a struggle with his mom. That expression involved a pout with the corners of the mouth turned down, and an avoidance of eye contact with his mother as he sat in her lap in the aftermath of a scolding for having jumped on her back.

Each child produced one mild expression of fear. Benjamin's occurred when he was standing near his mother, but with his back to her, and looking up and smiling at the cameraman. His mother moved slightly to her left, and as he reached back to touch her and felt the empty air, his lips pulled back tensely into a fear mouth for .40 of a second. His mouth relaxed as he made contact with his mother again. Billy tensed and pulled back his lips and widened his eyes as he let go of the top of a slide. The expression stayed on his face for the full 1.43 seconds that it took him to reach the bottom of the slide. Billy also produced two fear blends. One involved a fear–disgust mixed blend, with lips tensed and pulled back combined with an upper-lip rise. This was accompanied by a whimper as his father put medicine on his sore bottom during a diaper change. The other blend involved a fear–distress blend that included the raised eyelids, giving the eyes a wide, staring appearance, combined with a distress mouth and a freezing of his body. This expression occurred when the cameraman accidently bumped into a piece of furniture and let out an audible "Ow!" Billy froze and held this expression for 4.16 seconds. He then squatted down behind the table he was near and continued staring wide-eyed at the cameraman for another 2.60 seconds. Finally he ran to his mother who was sitting in a chair across the room, and once he was safely in the chair, he smiled shyly at the cameraman.

Benjamin did not produce any unblended expressions of anger and only the four distress–anger blends previously described. Billy produced the enjoyment–anger blends already described as well as the two pure angry expressions that alternated with these blends. He also produced one other unblended anger expression that followed a distress–anger blend. On several occasions he either expressed anger vocally, without a facial component—such as screams or protest vocalizations—or behaviorally by throwing toys. He did produce one tantrum in which he threw his body on the floor and loudly protested his mother's removal of the crayons.

However, because his face was turned towards the floor, we were unable to see the expression on his face.

There was only one full-faced expression of disgust which was produced by Benjamin as he turned his face directly into the wind.

To summarize the data on the two oldest children, we observed a striking difference in their smiling behaviors. Benjamin's smiles were similar to those observed in the younger children in that the majority were unblended, simple smiles, and the most common blend was the jaw-drop smile. Benjamin's record differed from that of the younger children in that his exchanges with his mother were more verbal, and he showed more variety in his blends and emblems, utilizing his eyebrows. Billy differed from all the other children in the sample in the degree to which his smiles were blended with components of tension and/or disgust, and in the production of an unusual enjoyment–anger blend. It was suggested that this difference was related to the transactional style of Billy's mother, which focused on maintaining a standard of behavior rather than on mutuality, shown by Benjamin's mother. Both children produced a majority of relatively mild, unblended distress expressions, and similar blends of distress–anger and distress–disgust, although the context for these expressions differed. Billy's occurred in struggles with his mother, whereas Benjamin's tended to occur when his mother was absent. Each child showed an expression of mild fear—one involved a violation of an expectation and the other, an enduring of a "scary" activity—and Billy produced two fear blends. Expressions of anger occurred primarily in blends. Billy also produced a few examples of vocal or behavioral expressions of anger, including one temper tantrum.

CONCLUDING DISCUSSION

We began this investigation with detailed information about adult facial expressions drawn from the work of Ekman and Friesen (1975), and asked how many of these phenomena would be true for young children, how would they relate to context, would we find individual expressive styles, and what would be the frequency of blended versus unblended expressions. What follows is a brief summary and discussion of these initial concerns:

1. When we looked carefully at all the facial expressions produced by these six children, we found that they did indeed fit the patterns of the specific facial movements designated by Ekman and Friesen for each discrete affect. For example, the inner corners of the brows were raised and pulled together in distress (e.g., when Dick was alone outside in the playpen and was crying for his mother), the corners of the lips were turned up and pulled back into the smile of enjoyment (e.g., when Benjamin was playing

with his mother), and the upper lip was raised and the nose wrinkled in disgust (e.g., when Tom ate food that was too hot).

There is, at this point in time, no way to demonstrate conclusively that these children were in fact experiencing the specific affect we saw on their faces; indeed, there is a sense in which we will never know what a preverbal child is experiencing. Nevertheless, it does not seem unwarranted to make the assumption that the expressive behavior and the inner experience go together when a child's face, voice, and behavior all create a unitary impression, thereby providing redundancy and intensity, and when the expression occurs in a reasonable context. At such times, not only does it seem clear, at the very least, that the experience for the child is qualitatively positive or negative, but it is difficult for the observer not to experience the same qualitative state. Thus it is difficult not to smile back at and enjoy a young child who is smiling and laughing and whose body is relaxed, or not to feel distress when seeing the distress face and tense body and hearing the distress cry of a young child. To continue to insist that we can know nothing of what an infant experiences is to deny the evidence of our senses, and becomes a pseudo scientific stance. The disciplined use and articulation of empathy in understanding another is not an unscientific endeavor (see Newson, 1977, for an intersubjective approach).

2. Even though the specific facial actions appeared to be lawful, nonrandom, patterned events, which looked smooth, well practiced, and coordinated, the timing of these actions, their duration, the number of specific facial actions involved, the strength of the muscle action, and the presence or absence of a vocalization all seemed to be more variable and less subject to predetermined patterns. For example, the experience of enjoyment probably always involves some kind of a smile, but the intensity, duration, and presence or absence of a vocalization or of other blended elements is variable. Ekman and Friesen have suggested that this variance is not random, but represents meaningful and subtle differences in the individual's experience. Yet it is not always possible to determine the connection between the event and the child's experience of it. Sometimes this connection is reasonably clear, as we stated previously, such as when the child's face, voice, body, and the context all go together. But that connection is less clear when the face expresses a blend, or the face expresses one thing and the voice another, or when the face and/or voice express something different than was expected given the context.

If one assumes that these subtle variations in facial movements are meaningful, then there remains the task of developing the methodological tools, both conceptual and technical, that will enable us to discover their meaning. We have proceeded by using an anatomically based, microanalytic technique for analyzing facial movements, developed by Ekman and Friesen, and then relating the patterns we observed in natural settings to the contexts. Yet even with the availability of such a fine-grained tool for coding facial movement, several problems remain. Many of these subtle variations occur infrequently; thus, there are often sampling problems that make the use of statistical analsis inappropriate. No criteria for establishing the validity of attaching a particular meaning to a particular pattern of facial movements have yet been developed. Also, we are not very far advanced in developing a systematic way of describing contexts. And finally, to analyze the data on facial expressions correctly even with current techniques requires an enormous commitment of time and effort. Yet the potential for learning a great deal more about the affective experience of young children is also enormous. We have barely begun to probe this area.

3. For five of the six children we observed, we found that the expression of discrete, unblended affects was more frequent than the expression of blended affects. However, it is generally asserted that the reverse is true for adults (Ekman & Friesen, 1975; Lewis, 1980). If these data are representative of early childhood, and the assertion about adult expressive behavior is correct, then there would appear to be a developmental shift in this phenomenon that takes place sometime after the age of 2. But, if it is possible to generalize from these few cases, the most striking developmental feature in the data was the increase in individual variation with an increase in age, and this variation did not always involve an increase in the frequency of blends. More data from both young children and adults are needed to clarify this issue.

4. When we did observe blends, they most frequently occurred with the smile—the jaw-drop smile, the jaw-clench smile, the upper-lip–rise smile, the raised-eyebrow plus jaw-drop smile, the excited, intense smile, and the smile with the lowered, angry brows. This variety may reflect our cultural preference for the smiling face (Tomkins, 1962, 1963). If so, then these findings demonstrate how early children begin to learn to express a range of feelings through variations in the culturally acceptable smile.

In the same vein of cultural influences, we observed a paucity of unblended, full-faced expressions of anger, and instead saw a predominance of anger blends—for example, distress–anger blends for Mary, and an unusual enjoyment–anger blend for Billy. This could, of course, represent a gap in our sampling. However, these results do correlate with the cultural pressure in American middle-class families to inhibit the direct expression of anger.

5. Although we have just suggested that these children were already learning some of the cultural rules about expressing affect, we saw only a few instances, and none until the age of 1, of children actually trying to deintensify or to control their affective expressions. These efforts occurred in relation to expressions of distress, and perhaps particularly to expressions of vocal distress, and involved lip sucks, lip presses, and lip funnels. We did not observe any direct parental efforts to suppress their child's expressions

of distress; however, the parents of the two children who showed these deintensifying behaviors tended to be less active in helping their distressed children. Thus the pressure to deintensify the expression, and by implication the experience, may have come from the children who were expected to fend for themselves.

We also speculated that holding the jaw open in the jaw-drop smile may have represented an inhibition of vocalization. However, in this case, inhibiting the vocalization seemed to be in the service of intensifying or exaggerating the suspense aspect of the enjoyment.

6. Every child we observed produced a facial emblem. The most common was the raised eyebrows to indicate a question. The next most common was the flirtatious nose wrinkle, and the closely related varieties of facial mugging signaling playful friendliness. How early these behaviors can be observed is an open question. We did not see them in our two youngest children until 8 months of age. But sampling once a month, as we did, is not sufficiently frequent to get a reliable developmental record of the onset of such events.

We also observed what we interpreted to be exaggerated expressions—Jane's prolonged nose wrinkles to express excitement, or Benjamin's prolonged surprise expressions functioning as emotional emblems. And we thought that Mary was using jaw clenches and upper-lip rises as qualifiers for some of her smiles. We are not necessarily implying that any of these actions were produced intentionally by the children. These behaviors, as well as the facial emblems, can function and convey meaning without their being consciously produced. However, the varieties of facial mugging are an exception to this statement. The children seemed very conscious of what they were doing, evidenced by the smiles and expectant looks that always followed these behaviors.

7. We made an attempt to relate the individual differences in expressive behavior that we observed to the transactional styles of the families. We were only able to do this in a suggestive and general way; by no means have we demonstrated a connection. But we are suggesting that some of these affective expressions could have occurred as reactions to or the result of rather stable transactional patterns that have created particular experiences or expectations in the child—examples are Mary's characteristic blend of distress and anger, or Billy's tendency to blend enjoyment and tension. It is equally possible that these blends could have been learned through imitating their parents' expressions. We did not have a sufficient record of the parents' facial expressions to study this possibility. Nevertheless, it remains as a viable explanation, and one that is not necessarily in conflict with the first explanation.

8. Closely related to the previous issue, we also noted what we thought might represent the beginnings of a characteristic affective sequence for

Dick that involved enjoyment–distress–enjoyment, and a characteristic coupling of the affects of distress and anger for Mary. Whether these will become enduring personality characteristics for these two children is, of course, impossible to determine at this point in time. However, the point we would like to make is that the process of socialization of affect involves the possibility of establishing such enduring sequences and couplings as well as affecting the expression and experience of discrete affects.

We would like to close with both a caution and a claim. The caution involves reminding the reader that these are descriptive data on only six children, and much more data are needed in order to verify the findings. The claim is that, nevertheless, we have made a useful beginning. The data are astonishingly rich and indicate that there is a wealth of information to be mined in the field of affective expressions.

ACKNOWLEDGMENTS

This chapter was written while the author was partially supported by the William T. Grant Foundation, grant number 8427-6, awarded to the Department of Pediatrics at Boston City Hospital. I would also like to acknowledge the assistance of Carolyn Verdaasdonk in coding the data, of Jane Freeman in editing and typing the manuscript, and of Alison Demos in drawing the sketches used to illustrate some of the blends.

REFERENCES

Charlesworth, W. R., & Kreutzer, M. A. Facial expressions of infants and children. In P. Ekman (Ed.), *Darwin and facial expression.* New York: Academic Press, 1973.

Darwin, C. *The expression of the emotions in man and animals.* New York: D. Appleton and Co., 1872. (Reprinted in Chicago: University of Chicago Press, 1965.)

Demos, E. V. *Children's understanding and use of affect terms.* Unpublished doctoral dissertation, Harvard University, 1974.

Demos, E. V. *The socialization of affect in early childhood.* Unpublished monograph, 1975.

Demos, E. V. The role of affect in early childhood: An exploratory study. In E. Tronick (Ed.), *Social Interchange in Infancy: Affect, Cognition, and Communication.* Baltimore: University Park Press, 1982.

Ekman, P. Universal and cultural differences in facial expression of emotion. In J.R. Cole (Ed.), *Nebraska symposium on motivation.* Lincoln: University of Nebraska Press, 1972, *19,* 207–283.

Ekman, P. Biological and cultural contributions to body and facial movement. In J. Blacking (Ed.), *Anthropology of the body.* London: Academic Press, 1977.

Ekman, P. Personal communication, 1980.

Ekman, P., & Friesen, W. *Unmasking the face.* Englewood Cliffs, N.J.: Prentice-Hall, 1975.

Ekman, P., & Friesen, W. Manual for the facial affect coding system. Palo Alto, Calif.: Consulting Psychologist Press, 1978.

Izard, C. Talk delivered at Society for Research in Child Development Meetings, Boston, 1981.

Izard, C., & Buechler, S. Aspects of consciousness and personality in terms of differential emotions theory. In R. Plutchik, & H. Kellerman (Eds.), *Emotion: Theory, research and experience, Vol. 1. Theories of emotion.* New York: Academic Press, 1980.

Lewis, M. *The socialization of affect.* Paper presented at Workshop "Infant affective displays and physiological correlates during normal, disturbed and manipulated social interactions." Mailman Center for Child Development, Miami, Florida, December 1980.

Newson, J. An intersubjective approach to the systematic description of mother–infant interaction. In H. R. Schaffer (Ed.), *Studies in mother–infant interaction.* London: Academic Press, 1977.

Oster, H. Facial expression and affect development. In M. Lewis, & L. Rosenblum (Eds.), *The development of affect.* New York: Plenum, 1978.

Oster, H., & Ekman, P. Facial behavior in child development. In W. A. Collins (Ed.), *Minnesota symposia on child psychology* (Vol. 11). Hillsdale, N.J.: Lawrence Erlbaum Associates, 1978.

Tomkins, S. *Affect, imagery, consciousness, Vol. 1. The positive affects.* New York: Springer, 1962.

Tomkins, S. *Affect, imagery, consciousness, Vol. 2. The negative affects.* New York: Springer, 1963.

Tomkins, S. Script theory: Differential magnification of affects. In *Nebraska symposium on motivation.* Lincoln: University of Nebraska Press, 1978.

Van Hooff, J. A. R. A. M. A comparative approach to the phylogeny of laughter and smiling. In R. A. Hinde (Ed.), *Non-verbal communication.* Cambridge, Eng.: Cambridge University Press, 1972.

Wexler, D. Method for unitizing protocols of descriptions of emotional states. *Journal of Supplemental Abstracts Service* (Catalogue of Selected Documents in Psychology), American Psychological Association, 1972, *2*, 116.

7

Affective Exchanges Between Normal and Handicapped Infants and Their Mothers

Jeanne Brooks-Gunn
Michael Lewis
Institute for the Study of Exceptional Children,
Educational Testing Service

INTRODUCTION

Susan, a 28-month-old physically impaired infant, is playing with her mother. She is engaged in trying to manipulate the surprise box following demonstration of the toy by her mother. Frustrated, she frets. Her mother, rather than responding to the fret, again demonstrates the surprise box.

Randy, an 8-month-old infant, is startled by the sudden appearance of the nurse at the waiting-room door during a pediatric examination. His mother exclaims, "Don't be frightened, nobody is going to hurt you." Randy then begins to fret, and his mother attempts to soothe him.

These examples of early mother–child interactions illustrate aspects of emotional development. Although the biological maturation of emotional expression has generated a great deal of research, until recently the role of socialization in emotional development (which includes emotional expression) has not received much attention. Even though Lewis and Michalson (Chapter 8, this volume) focus on issues related to the early socialization of emotions, research with young infants and children is still unusual (Malatesta, Chapter 1, this volume). Ekman, Friesen, and Ellsworth (1972) have outlined a variety of possible strategies (that are probably related to socialization) in the display of emotions or at least components of emotional behavior. They suggest that individual and group differences as well as ontogenetic trends be examined in terms of strategies used to mask facial expressions. These rules include such factors as *neutralization, exaggeration, minimization,* and *dissimulation.*

Little research on emotional displays and socialization rules has been conducted. A notable exception is the work of Saarni (1978, 1979), who has investigated the rules of emotional display in 6- to 10-year-olds. Saarni reports an age-related increase in children's understanding of display rules. In 1980, Saarni extended her research by observing children's spontaneous use of display rules. Both children's knowledge and use of complex display rules increased with age over the 6- to 11-year-old period. Sex differences were found for at least one display rule, which may be described as "look pleased and smile when someone gives you something they expect you to like *even* if you do not like it." Girls were more likely to subscribe to this rule than were boys, especially at the older ages.

Work such as Saarni's represents an important beginning in the study of the socialization of affect display rules. Unfortunately, comparable work has not been conducted in infancy and early childhood. Thus, the origins and developmental course of socialization rules have not been explored in much detail. Observations of children in interaction with others, especially during affective exchanges suggest, however, that differences in dyads and in individual children exist (Demos, Chapter 6, this volume). Cultural differences are also apparent (Field, Sostek, Vietze, & Leiderman, 1981). For example, cultures that discourage their children from crying or do not allow their children to cry (in terms of removing all frustrating situations) socialize their infants quite differently than do cultures that permit crying or provide mildly frustrating experiences. Studies of Japanese–American families suggest that different types of affective expressions and interactions are encouraged in the Japanese culture. These differences are probably a function of cultural rules, and socialization practices are probably in the service of these rules (Caudill & Weinstein, 1969). Such results reinforce our belief that cultural values (in this case, affective behavior) are imparted through the particular socialization practices of the caregivers vis-a-vis the young child.

In this chapter, differences in socialization practices related to affective expression are explored by focusing on interactions between mothers and infants in families with normal and handicapped young children. Our focus on emotional interchanges is predicated on the premise that the integration of emotional expression and even emotional experience[1] arises, in part, out of the interaction of the child and the caregiver's behavior and the caregiver's response to the child's behavior (Lewis, 1981).

The socialization practices of families are best studied via interaction. Internal meaning is developed through behavior in context. Infants and adults construct meaning through affective exchanges (Lewis & Michalson, 1982).

---

[1]The distinction between emotional expression and emotional experience has been made repeatedly. Emotional behavior may be studied in terms of elicitors, receptors, states, expressions, and experiences (Lewis & Brooks, 1978; Lewis & Michalson, 1982.)

The meaning of an emotional expression (or state) is inferred from facial, vocal, and bodily acts as observed in a particular context. For both receiver and sender (whether infant or adult), meaning is derived through internal conditions, contextual variables, and recipient's response, the anticipated responses based on previous experience, and the actual intent of the sender (and receiver's perception of that intent). In addition, both may use the cues made salient by the situation, the interpretation of the signal, and the individual's idiosyncratic features. Demos (Chapter 6, this volume), for example, presents evidence of individual patterns of affective experience in response to particular situations.

In the discussion to follow, systematic patterns of affective exchange between mothers and their infants are observed in order to study how affective expression can be influenced through socialization. The use of dysfunctional infants is particularly important in this regard because one may contrast systematic differences in interaction exchanges between handicapped and normal dyads in order to study the impact of these differences on the socialization of emotional development. In the study of dysfunctional and normal infants' emotional development, there are a variety of possible differences: (1) the dysfunctional child's expression of emotion may differ—that is, the facial, postural, and vocal behaviors may not be available, may be delayed, or may be different (Gallagher, Jens, & O'Donnell, in press); (2) the mother's interpretation of the behavior may be affected—that is, her expectations may be affected; (3) the socialization rules may be different for parents with dysfunctional versus normal infants. In addition, differences in emotional development among different groups of dysfunctional children are of interest, as is the relationship between cognitive growth and emotions.

That different patterns of affective exchanges may exist for the handicapped child and the mother is suggested by several lines of research. This literature indicates that not only may a handicapped child's expression be different or delayed, but the mother's interpretation of that response and her subsequent behavior may be different. Parents may experience a tumultuous sequence of emotional reactions following the birth of a handicapped child—depression, rejection, anger, and finally acceptance of the child (Broussard & Hartner, 1970). Parents may need to mourn the death of the ideal child that they had expected before accepting their handicapped child (Solnit & Stark, 1961). The birth of a handicapped or high-risk infant is a stressful event, one that may lead the mother to inadequate coping styles, difficulties in other relationships, or severing of ties in the social-support network, all of which may result in negative affective experiences (Lewis, Brooks-Gunn, & Fox, 1981).

How might these feelings be translated into maternal interaction with the child? Research suggests that mothers of blind babies often feel less "attached" to them, presumably because of the lack of eye-to-eye contact and mutual gaze patterns (Fraiberg, 1975). Mothers of sick neonates exhibit less overall interaction than mothers of healthy neonates, possibly because of the fear of losing or harming the child rather than due to any intrinsic feature of the illness (Fox & Lewis, 1981).

Additionally, the fact that handicapped or high-risk infants are often different from normal infants in some skills may intensify affective interaction difficulties. Mothers of premature infants with a delay in smiling interacted less than mothers with normal children (Field, 1980). This also may be true of handicapped infants, especially because there is evidence to indicate that the birth of a handicapped child results in depression in the parents. Harmonious interchanges may be disrupted by negative affect on the part of the infant as well as by delayed positive emotional expression. Handicapped infants tend to be more difficult temperamentally than normal infants (Brooks-Gunn & Lewis, 1981; Cicchetti & Bridges, in press; Greenberg & Field, in press), and handicapped infants with more difficult temperaments have disruptive vocalization exchanges with their mothers, and the mothers are much less responsive vocally (Brooks-Gunn & Lewis, 1981). In brief, handicapped infants and their mothers may exhibit different patterns of affective exchanges than normal infants and their mothers, and both the affective meaning conveyed to the child and the parental methods of managing the child's affect are influenced.

METHOD

Subjects

One hundred and ten handicapped children (64 males and 46 females) ranging in age from 3 to 36 months of age were seen. These children were part of a project on the development of competencies in young handicapped children, were recruited through infant-stimulation programs in New York City and New Jersey, were receiving some form of intervention at the time of testing, and were tested primarily in the field (i.e., in a small room at their program site). Of the 110 subjects, 56 were children with Down's syndrome (DS), 34 were children with a primary motor impairment (typically cerebral palsy, PI), and 20 were developmentally delayed infants (who had no known organic problem but whose cognitive and/or physical development was slower than normal; DD). Classifications were based primarily on diagnoses of physicians and interdisciplinary evaluation teams. Down's syndrome was identified by cytogenetic testing: Of the 39 children for whom we had karyotype information, two children had translocations and the rest had trisomy 21 abnormalities. Trisomy 21 abnormalities typically account for 90% of Down's syndrome cases, translocations for 5%, and mosaicism and other abnormalities for about 5% (Donnell, Alfi, Rublee, & Koch, 1975).

For the following analyses, the sample was divided into four age groups—2 to 7 months (N = 16), 8 to 16 months (N = 27), 17 to 27 months (N = 39), and 28 to 36 months (N = 28). These groupings were based on the age composition of the sample and the ages at which our normal comparison group had been seen. The mean ages for the four groups are as follows: 5.5, 12.1, 22.2, and 32.5 months of age. Table 7.1 presents the number of subjects divided by age group and handicapping condition. In-

TABLE 7.1
Number of Subjects for the Normal and
Handicapped Sample by Age and Handicapped Group

| Group | Age in Months | | | | |
	2-7	8-16	17-27	28-36	Total
Normal[a]	193	167	156	0	156
Handicapped	16	27	39	28	110
Down's syndrome	16	13	14	13	56
Developmentally delayed	0	4	9	7	20
Physically impaired	0	10	16	8	34

[a] The normal infants are part of a longitudinal study in which these infants were tested at ages 3, 12, and 24 months of age; 156 were seen at all three ages (Lewis, 1978).

cluded in the table are 156 normal infants who were seen at 3, 12, and 24 months of age as part of a longitudinal study on the effects of gender, birth order, and social class upon early development (Lewis, 1978). The mean ages of the handicapped and normal samples are comparable.

As can be seen in Table 7.1, the youngest age group is comprised of Down's syndrome infants, which is not surprising, as these children are usually identified at birth. This fact should be remembered in the interpretation of the age-related comparisons. The overall comparisons made among the three handicapped groups in this chapter only include infants 8 months of age and older (because the three groups are only comparable in age if the 2 to 7 month olds are excluded). The mean age of all three handicapped groups was the same—21 to 23 months of age.

Using Hollingshead's system for the determination of the family's socioeconomic status (Hollingshead, 1957), fairly even distribution among the highest four of the five SES categories was found. Additionally, most of the mothers had a high-school education or better. Approximately 90% of the sample was Caucasian, 5% black, and 5% Hispanic. Children were equally divided between first- and later-born.

Mother–Infant Observation

Infants and their mothers were escorted to a small playroom (10 × 6 feet) that contained eight toys, a chair, and several magazines and the mothers were told to do as they wished. They were observed for 15 minutes through a one-way mirror and the observer dictated on-going behaviors and interactions onto an audiotape that was later transcribed and coded. These transcriptions were divided into 10-second periods.

Eleven maternal and 16 infant behaviors, representing distal, proximal, and toy-play categories were recorded. Using the system of recording interaction developed by Lewis (Lewis, 1972; Lewis & Lee-Painter, 1974), three types of behavior were recorded: (1) *occurrence,* an on-going or noninteractive behavior that serves neither as an initiation nor as a response to the other dyad member; (2) *initiation,* any behavior that results in a response from the other dyadic member; and (3) *response,* any behavior that immediately follows and is linked in a meaningful way to behavior emitted by the other dyad member. An interaction is defined as at least one initiation that is followed by at least one response. More than one interaction could be recorded within a 10-second period.

Interobserver reliabilities were calculated twice during the course of the study; each time, videotapes of mother–infant free play were observed by two observers. Number of agreements as a proportion of disagreements and agreements for each behavior in each of the 10-second periods was calculated with the range across behaviors being .70 to .81 (Mean .75). These reliabilities are comparable to those reported in the normal comparison sample, as well as in other studies using this coding system (Lewis, 1972; Lewis & Coates, 1980).

Sample Characteristics

Handicapped sample and age-equivalent groups. Each child was assessed with the Bayley Scales of Mental Development in order to obtain, among other measures, age-equivalent scores. In subsequent analyses, the handicapped infants were classified into age-equivalent groups as well as chronological age groups; the number of children in each handicapped and age group when categorized by age equivalent is listed in Table 7.2. None of the infants had age-equivalent scores of more than 28 months; therefore, only three age groups are included in the age-equivalent comparisons (2 to 7 months, 8 to 16 months, and 17 to 27 months of age). All of the normal children had Bayley scores appropriate for their age.

TABLE 7.2
Number of Subjects in Each Handicapped Group by Age Equivalent[a]

| Group | Age Equivalent | | | |
	2-7	8-16	17-27	Total
Handicapped	33	35	19	87
Down's syndrome	21	21	8	50
Developmentally delayed	3	7	5	15
Physically impaired	9	7	6	22

[a] Not all subjects could be given an age equivalent because they were too handicapped to be given all the relevant Bayley items for a particular age-equivalent point.

Normal Sample

A normal sample of over 150 children was seen longitudinally over the first 3 years of life (Lewis, 1978). This sample was equally divided with respect to sex of child, birth order (first, second, third, and fourth plus), and family socioeconomic status (Hollingshead's class 1 and 2 versus 3 and 4). Of interest here is that these infants were observed with their mothers at 3, 12, and 24 months of age in a free-play setting similar to the one described for the handicapped sample. The only difference involved the observation at 3 months when infant–mother dyads were seen in the home for 2 hours of awake time rather than in a laboratory for 20 minutes. Consequently, proportion measures (i.e., proportion of time spent vocalizing as compared to the total number of behaviors emitted) but not frequency of occurrence measures are presented when a 3-month normal comparison is of interest.

Target Behaviors

In order to examine affective interchanges, three infant behaviors and two maternal behaviors in the free-play session were observed; these represent a positive affect, a negative affect, and a frequently occurring communicative behavior.

Infant smiles (as operationalized by facial expressions, primarily corners of the mouth turned up, mouth either open or closed), infant frets or cries (including all negative vocalizations, whines, frets, whimpers, cries, or screams), and infant vocalizes (including cooing, babbling, or talking but excluding grunts, sighs, and so forth) were observed and coded in one of the three categories described earlier (initiation, response, or occurrence). Maternal behavior included smiles and vocalizes. Because mothers typically exhibit little or no negative behavior when being observed, no negative affective maternal behavior was included in the data analysis.

Levels of Analysis

Several levels of analysis were of interest. The first involved the frequency of occurrence of each behavior as a proportion of the total behaviors exhibited. Second, differences as a function of age, handicapped group, and age equivalence were examined in terms of the number of subjects exhibiting a specific behavior. These analyses are particularly relevant for behaviors with a low incidence rate. (In this sample, smiles and frets were highly salient but infrequent infant behaviors.) Third, how much of the time that was spent in interaction as a proportion of the total amount of the specific behavior emitted was examined. Fourth, initiation and response proportions were analyzed separately to investigate the nature of the interaction. For all levels of analyses, differences among the four age groups and between the age-equivalent and chronological age groups were examined.

RESULTS

Positive Affective Interchange

Positive affect as evidenced by smiling is an infrequent infant behavior in the free-play setting. Correcting for the time in the play situation, the frequency of smiling varied between 3.9 to 8.0 times for the handicapped and 3.2 to 6.6 times for the normal sample. Fig. 7.1 presents the proportion of infant smiles as a function of total infant behavior for the normal and handicapped samples, both by chronological age and age-equivalent groups. Smiling comprised 3% to 6% of the handicapped infants' behavior and no significant age trends were found for these infants by chronological age or age equivalent. When we examined the percentages for normal and handicapped subjects, the normal sample smiled more (as a proportion of their total behavior) than did the handicapped sample. Smiling increased with age in the normal sample, increasing from 7% at 3 months to 12% at 24 months. Comparisons across age groups indicate that differences between the handicapped and normal samples occurred at 12 months (3% versus 10%) and 24 months (3% versus 12%), but not at 3 months. Finally, differences among the handicapped groups were seen. Smiling comprised 2% of the Down's syndrome infants' total behavior, 3% of the developmentally delayed infants' total behavior, and 6% of the physically impaired infants' behavior.

We also examined the percentage of subjects who never smiled, smiled once or twice, and smiled more than three times during the free-play situation. For the total handicapped sample, 29% never smiled, 21% smiled

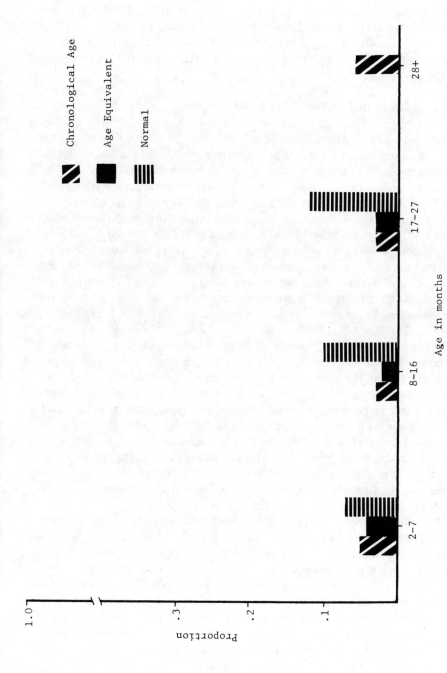

FIG. 7.1 Infant smiles as a proportion of all behaviors: age trends.

once or twice, and 50% smiled more than three times. One-third of the sample never smiled in the first 2 years, with the percentage dropping to 14% in the third year. By the third year of life, 79% of the handicapped infants were frequent smilers. The Down's syndrome infants were the least frequent smilers.

Socialization of Positive Affective Interchanges

How much of the infants' smiling was exhibited in interaction rather than just as an occurrence? Fig. 7.2 presents the proportion of infant smiles exhibited in interaction as a function of total infant smiles. As can be seen, interactive smiling decreased with age for the handicapped sample (from 50% to 35%). This decrease was also seen using the age equivalents rather than chronological age. Conversely, the normal infants increased their interactive smiling over age; the 12-month-olds exhibited the highest proportion. At 3 months of age, the handicapped infants exhibited more interactive smiling than did the normal infants, whereas the reverse was true at 12 and 24 months of age. Handicapped group differences were seen: The physically impaired infants spent more time in interactive smiling than the developmentally delayed or Down's syndrome infants (PI = .52; DS = .30; DD = .28).

Within an interaction, infant smiling can be an initiation or a response to a maternal behavior. Table 7.3 presents, for the handicapped and normal samples by age, the proportion of infant smiles that were responded to by the mother or were the response of the infant. The proportion of infant smiling as a response to maternal behavior decreased with age in the handicapped sample (both for chronological age and age equivalent) and in the normal sample (Table 7.3-A). Sample differences were only seen at 24 months of age where handicapped infants had higher smiling response proportions than did the normal infants. Higher response proportions were seen for the physically impaired infants as compared to Down's syndrome and developmentally delayed infants (PI = .35; DS = .17; DD = .19).

Maternal responses to their handicapped infants' smiling behavior comprised 11% to 17% of the total smiles, as is shown in Table 7.3-B, with no age trends being found for either chronological age or age equivalent. In contrast, mothers of normal infants dramatically increased their responsivity to their infants' smiles over age (7% at 3 months to 27% at 24 months). Thus, as the normal children became older, their mothers became much more responsive to their smiles whereas the mothers of the handicapped children did not become more responsive to their infants' expressed positive affect. This difference in maternal responsivity cannot be accounted for by delays in cognitive ability because the age-equivalent and chronological age data were the same. Somewhat paradoxically, however, the handicapped in-

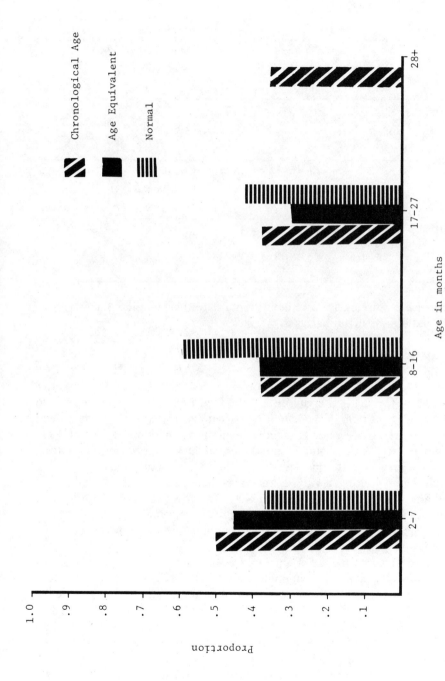

FIG. 7.2 Proportion of infant smiles exhibited in interaction: age trends.

TABLE 7.3
Infant Smiling by Age and Handicapped Group

A. *Proportion of Infant Smile as a Response to Maternal Behavior*

	Age in Months			
	2-7	8-16	17-27	28-36
Handicapped sample				
Chronological age	.39	.21	.28	.21
Age equivalent	.33	.22	.14	–
Normal sample	.30	.29	.15	--

B. *Proportion of Maternal Responses to Infant Smile*

	Age in Months			
	2-7	8-16	17-27	28-36
Handicapped sample				
Chronological age	.11	.17	.10	.14
Age equivalent	.12	.14	.15	–
Normal sample	.07	.23	.27	–

fants were more likely to smile in response to their mothers than were the normal infants of similar ages.

Negative Affective Interchanges

Like the positive affective behavior examined, the incidence of negative behavior (fretting and crying) was quite low. Frets/cries comprised 2% to 5% of all behaviors in the handicapped sample, 1% to 11% in the normal sample. Fretting decreased dramatically in the normal sample, from 11% at 3 months to 1% at 12 and 24 months; in the handicapped sample, fretting did not decrease to this level until 28 to 36 months. Using the age equivalents, fretting/crying decreased systematically from 6% at 2 to 7 months to 1% at 18 to 27 months. No differences between the normal and age-equivalent samples at 12 or 24 months were found, although fret/cry was highest for the normal group at 3 months. No differences among the handicapped groups were found.

Given that fretting and crying in a free-play setting are frequently occurring infant behaviors, the number of subjects who never fretted, fretted once or twice, and fretted more than three times was examined. Almost two-thirds of the handicapped infants never fretted or cried, 10% cried or fretted once or twice, and one-quarter fretted or cried more than three times during the session. When the infants over 8 months of age were classified by handicapped group, no differeces were found. Using the age equivalents, fewer infants cried at each age point than when using the chronological age groups.

Socialization of Negative Affective Exchanges

Only maternal responses to infant fret/cry were examined, because infants responded with a fret/cry to their mothers' behavior very infrequently (1% of the total infant fret/cry behavior) and because mothers do not exhibit this particular negative behavior in response to their infants' behavior. Fig. 7.3 presents the maternal response to infant fretting data for the normal and handicapped samples by chronological age and age equivalence. Maternal responsivity to their infants' fretting decreased over age in the handicapped sample (31% versus 13%). Similar decreases were seen in the normal samples (22% to 7%). The mothers of handicapped infants responded more at 2 to 7 months than did the mothers of normal infants; no differences occurred thereafter. When age equivalence is taken into account, these differences disappeared.

Thus, mothers were more responsive to their infants' fretting in the first half of the first year than later on. This is true in the handicapped sample even though the infants did not decrease their fretting and crying proportionately until 28 to 36 months of age.

Communicative Interchanges

Infant vocalization was a much more frequently occurring behavior than the positive or negative affective behaviors. As illustrated in Fig. 7.4, vocalization increased with age in the handicapped sample: from 8% at 2 to 7 months to 19% at 28 to 36 months. Using age equivalents, this increase was 9% to 23%. The normal sample exhibited more vocalizing at all three ages and overall exhibited dramatic age increases (17% to 67% versus 8% to 19%). Differences appeared at all ages, doubling at each of the three ages (9% at 2 to 7 months, 20% at 8 to 16 months, and 39% at 17 to 27 months). No handicapped group differences were found in vocalization.

Socialization of Communicative Interchanges

The proportion of interactive vocalization to total vocalization remained relatively constant across age for the handicapped sample (33% to 44%). This was unaffected by the use of age equivalence. In contrast, in the normal sample, the proportion increased consistently and dramatically from 22% of all vocalization at 3 months to 40% at 12 months to almost 75% at 24 months of age. At the youngest age, more interactive vocalizing was seen in the handicapped than the normal sample (44% versus 22%); in the first year, no differences were found; and in the second year, interactive vocalizing was much higher in the normal sample (75% versus 41%). These trends also were found using the age equivalents in comparison to the normal sam-

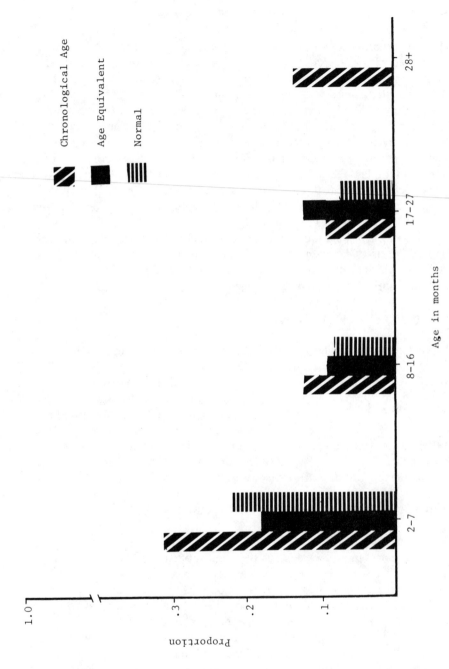

FIG. 7.3 Maternal response to infant fret/cry as a proportion of total fret/cry behavior: age trends.

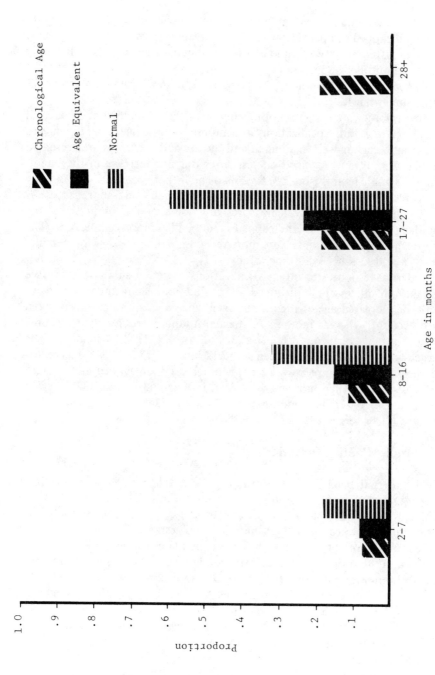

FIG. 7.4 Infant vocalizations as a proportion of all behaviors: age trends.

175

ple. Thus, communicative interchanges were higher in the normal than in the handicapped sample even when age equivalence was taken into account.

Small differences were found among handicapped groups. The physically impaired and developmentally delayed infants exhibited the most interactive vocalization (41% and 40%, respectively), and Down's syndrome infants somewhat less (35%).

To explore who was promoting the vocalization interaction, maternal responses to infant vocalizations and infants' vocalizing as a response to maternal behavior were examined, and the proportion scores are presented in Fig. 7.5. Infant vocalization responses did not increase in the handicapped sample (comprising 7% to 15% of all infant vocalizations) but they increased dramatically in the normal sample (from 8% at 3 months to 26% at 24 months). Age-equivalent scores did not alter the findings for the handicapped infants. Handicapped group differences appeared: The physically impaired infants were more responsive than the developmentally delayed and Down's syndrome infants (PI = .17; DS = .08; DD = .09).

Maternal responses to infant vocalizations present a similar picture (see Fig. 7.6). Mothers of handicapped infants did not become more responsive with the increased age of the infant, even when age equivalence was taken into account, whereas mothers of normal infants increased their responsivity to infant vocalization (13% at 3 months to 49% at 24 months). The largest increase occurred between 3 and 12 months (12% to 34%). Age differences between samples were seen: Mothers of handicapped infants were more responsive than mothers of normal infants at 3 months (33% versus 13%), but they were less responsive at 12 months (26% versus 34%) and 24 months (28% versus 49%).

Maternal Affective Behavior

Two maternal behaviors were examined—maternal smiles and vocalizations. As with the infancy results, proportions of materal behaviors were examined in terms of proportion of total behavior, proportions exhibited in interaction, and proportions of initiation and responses.

Table 7.4 presents the proportion of all maternal behaviors that are smiles and the proportion of maternal smiles that are exhibited in interaction (initiation and response). Mothers of handicapped infants smiled proportionately about the same amount as did their infants: Mothers' smiles comprised 3% to 5% of their behavior. Maternal smiling did not increase with the age of the infant, either chronological age or age equivalent. In the normal sample, maternal smiling comprised more of the total behavior than in the handicapped sample. Maternal smiling increased as the infants became older (8% at 3 months, 24% at 12 months, and 19% at 24 months). The mothers of handicapped infants exhibited less smiling at 12 and 24

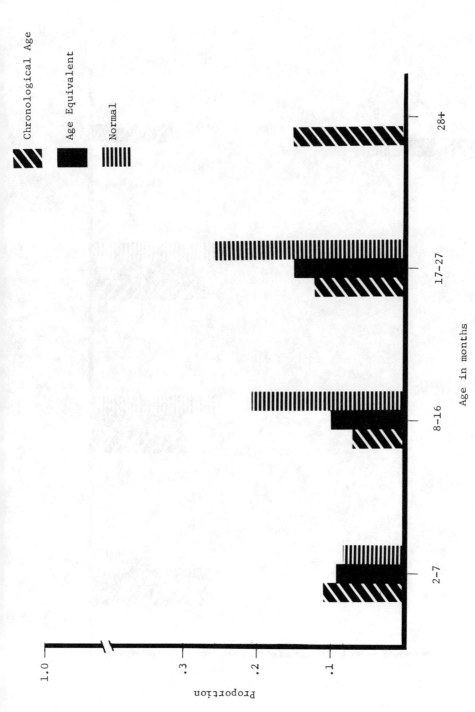

FIG. 7.5   Infant vocalization as a response to maternal behavior as a function of total vocalizations: age trends.

177

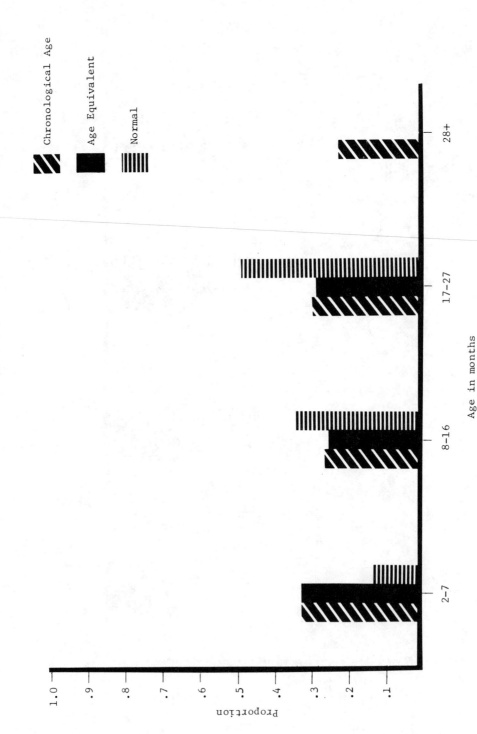

FIG. 7.6   Maternal responses to infant vocalizations as a proportion of total vocalization behavior: age trends.

TABLE 7.4
Maternal Smiling by Age and Handicapped Group

A. *Proportion of Smiles to Total Behavior*

| | Age in Months | | | |
	2-7	*8-16*	*17-27*	*28-36*
Chronological age	.03	.05	.04	.04
Age equivalent	.03	.05	.04	.04
Normal	.08	.24	.19	–

B. *Proportion of Interactions to Total Smiles*

| | Age in Months | | | |
	2-7	*8-16*	*17-27*	*28-36*
Chronological age	.12	.36	.37	.38
Age equivalent	.24	.40	.40	–
Normal	.30	.57	.56	–

C. *Proportion of Maternal Smiles as a Response to Infant Behavior*

| | Age in Months | | | |
	2-7	*8-16*	*17-27*	*28-36*
Handicapped sample				
Chronological age	.11	.29	.33	.36
Age equivalent	.18	.37	.38	–
Normal sample	.14	.46	.53	–

months than did the mothers of normal infants (5% versus 24% and 4% versus 19%, respectively).

The proportion of mother smiles exhibited in interaction also shows some parallels with the infant data. Interactive smiling increased with the age of the infant in the handicapped sample, from 12% to 38% for chronological age and from 24% to 40% for age equivalents, as well as in the normal sample, from 30% to 56%. Smiling was more likely to be exhibited in interaction in the normal than the handicapped sample at all ages. Age equivalence removed the normal–handicapped differences seen at 3 months of age. The mothers' smiling behavior did not differ as a function of handicapping conditions.

Maternal smiles as a response to infant behavior also increased with age in both samples (see Table 7.4-C), from under 15% at 3 months to 33% to 53% at 24 months. Mothers of normal infants were more responsive (vis-a-vis smiling) at 12 and 24 months than were mothers of handicapped infants.

In brief, mothers of normal infants were more likely to smile as a proportion of total behavior and were more likely to smile within interaction sequences than were mothers of handicapped infants. Age trends suggested that normal–handicapped differences were most dramatic in the first half of the first year and that the use of age equivalents decreased the difference between normal and handicapped.

Maternal Vocalization

Maternal vocalization was examined in three ways: (1) as a proportion of all mother behaviors; (2) as a proportion of interactions to all maternal vocalizations; and (3) as a maternal response to all infant behavior. Maternal vocalization was the most frequent maternal behavior in both samples, as seen in Table 7.5-A. The proportion of maternal vocalization increased over age in the handicapped sample (27% at 2 to 7 months and 40% at 28 to 36 months) and in the normal sample (21% at 3 months and 65% at 24 months). Differences between the samples were not seen until 24 months of age (65% in the normal and 42% in the handicapped sample). No differences among mothers of different handicapped groups were found.

The proportion of maternal vocalization in interaction exhibited age-related increases in both samples, as is seen in Table 7.5-B. Although these trends were the same in both samples, infant handicapped–normal differences only occurred at 8 to 16 months (54% versus 37%). The age

TABLE 7.5
Maternal Vocalization by Age and Handicapped Group

A. *Proportion of Vocalization to Total Behavior*

| | Age in Months | | | |
	2-7	8-16	17-27	28-36
Chronological age	.27	.30	.42	.40
Age equivalent	.29	.36	.43	–
Normal	.21	.37	.65	–

B. *Proportion of Interactions to Total Vocalization*

| | Age in Months | | | |
	2-7	8-16	17-27	28-36
Chronological age	.21	.37	.49	.51
Age equivalent	.28	.47	.60	–
Normal	.29	.54	.56	–

C. *Proportion of Responses to Total*

| | Age in Months | | | |
	2-7	8-16	17-27	28-36
Chronological age	.14	.27	.33	.37
Age equivalent	.18	.35	.41	–
Normal	.19	.46	.65	–

equivalents narrowed but did not ameliorate the differences between samples. Interestingly, the mothers spent somewhat more time in interactive vocalization with their developmentally delayed (54%) than their Down's syndrome (46%) or physically impaired (43%) infants.

Maternal vocal responses to an infant behavior as a proportion of all maternal vocalization is presented in Table 7.5-C. Maternal responsivity increased in both samples over age; increases were much more dramatic in the normal than the handicapped sample. In the first half of the first year, maternal vocal responsivity was the same in both samples (14% versus 19%); from this point, however, mothers of normal children increased their vocalization faster than mothers of handicapped children (at the first year, 46% versus 27%; at the second year, 65% versus 33%). The use of age equivalents decreased these differences. As before, mothers of developmentally delayed infants were more vocally responsive to their children (39%) than were mothers of the Down's syndrome (32%) and physically impaired infants (28%).

In brief, mothers of infants in the first half of the first year vocalize the same amount of time to their handicapped and normal infants; by the end of the first year, however, mothers of handicapped infants are vocalizing somewhat less in interaction sequences and in response to their infants' behavior in comparison to mothers of normal infants. These differences were reduced by the use of age equivalents but continue to persist at the end of the second year.

DISCUSSION

Comparing Handicapped and Normal Infants

The data just presented suggest that differences between normal children and children with known handicapping conditions may not be understood unless several groups of dysfunctional children are studied (Lewis & Brooks-Gunn, in press). For example, if we compare a group of normal and Down's syndrome infants, finding the former to be functioning better, we do not know if being Down's syndrome, being dysfunctional (i.e., different from normal), or just being cognitively delayed accounts for the group's difference. If a third group of handicapped children is included, our task is easier, as comparisons between the two groups as well as with the normal group provide valuable information as to what differences are associated with being handicapped versus having a specific handicapping condition. In addition, gathering mental-age equivalence information allows for an examination of the effects of cognitive delay versus other aspects of being handicapped upon functioning. Finally, comparing different groups of handicapped infants and examining mental-age equivalents allows the most detailed exploration of the nature of a specific dysfunction as well as the nature of dysfunction in general.

Age equivalents themselves may differ, given the fact that infants, especially dysfunctional ones, often exhibit uneven profiles across developmental domains and measures. It would not be surprising for different equivalent scores to yield different patterns in relation to maternal or infant behavior. For example, infant linguistic competence may be more directly influencing maternal vocalization or vocalization exchanges than general intellectual competence. Research indicates, for example, that mothers adjust their speech in accordance with their normal children's developing linguistic competence (Moerk, 1974; Shatz & Gleitman, 1973; Snow, 1972). When examining dysfunctional children and their mothers, maternal language usage is bounded by child's Mean Length of Utterance (Rondal, 1978). When matching Down's syndrome children on chronological age and language (MLU), maternal question asking was related to the MLU of the child rather than to chronological age (Leifer & Lewis, 1980).

Positive Affective Exchanges

Positive affective exchanges were different for handicapped infants and their mothers as compared to normal dyads, and these differences involved both mothers and infants. The handicapped infants smiled less overall. Others have reported delays in smiling although frequencies are typically not examined (Gewirtz, 1965; Lewis, 1969). These delays are usually believed to be maturational or cognitive in origin. However, our age-equivalence data suggest that developmental age does not totally account for the less frequent smiling of the handicapped children. Additionally, differences among handicapped groups were found: Down's syndrome infants smiled less than the physically impaired and the developmentally delayed infants, even after taking age equivalence into account. This counters the stereotype of the Down's syndrome child as typically exhibiting high positive affect (Baron, 1972) and corroborates our findings on Down's syndrome infants' temperament profiles (Brooks-Gunn & Lewis, 1981).

Another finding of interest is the dip in smiling seen in the normal and the handicapped sample when comparing the age groups. Decreases in smiling at the end of the first year have been reported by others (Gewirtz, 1965) and are presumably due to the increase in differentiation of objects and persons, recognition of familiar and unfamiliar, and awareness of social dimensions (Brooks-Gunn & Lewis, 1978; Lewis & Brooks-Gunn, 1979).

Mothers of handicapped infants, like their children, smiled less than did mothers of normal infants. In the normal sample, the proportion of maternal smiles as a proportion of mother behavior tripled when their children were between 3 and 12 months of age and was higher than their infants' smiling proportions. This suggests that the maternal smiling behavior is facilitated by the infants' rise in smiling. As the infants exhibit more positive emotion, mothers become even more affective. Conversely, mothers of handicapped infants are not smiling more as their children become older, in part because their infants are not increasing their smiling rapidly. At the same time, they are not responding to the increases that do occur. For example, the large increase in the number of frequent smilers occurred in the third year of life for the handicapped sample; this was not paralleled by an increase in proportional or interactive maternal smiles. This finding suggests that these mothers were not responding to the positive affective increase seen in the third year, perhaps because the increase came later than what mothers expect (at least in terms of normal development) or perhaps because maternal positive affect is suppressed due to their perceptions (or feelings) about having a handicapped child.

Across handicapped groups we find that Down's syndrome infants were not only less likely to smile than physically impaired or developmentally delayed infants, but the physically impaired infants exhibited more responsive and interactive smiling than did the other two groups. These trends were seen even when age equivalence was taken into account. Interestingly, the mothers of different handicapped groups did not differ in terms of affective responses, even though their infants did.

Negative Affective Exchanges

Infant negative affect does not occur frequently in free-play settings but is very salient to mothers. Handicapped infants did cry more than normal infants. Mothers of handicapped and normal children decreased their responses to infant fret/cry after 2 to 7 months of age. The age-related decrease in responses by mothers of handicapped children was much more rapid than the age-related decrease in the children themselves. These data suggest that maternal response to fret/cry is based on the social rule that fret/cry is an accepted behavior in the first 6 months, probably indicating a biological need of the child (hunger, dampness, abdominal pain and gas, fatigue). Around the first year, however, an infant's fret may not be interpreted this way, but is seen as more inappropriate, less tied to biological need, and/or more amenable to shaping. At this time maternal responsivity decreases regardless of handicapping condition, infant maturity, or amount of crying.

High infant fretting may be related to more general temperamental characteristics. In another study we found that infants characterized as difficult temperamentally, based on the Carey Scale, were more likely to fret with free-play settings than were "easier" infants (Brooks-Gunn & Lewis, 1981). Thus mothers may be decreasing their responsiveness as they discover that their child is difficult. Interestingly, difficult infants are not necessarily less responsive, although the mothers may perceive them as such.

Vocalization Exchanges

Vocalization patterns differed as a function of age and infant dysfunction. Not surprising was the fact that proportion of infant vocalization and of interactive vocalizing was much more prevalent in the normal than in the handicapped sample, especially after the 2 to 7 month period and even when age equivalents are taken into account. Interestingly, mothers of handicapped infants did not become more responsive to their infants' vocalizations over age (even with age equivalence), whereas mothers of normal infants did. However, maternal vocal response did increase in both samples, although much more dramatically than in the normal sample.

What is surprising is that normal–handicapped vocalization differences are not erased by looking at age equivalents, nor are mothers of handicapped infants becoming more responsive to their children's increasing vocalizations. Thus, vocalization differences do not seem to be accounted for by general developmental delay or solely by infant differences. This finding, like that for smiling, may reflect depressed maternal behavior towards her infant as a function of lower expectations about her child's course of development.

Handicapped group vocalization differences focused on the mothers, who were more vocally responsive and spent more time in interactive vocalization with their developmentally delayed than with their Down's syndrome or physically impaired infants. Infant differences suggested that Down's syndrome infants were less vocally responsive than the other two groups.

Management of Emotions

As discussed earlier, major socialization tasks of the mother include helping the child manage his or her emotions, as well as interpreting and attaching meaning to the expressed emotions of the child. In terms of emotional management, the mother may modulate the child's emotional responses and facilitate emotional expression.

Modulating emotions includes such processes as inhibition of a response or dampening of a response. Modulation may be especially important for the handicapped or high-risk infant, who often has difficulty in this aspect of emotional expression. For example, premature infants tend to exhibit disorganized sleep–wake patterns (Dreyfuss-Brisac, 1970) and a high degree of irritability and dampening deficits (Brachfeld, Goldberg, & Sloman, 1980). Down's syndrome infants have longer latency to cry in free-play settings but, once negative affect is elicited, take much longer to calm down. Serafica and Cicchetti (1976; Cicchetti & Serafica, 1981) suggest that Down's syndrome infants have deficits in dampening and arousal mechanisms. Given these problems, we might expect mothers of high-risk infants to alter their behavior to help their infants. Typically, however, mothers do not spontaneously alter their behavior, as our data on mothers' responses to negative affect and the data from early-intervention programs suggest. With intervention, mothers tend to change their styles of interaction. For example, Bromwich and Parmelee (1979) found that parental involvement in a program for high-risk infants increased maternal enjoyment and responsivity to the infant. Others have reported similar results with premature infants and their mothers (DiVitto & Goldberg, 1979; Field, 1979, 1980). Taken together, the findings from observations of dyads and from specific interventions suggest that alteration of maternal interactive patterns may be more difficult than previously thought, especially because they may be based on expectations rather than on simple exchange rules. Although the mother–infant exchange has been described as synchronous and finely tuned (Stern, 1974), mothers of risk children may not only require specific instruction on how to alter interaction patterns (rather than changes just "naturally" occurring in the tuning process), but also must be sensitive to how their beliefs and expectations are translated into behavior vis-a-vis the child.

Facilitation of emotions is another area in which mothers may be of assistance to their children. We have seen that handicapped infants have a lower incidence of positive affect than normal infants. However, mothers do not seem to facilitate positive emotional expression as evidenced by their responsivity to infant smiles. If anything, mothers of handicapped infants are *less* responsive to their children's smiling behavior. Similar findings are reported by Bromwich and Parmelee (1979) for premature infants whose smiling is delayed. Maternal disappointment, frustration, or expectations again may be mediating factors in this relationship. The point here, however, is that mothers of handicapped infants, at least in this study, are less facilitative of their infants' positive affect than are mothers of normal infants.

In summary, the infant's capacity in part determines maternal responsivity to affective expression. However, the mother's perception of capacity or rate of acquisition also influences her behavior. Expectations for certain behaviors in specific situations and for age-related behaviors may be based on beliefs about appropriate exchanges or parenting behavior. Affective exchanges seem to be more difficult and disharmonious when handicapped or high-risk infants are involved, which may be related to the affectual difficulties sometimes seen in these groups later in childhood.

ACKNOWLEDGMENTS

This chapter was presented at a Conference on Affective Displays of High Risk Infants, Mailman Center for Child Development, Miami, 1980. The research reported in this chapter was supported by a grant from the Bureau for the Education of the Handicapped and by an Early Childhood Institute, supported by the Bureau for the Education of the Handicapped, Department of Education. We wish to thank Aileen Wehren and Pamela Ritter for their help in data collection and John Jaskir for his assistance in data analysis.

REFERENCES

Baron, J. Temperament profile of children with Down's syndrome. *Developmental Medicine and Child Neurology,* 1972, *14,* 640–643.

Brachfeld, S., Goldberg, S., & Sloman, J. Parent–infant interaction in free play at 8 and 12 months: Effects of prematurity and immaturity. *Infant Behavior and Development,* 1980, *3,* 289–305.

Bromwich, R., & Parmelee, A. An intervention program for pre-term infants. In T. Field, A. Sostek, S. Goldberg, & H. Shuman (Eds.), *Infants born at risk: Behavior and development.* New York: S.P. Medical & Scientific Books, 1979.

Brooks-Gunn, J., & Lewis, M. Early social knowledge: The development of knowledge about others. In H. McGurk (Ed.), *Childhood social development.* London: Methuen, 1978.

Brooks-Gunn, J., & Lewis, M. *Temperament characteristics of handicapped infants.* Paper presented in a symposium on Temperament Characteristics of Atypical Infants at the Society for Research in Child Developoment Biennial Meetings, Boston, April 1981.

Broussard, E. R., & Hartner, M. S. S. Maternal perception of the neonate as related to development. *Child Psychology and Human Development,* 1970, *1,* 16–25.

Caudill, W., & Weinstein, H. Maternal care and infant behavior in Japan and America. *Psychiatry,* 1969, *32,* 12–43.

Cicchetti, D., & Bridges, F. Temperament in Down's syndrome infants. *Developmental Psychology,* in press.

Cicchetti, D., & Serafica, F. C. Interplay among behavioral systems: Illustrations from the study of attachment, affiliation, and wariness in young children with Down's syndrome. *Developmental Psychology,* 1981, *17,* 36–49.

DiVitto, B., & Goldberg, S. The effects of newborn medical status on early parent–infant interaction. In T. Field (Ed.), *Infants born at risk: Behavior and development.* New York: S. P. Medical & Scientific Books, 1979.

Donnell, G. N., Alfi, O. S., Rublee, J. C., & Koch, R. Chromosomal abnormalities. In R. Koch, & F. la Cruz (Eds.), *Down's syndrome (Mongolism): Research, prevention and management.* New York: Brunner/Mazel, 1975.

Dreyfuss-Brisac, C. Sleep ontogenesis in human prematures after 32 weeks of conceptional age. *Developmental Psychobiology,* 1970, *3,* 91–121.

Ekman, P., Friesen, W. V., & Ellsworth, P. *Emotion in the human face: Guidelines for research and an integration of findings.* New York: Pergamon, 1972.

Field, T. Interaction patterns of preterm and term infants. In T. Field, A. Sostek, S. Goldberg, & H. Shuman (Eds.), *Infants born at risk: Behavior and development.* New York: S.P. Medical & Scientific Books, 1979.

Field, T. Interactions of preterm and term infants with their lower- and middle-class teenage and adult mothers. In T. Field, S. Goldberg, D. Stern, & A. Sostek (Eds.), *High-risk infants and children: Adult and peer interactions.* New York: Academic Press, 1980.

Field, T., Sostek, A., Vietze, P., & Leiderman, A. H. (Eds.). *Culture and early interactions.* Hillsdale, N.J.: Lawrence Erlbaum Associates, 1981.

Fox, N., & Lewis, M. The role of maturation and experience in preterm development. In J. Gallagher (Ed.), *New directions in special education.* San Francisco: Jossey-Bass, 1981.

Fraiberg, S. Intervention in infancy: A program for blind infants. In B. Z. Friedlander, G. M. Sterritt, & G. E. Kirk (Eds.), *Exceptional infant: Assessment and intervention* (Vol. 3). New York: Brunner/Mazel, 1975.

Gallagher, R. J., Jens, K. G., & O'Donnell, K. J. The effect of physical status in the affective expression of handicapped infants. *Infant Behavior and Development,* in press.

Gewirtz, J. L. The course of infant smiling in four childrearing environments. In B. M. Foss (Ed.), *Determinants of infant behavior* (Vol. 3). New York: Wiley, 1965.

Greenberg, R., & Field, T. Temperament ratings of handicapped infants during classroom mother and teacher interactions. *Pediatric Psychology,* in press.

Hollingshead, A. B. *Two-factor index of social position.* New Haven: Author, 1957.

Leifer, J., & Lewis, M. *Maternal speech to normal and handicapped children: A look at question-asking behavior.* Paper presented at the International Conference on Infant Studies, New Haven, April 1980.

Lewis, M. Infants' responses to facial stimuli during the first year of life. *Developmental Psychology,* 1969, *1,* 75-86.

Lewis, M. State as an infant-environment interaction: An analysis of mother-infant interaction as a function of sex. *Merrill-Palmer Quarterly,* 1972, *18,* 95-121.

Lewis, M. *Effects of birth order on the mother-child relationship.* Unpublished manuscript, Educational Testing Service, Princeton, N.J., 1978.

Lewis, M. *The socialization of emotions.* Paper presented at the meetings of the Society for Research in Child Development, Boston, April 1981.

Lewis, M., & Brooks, J. Self-knowledge and emotional development. In M. Lewis, & L. A. Rosenblum (Eds.), *The development of affect.* New York: Plenum, 1978.

Lewis, M., & Brooks-Gunn, J. *Social cognition and the acquisition of self.* New York: Plenum, 1979.

Lewis, M., & Brooks-Gunn, J. Developmental models and assessment issues. In N. Anastasio, W. Frankenburg, & A. Fondel (Eds.), *Identifying the developmentally delayed child.* College Park: University Park Press, in press.

Lewis, M., Brooks-Gunn, J., & Fox. N. Socio-affective dysfunction in high risk infants and mothers. Unpublished manuscript, Educational Testing Service, Princeton, N.J., 1981.

Lewis, M., & Coates, D. Mother-infant interaction and cognitive development in twelve-week-old infants. *Infant Behavior and Development,* 1980, *3,* 95-105.

Lewis, M., & Lee-Painter, S. An interactional approach to the mother-infant dyad. In M. Lewis, & L. Rosenblum (Eds.), *The effect of the infant on its caregiver: The origins of behavior* (Vol. 1). New York: Wiley, 1974.

Lewis, M., & Michalson, L. *Children's emotions and moods: Theory and measurement.* New York: Plenum, 1982.

Moerk, E. Changes in verbal mother-child interaction with increasing language skills of the child. *Journal of Psycholinguistic Research,* 1974, *3,* 101-116.

Rondal, J. Maternal speech to Downs' syndrome and normal children matched for mean-length-of-utterance. In C. E. Myers (Ed.), *Quality of life in severely and profoundly retarded people: Research foundation for improvement.* Washington, D.C.: American Association on Mental Deficiency, 1978.

Saarni, C. Cognitive and communicative features of emotional experience of do you show what you think you feel. In M. Lewis, & L. A. Rosenblum (Eds.), *The development of affect.* New York, Plenum, 1978.

Saarni, C. Children's understanding of display rules for expressive behavior. *Developmental Psychology,* 1979, *15,* 424–429.

Saarni, C. *Observing children's use of display rules: Age and sex differences.* Paper presented at the Annual Meeting of the American Psychological Association, Montreal, September 1980.

Serafica, F. D., & Cicchetti, D. Down's syndrome children in a strange situation: Attachment and exploration behaviors. *Merrill-Palmer Quarterly,* 1976, *22,* 137–150.

Shatz, M., & Gleitman, R. The development of communication skills: Modifications in the speech of young children as a function of the listener. *Monographs of the Society for Research in Child Development,* 1973, *38* (5, Serial No. 152).

Snow, C. Mother's speech to children learning language. *Child Development,* 1972, *43,* 549–565.

Solnit, A. J., & Stark, M. H. Mourning and the birth of a defective child. *Psychoanalytic Study of Children,* 1961, *16,* 523–537.

Stern, D. Mother and infant at play: The dyadic interaction involving facial, vocal, and gaze behaviors. In M. Lewis, & L. Rosenblum (Eds.), *The effect of the infant on its caregiver: The origins of behavior* (Vol. 1). New York: Wiley, 1974.

8 The Socialization of Emotions

Michael Lewis
Linda Michalson
Educational Testing Service

"Not only ideas, but emotions too, are cultural artifacts..."
(C. Geertz, 1973, p. 81).

In the study of emotions, most attention has been given to issues related to the measurement and development of emotional behavior. In general, the implicit theory governing these studies is derived from a biological model based on the Darwinian notion of the fixity and universality of affective expressions. Following the work of Darwin (1872), Tomkins (1962, 1963), Ekman (Ekman, Friesen, & Ellsworth, 1972), and Izard (1977), investigators have focused on the measurement of facial expressions, the relationship of expressions to physiological responses, and, on occasion, the connection between situations and emotions as expressed in the face. Less often, the affective qualities of vocal behavior and bodily responses are examined (e.g., Argyle, 1972; Scherer, 1979, 1982).

Although the neuromusculature involving facial expressions and the relationship of emotional expressions to particular situations are important topics for study, the ways in which emotions are socialized have been neglected for the most part. It is towards a consideration of the socialization of emotions, particularly through the interaction of the child with the social environment, that the present chapter is focused. In order to understand the particular role of the parent–child interaction in the socialization of emotions, it is necessary to consider first some of the general issues surrounding this topic. Following this discussion special attention is given to one particular study on the socialization of the child's affect lexicon and to the ways in which such socialization practices might impact on developmental psychopathology.

ISSUES IN THE STUDY OF THE SOCIALIZATION
OF EMOTIONS[1]

The first task is to explore the ways affects in general and emotions in particular are socialized. Underlying this discussion is a contrast between two prototypic models of emotional development. Although drawing too gross a distinction between the model, Hochschild (1979) provides a good starting point for analyzing the socialization of emotions. Hochschild contrasts the organismic or biological model with the interactive or socialization model, arguing that the first is concerned primarily with the relationship of emotions to biologically given instincts or impulses. She sees this model raising most of the critical questions now posed. Thus, the measurement of emotional expressions focuses mainly on the fixity and universality of expression rather than on socialization factors that may account for individual or group differences. Moreover, when they are recognized, socialization factors are considered only in regard to how emotions are stimulated and expressed within the constraints of fixity and universality. To quote Hochschild (1979):

> the image that comes to mind [in considering the organismic view] is that of a sudden automatic reflex syndrome—Darwin's instant snarl expression; Freud's tension discharge at a given breaking point of tension overload; James and Lange's notion of an instantaneous unmediated visceral reaction to a perceived stimulus, the perception of which is also unmediated by social influences [pp. 553–554].

In other words, emotions are viewed as analogous to knee jerks or sneezes, unlearned, biologically controlled, and subject to relatively little socialization influence.

In the interactive or socialization view, attention is focused on how social influences affect "feeling rules." Feeling rules imply something more active than a reflex and must be considered because, according to Hochschild (1979), "we do feel, we try to feel, and we want to try to feel [p. 563]." Thus, rather than talking about emotions as fixed or universal phenomena, or about emotional development as the unfolding of various and combinatorial maturational systems, including physiological, social, and cognitive, we need to focus on the problem of how emotions are socialized. This is not to say that such organismic functions are unimportant but rather to stress the equally important role of socialization and learning in emotional development.

Specifically, five questions on the socialization of emotions can be raised,

---

[1]In the following discussion, little differentiation is made between the terms "affect" and "emotion," although we recognize that such a distinction is possible (Izard, 1977). Because we are primarily interested in issues related to the acquisition of a lexicon, we are prepared to consider all relevant phenomena and thus we make no distinction between the two terms.

and it is towards one of these that we eventually turn our attention. These five socialization issues are: (1) how to express emotions; (2) when to express emotions; (3) how emotions are managed; (4) how emotions are labeled; and (5) how emotional states are interpreted. Each of these issues is discussed briefly here. (For a more complete review, see Lewis & Michalson, in preparation, Chapter 6 and Chapter 7).

How to Express Emotions

How to express emotions is an important feeling rule that all members of a culture must learn. There is no good evidence to indicate when children start to learn particular rules of affect expression, although observations of mother–child interaction patterns suggest that some of the socialization of these rules occurs in early mother–infant interactions (see Brooks-Gunn & Lewis, Chapter 7, this volume).

When to Express Emotions

Situations have associated with them expectations about how people should feel. The acquisition of this knowledge is critical to children's adaptation to their social environment. This being the case, it becomes important to study where the knowledge comes from, how it is acquired, and what its developmental course might be. That very young children show some understanding about the experiences of others (Borke, 1971; Halliday, 1973) and about the social requirements of different situations (Edwards & Lewis, 1979) suggests that the transmission of these feeling rules takes place early and constitutes one of the important socialization lessons of early childhood.

How Emotions are Managed

Children are taught early in life to manage emotions by modifying or suppressing expressions that society deems inappropriate and expressing responses suitable to the occasion. There is evidence that children as young as 10 months learn to manage emotions through the use of significant others either in direct interactions or through more indirect processes (Feinman & Lewis, 1981; Lewis & Feiring, 1981; Lewis & Weinraub, 1976). Whether the socialization rules governing the management of emotions need to be learned for each situation or whether the rules once learned are generalizable is not known.

How Emotions are Labeled

One important aspect of the socialization process that has received little attention concerns the acquisition of labels for specific emotions and the effect of the label on the child's affective experience. If a relationship exists between language and the way in which we perceive and experience our world (Cole & Scribner, 1974), then children's acquisition of emotional terminology becomes an important area of research. We discuss this topic in detail later in this chapter.

How Emotions are Interpreted

The expressive behavior of young organisms may indicate that they have emotional states. The question is how these emotional states become associated with specific emotional experiences. Data indicate that parents attribute emotions to their infant prior to the infant's ability to *experience* those emotions (Pannabecker, Emde, Johnson, Stenberg, Davis, 1980). Such attributions may help children learn to interpret their own states. This socialization can occur through the specific labels parents apply as well as through the behaviors parents exhibit in response to the infant's emotional expressions or behaviors.

A DEFINITION OF EMOTION

In order to explore the role of socialization factors in emotional development, it is necessary to review what we have referred to as the five features of affects or emotions (Lewis & Brooks, 1978; Lewis & Brooks-Gunn, 1979; Lewis & Rosenblum, 1978). These include elicitors, receptors, states, expressions, and experiences. *Emotional elicitors* refer to events that trigger emotional receptors. *Emotional receptors* are relatively specific loci or pathways in the central nervous system that mediate changes in physiological and/or cognitive states of the organism. *Emotional states* are the particular constellations of changes in somatic and/or neuronal activity that accompany the activation of emotional receptors. "Change in" is the critical aspect of this definition. *Emotional expressions* are those potentially observable surface features of changes in face, body, voice, and activity level that accompany emotional states. Finally, *emotional experiences* are individuals' conscious or unconscious interpretations and evaluations of their perceived emotional states and expressions.

In the organismic view, the connection between elicitors, receptors, expressions, and states is biologically determined. Thus, elicitors are connected to receptors, which in turn produce certain states. Moreover, states can be directly inferred from expressions. Emotional experiences (i.e., the interpretation of states) are often not considered aspects of emotion. This is somewhat surprising in light of James' (1884) definition of emotion as (1) somatic change (what we call state) and (2) the experience of that change.

Although the organismic view allows for the effect of socialization, its basic premise is that these connections are fixed. Arguments for the fixity are based on cross-cultural evidence of the universality of the fundamental emotions (Darwin, 1872; Ekman, 1973; Izard, 1971; Sorenson, 1975).

In the interactive or socialization view, these components of emotion are seen as less fixed and potentially open to socialization influences. Indeed the connections between these components may derive from the socialization process itself. In other words, emotional states and experiences may be linked together through the particular socialization experiences of the child. Moreover, an emotional experience may not be connected in any fixed one-to-one fashion to expression and the socialization task is to connect them. That is, the culture must match what it expects one to experience given both a particular emotional expression (presumed to reflect an emotional state) and a set of elicitors.

For example, a 1-year-old child might cry because a tower of blocks has fallen over or because he or she has struck a leg against a pointed object. In both cases the expression and presumed state is one of distress. The interactive model suggests that socializing agents act to define the child's emotional experience, both through labeling the child's experience as well as through their behavior towards the child. In the first instance, when the tower of blocks falls down, the child's mother is likely to say to the child "you are frustrated" and then help the child build the tower again. Both verbal and nonverbal actions may serve to socialize feelings of frustration in the child. In the second case the mother as the socializing agent may say to the child, "you are in pain" (instead of frustrated) and accompany the labeling with a different set of behaviors, such as holding and comforting. Thus, the emotional state as referenced by external behavior such as crying may be linked to two totally different emotional experiences through differential socialization practices. From a psychopathological point of view, "incorrect" labeling and behavioral responses in the face of particular elicitors and particular expressions (and presumably states) may produce "inappropriate" emotional experiences. The experience is "inappropriate" or psychopathological *only to the degree that it is unique and incompatible to what others might feel in similar situations.*

Such issues should direct our attention to a dynamic socialization model in which the socialization experiences of the child play a critical role in all aspects of emotional development. Although there certainly is a biologically determined universality and fixity between expressions and elicitors, especially in young organisms, the role of socialization in the development of emotions is as critical and in need of examination.

We now turn to two specific issues that are important in studying the socialization of emotions: how emotions are labeled and interpreted. We also prevent several models of developmental psychopathology as a consequence of the misinterpretation of emotional states.

THE SOCIALIZATION OF EMOTIONS THROUGH
AFFECT LABELING

One aspect of the socialization process that is seldom investigated is the acquisition of a lexicon of emotions. Although we and others (e.g., Ekman & Friesen, 1975; Izard, 1977; Lewis, 1981; Plutchik, 1970, 1980) recognize the existence of complex mixtures of emotions, such mixtures are usually not part of our affect lexicon. Indeed, we know very little even about the labeling and use of specific affect terms. If we adopt the position of social anthropologists who believe that cognitive concepts and language are intimately related (for example, consider the well-known case of the ability of Eskimos to differentiate types of snow and the nature of their language, which encodes many types of snow), then the study of the child's acquisition and use of affect terms becomes quite important. Recently it has been shown that even the experience of smell may depend on the labels available to describe it. Not only do the labels given to different odors help people remember them but they also appear to influence how people actually perceive the smell. Having a name transforms the smell from the vague to the clear (Cain, 1979).

There is evidence that children have some understanding of their emotional experiences and the emotions of others prior to the acquisition of specific linguistic labels for those emotions. For instance, an 18 month old who exhibits empathic behavior by patting a bereaved parent indicates to us through appropriate behavior that the child has at least a rudimentary understanding of the parent's particular experience although he or she is unable to put a label on that experience (Borke, 1971).[2]

Even when the child's linguistic abilities emerge, the child may be unable to use the appropriate lexical term although he or she may have other emotional expressions. For example, Lewis and Brooks (1978) give an example of Benjamin, whose family moved from one house to another when he was 2 years and 9 months old. Benjamin had spent all of his life in the first house. One week after moving to the new house he was asked whether he liked the new house. "This house doesn't taste good," he said, as he stuck out his tongue. Such examples as this again reflect the fact that children may well have emotional experiences that can be articulated through their behaviors even without the appropriate linguistic labels.

The acquisition of affect terms by the individual may certainly reflect the interface between language acquisition, cognitive capacity, and emotion in

---

[2]Although Borke argues that this behavior represents a child's understanding of the parent's experience, others have suggested that such behavior might be a conditioned response to a particular elicitor or a reflexive-like behavior, neither of which would necessarily imply any understanding on the part of the child.

a manner similar to the way the affect terms of a culture may reflect important underlying properties of the social experience of that culture (Geertz, 1959; Shott, 1979). Kagan (1981) has described the way in which cultures differ in the availability of affect terms and their referents. However, the relationship between the use of such affect terms by particular cultures and cultural differences in experiences has not been studied. Elsewhere we have shown that within our own culture (at least within the academic part of that culture) affect terms and the study of emotions in general focus on the negative end of the emotional spectrum. For example, textbook discussions of children's emotions contain more about sorrow, gloom, and sadness than about laughter and humor, and more about jealousy than about sympathy. Without question the most lengthy discussions have revolved around topics of fear and anger. In every textbook we surveyed, one or both of these feelings were allotted the largest number of pages of discussion (Lewis & Michalson, in preparation).

How this bias towards certain aspects of emotional experience rather than others relates to the particular goals and values of a society is not clear. The Puritan background and the northern European influence of the dominant group in our culture, with its emphasis on impulse control, work, and guilt, imply it may be no accident that our intellectual search lights are focused on negative feelings rather than on whimsey, playfulness, or delight. Even within the study of positive affects such as humor our interests are often related to topics of its psychopathological implications (e.g., Freud, 1960; Levine, 1979). Unfortunately, too little information on cultural differences in the psycholinguistics of emotion is available for us to do more than suggest an interconnection between the use of affect terms in general and important cultural phenomena.

In the same way that knowledge of cultural rules about the use of affect terms may be valuable for understanding the structure of particular cultures, knowledge of how a child acquires and uses affect terms may be of some importance in understanding the structure of the child's emotional experience. Although studies on children's acquisition of language are numerous (to say the least), there are almost no studies on children's acquisition of emotion labels. Researchers have studied the acquisition of nouns, verbs, pronouns, and more recently personal pronouns, but the acquisition of emotion labels is not usually considered. Even though some studies have dealt with the language of emotion—that is, how children and adults talk about their feelings (e.g., Davitz, 1969; Lewis, Wolman, & King, 1972a, 1972b; Wolman, Lewis, & King, 1971, 1972a, 1972b)—very little is known about how children acquire labels for these feelings. Amen (1941) found that by 4 years of age, children have already acquired a limited number of affect terms, including "happy," "sad," "mad," "angry," and "scared." Izard (1971) reports that infants can discriminate emotions earlier than they can label them and that although the recognition and discrimination of emotions increase between 2 1/2 and 9 years of age, emotion labeling is not strongly related to age. The recognition and labeling of the basic emotions of joy, sadness, anger, and fear develop earlier than of emotions such as contempt and shame. Izard concludes that the ability to recognize emotions exceeds the ability to produce appropriate labels for them. More recently, Zahn-Waxler, Radke-Yarrow, and King (1979) have found that as early as 2 years of age children begin to understand and even produce verbal labels for affective displays such as crying and laughing and for emotions they express. Where there terms come from and how they relate to the children's experiences of these emotions is not clear, however.[3]

Language development, in particular the acquisition of phonetic and lexical abilities, appears to be related to the use of language by people around the child, including parents, siblings, and peers (Lewis & Rosenblum, 1977). If we are interested in studying the acquisition of affect language, an important place to start is by studying the use of such language by children's principal caregivers. Through determining the context of the use of affect labels around children we may be better able to relate that both to children's use of affect terms and to their expressions and experiences of those affects.

There are many methods for recording the language of mothers towards their children. In most, the mother is asked to behave naturally and talk to her child either in a nonstructured situation or around a teaching activity. The corpus of the mother's language is gathered from these situations and particular features of her language are studied. Such methods are favored because they capitalize on the spontaneous use of language by the mother (and child) and because a large corpus of naturally occurring language is usually obtained. The disadvantage of these techniques, however, is that they do not tap aspects of language usage that are related to situations unlikely or only likely with low probability to occur when the language corpus is being recorded. In particular, the mother's affect language is less apt to be observed in some situations than in others. Therefore, in order to

---

[3]After this chapter was written, it came to our attention that Greif, Alvarez, and Ulman (1981) have some data on how parents provide information about emotions to their preschool children during a task in which parents read a picture book to their children. Parents' references to emotions were coded according to whether they were statements, questions, explanations of emotions related to causal/situational factors, or information about the ways in which emotions can be inferred from body or facial cues. The investigators found that 71% of the parents mentioned emotions to their children, usually in the form of a statement or a question. The most frequently labeled emotions were anger, joy, and distress. Whereas mothers showed no difference in their use of affect labels to sons and daughters, fathers were twice as likely to emphasize affect to daughters compared to sons. Although not significant, there was a tendency for mothers to mention anger to sons more often than to daughters. Finally, when instances of the children's spontaneous use of affect terms were coded, it was found that of the 20 instances that occurred, 17 of the labels were produced by girls.

study the use of such language it becomes necessary to restrict or to focus the situations in which the language corpus is gathered. As a consequence, the language data collected are likely to be highly restricted to the particular situation. In order to counter this fault, it is necessary to look not only at restricted situations but at situations that have general importance in the child's life.

Specific situations with such properties are not easily produced because our analyses of situational constraints, especially within a developmental perspective, have been limited (Lewis, 1978). However, one situation in which affect terms are likely to occur is the "attachment situation." The attachment situation seems to meet the requirements previously outlined because by its nature it is: (1) a restricted situation eliciting a spontaneous sample of the mother's language; (2) more likely to elicit affect terms because of its stress on child and parents; (3) a prototypic measure of an important affect (attachment); and (4) generalizable and predictive to other situations (Ainsworth, Blehar, Waters, & Wall, 1978).

It seems reasonable, therefore, to use this situation to study the principal caregiver's (in this case the mother's) language as it relates to the use of affect terms. Even here, however, there is a limit on the types of affect expressions to be found. The enormous literature on the attachment situation leads us to believe that the emotions that mothers are likely to discuss are those of fear, anger, and unhappiness rather than joy, delight, and interest. Thus, it is important to keep in mind that the emotions produced in this situation cannot be contrasted to emotions either not present or elicited with very low frequency because of the situation.

MATERNAL AFFECT LABELING: A STUDY OF INFANT DISTRESS

Few studies have yet looked at maternal affect labeling. The present study represents an attempt to understand at least some aspects of affect labeling that occur during mother–infant interaction. Our discussion has made clear that affect usage will be highly dependent on the type of situation in which we collect our language data. Such limitations require that the situation possess the attributes previously outlined and imply that the study of affect labeling in the attachment situation, particularly during the mother–infant reunion following a separation, constitutes a reasonable starting point for our inquiry.

The data presented are from an unpublished study by Lewis and Michalson (1981). In order to investigate maternal affect labeling in response to infant distress 111 1-year-old infants and their mothers were observed during a 5-minute reunion period. This reunion period occurred after a 15-minute free-play episode in which the mother and infant engaged in unrestricted play and after the mother's departure from the playroom for not more than 2 minutes. This free-play, departure, separation, and reunion situation constitutes a modified "strange situation" in which attachment behaviors can be observed. A similar modified version, using one separation and one reunion episode, has also been used by Waters, Wippman, and Sroufe (1979). The infants observed were a subsample of children followed longitudinally and were included in the present sample if they were also seen at 2 years of age in the same situation. The sample was composed of 58 males, 53 females, 56 upper SES, and 55 lower SES children.

Use of Affect Terms

Of the 111 mothers only 29 (26%) used any affect labels during the 5-minute reunion, and 82 (74%) used no affect labels. Four categories of affect labels were used by the 29 mothers. Seven mothers said that their child was "tired/sad"; 7 said "angry/mad"; 7 said "scared/upset"; and 8 said "missed me." Thus, even though most mothers used no affect labels, those that did used only four different ones that were appropriate to the situation. This finding confirms our view that particular situations will limit the number of different affects observed. In this situation the emotions elicited were not positive. Because all mothers faced an upset child when they returned to the room, the next question we asked was whether there were any maternal variables that distinguished the 29 mothers who labeled ("labelers") from the 82 who did not ("nonlabelers").

Labelers versus Nonlabelers

Maternal variables available for study included SES level, WAIS verbal subscale score, and maternal internality–externality measured by the Rotter Internality–Externality Scale (Rotter, 1966). A chi-square analysis on each of these variables failed to indicate any significant differences between mothers who labeled and those who did not, although higher SES mothers were somewhat more likely to use affect labels than lower SES mothers. Others have also found the use of affect concepts to be more prevalent in the language of the middle class than that of the lower class (e.g., Bernstein, 1961; Hess & Shipman, 1965). There was also a tendency for maternal verbal performance on the WAIS to be related to label usage; labelers obtained higher WAIS verbal scores ($X^2_{(1)} = 2.90$, $p < .08$).

Labeling and nonlabeling mothers were also compared by looking at specific maternal behaviors towards infants during reunion, including vocalizing, looking, smiling, teaching, holding, approaching, and establishing proximity (moving within arms' reach of the child). Also compared were maternal initiations and maternal responses, which measured whether or not mothers initiated contact with the child or responded to the child's initiation. No differences between labelers and nonlabelers were found for any behavior except maternal response. Here, the nonlabelers were more likely to respond to their infants than the labelers ($X^2_{(1)}$ = 4.96, $p < .03$).

Differences Within Labelers

Because few differences between labelers and nonlabelers were found, we sought to determine whether there were any differences within the group of mothers who labeled their children in terms of the labels they used. Mothers with higher verbal WAIS scores more frequently labeled their children "scared/upset" or "miss me" compared to mothers with lower verbal WAIS scores, who used the terms "angry/mad" and "tired/sad" ($X^2_{(3)}$ = 8.09, $p < .05$). We also found that lower SES mothers tended to use "angry/mad" relatively more often than did higher SES mothers ($X^2_{(1)}$ = 2.64, n.s.). The SES difference in the use of "angry/mad" is intriguing in light of findings from other studies showing social-class differences in the expression and acting out of anger and aggression: Lower SES mothers and children tend to show more physical aggression than higher SES mothers and children (Feshbach, 1970; Zigler & Child, 1969). Whether or not the differential use of affect labels on the part of the mother serves to facilitate such social-class differences is highly speculative; still, the labeling of specific emotions as a function of social class is provocative. Additional evidence of the differential use of anger labels is provided by the Greif et al. (1981) finding that mothers tend to label anger more in talking to sons than daughters (see Footnote 3). Also, Izard (1971) reports that American children are more likely than French children to recognize and label anger.

Finally, mothers of males used "miss me" more than mothers of females ($X^2_{(1)}$ = 4.07, $p < .05$). The use of the term "miss me" more for male than female infants may also have important implications, especially from a psychoanalytical point of view, which suggests that mothers may be more seductive towards their male than female children (Sroufe & Ward, 1980). As we see here, "miss me" is an intriguing label because mothers tended to use it when they first returned to the room. Thus, the use of this particular label may have more to do with the feeings of the mother than the feelings of the child.

What about other maternal behaviors, besides labeling, which might have covaried with the children's behaviors and with maternal labeling behavior? Did the mothers' reunion behaviors differ as a function of how they labeled their children's distress? Mothers who labeled their children "scared/upset" held their children more than the mothers of the other three groups

$(X^2_{(3)} = 7.69, p < .05)$. Mothers who showed less proximal behaviors labeled their children "miss me" more than the other mothers $(X^2_{(3)} = 9.40, p < .02)$. Mothers who were more responsive to their children's behavior used "scared/upset" and "tired/sad" more than "miss me" and "angry/mad" $(X^2_{(2)} = 7.52, p < .05)$. The reason "miss me" and "angry/mad" children are similar in terms of eliciting low levels of maternal responsivity may have different causes. In the latter case "angry/mad" children were characterized by throwing themselves about and pushing and throwing toys, behaviors that were not conducive to maternal responsivity. In contrast, the use of "miss me" did not appear related to children's distress.

Labeling as a Function of Infant Differences

Having examined maternal differences in labeling behavior, we next examined whether there were any infant variables that might have caused the mothers to produce the particular affect terms they did. Infant variables of IQ (Bayley Mental Development Index) and sex were first examined by a chi-square analysis and found not to be related to the mothers' use of affect terms. Maternal labelers did not have children who were more upset than nonlabelers, because all infants were upset when the mothers left the room.

Although infant behaviors did not affect whether or not a mother used an affect label, they did influence the specific label she used. Mothers labeling their children "angry/mad," in fact, had children who tended either to throw themselves about on the ground or to throw and push toys around. The use of the label "tired/sad" was applied to children who showed depression, which was expressed in behavioral terms by a marked reduction in activity as well as a "tired appearance." The use of "scared/upset" was applied to children who cried and often assumed a bodily posture of wishing to be picked up, accompanied by a pleading look at the mother. In these cases, then, maternal labeling behavior appeared to be related to behavioral characteristics of the infants. Although the infants labeled "miss me" showed no consistent behavioral pattern, the central feature of their response was looking away from the mother or looking at a toy and not paying attention to the mother as she entered the room.

Mothers, it seems, label their infants' experiences according to the eliciting situation and according to the infants' behavior in that situation. Moreover, their labeling behaviors covaried with their other behavioral responses to distress. Not all cases of maternal labeling followed these patterns, however. These exceptions are the focus of a later section on developmental psychopathology.

One reason that the 29 mothers may have labeled their children's emotional behavior and the other 82 mothers did not is that these children may have expressed certain behaviors other than distress that facilitated maternal affect labeling. To examine this question, 30 nonlabeling mother–infant dyads were selected at random from the 82 dyads in the nonlabeling group for a comparison with the 29 labeling mother–infant dyads to see if any differences in infant behaviors could be found. Of the 30 nonlabeling dyads, 26 children exhibited behaviors similar to 29 of the children who were labeled. These 26 infants showed behaviors that fit into three affect categories: scared/upset (16 children), miss me (6 children), and angry/mad (4 children). None of the children appeared tired or sad and four showed no affect patterns. There appeared to be no differences in maternal nonverbal behaviors between these 30 nonlabelers and the 29 labelers. Thus, the results suggest that whether or not mothers applied affect labels was not attributable to infant behaviors, although the particular label used was influenced by the infant's behavior.

INDIVIDUAL DIFFERENCES IN THE USE OF AFFECT LABELS

Although limited in terms of the number and kinds of different affect labels studied, this investigation demonstrates that mothers of children use affect labels prior to their children's acquisition of language. Of interest is that the mothers' use of affect labels in this particular situation designed to produce stress was rather infrequent. Only 26% of the mothers used affect labels of any sort. That is not to say that mothers did not express any emotion towards the children; indeed, they did. In most cases they picked up and comforted their children either through direct physical contact or through distractions. Mothers neither scolded nor hit their children when they showed distress. Thus, the mother–child interaction appeared synchronous vis-a-vis the child's emotional expression and the mother's nonverbal response. For the most part, however, these mothers did not use affect labels. Whether this infrequent usage was due to the relatively infrequent use of affect labels by mothers in general or was due to the fact that their children were only 1 year old and without language remains unknown. Even so, the use of affect labeling in emotion-eliciting situations is an important finding in need of further exploration. This is especially true in light of data suggesting that mothers *attribute* the three affects as described here (sad/tired, angry/mad, scared/upset) to children of this age (Pannabecker et al., 1980) even though they may not *apply* these labels to their children's behavior.

Most of the mothers who used affect labels in the attachment situation used them in a way that appears to be related to the behaviors produced by the child. Thus, some mothers are providing affect terms for their children that are a function of the child's own behavior. Even though we could not detect maternal characteristics that distinguished labelers from nonlabelers, it can be hypothesized that mothers who produced these labels provide their child with a linguistic experience that should facilitate the child's acquisition of affect terms. Although there are no data on this topic, there is some evidence that mothers who use a more elaborated language have children who are able to differentiate their environment better than children of mothers who use a more restricted language (Bernstein, 1961; Hess & Shipman, 1965). Generalizations from these data allow us to speculate that the same may be true in the realm of affect. Mothers who use a greater number of and more differentiated affect terms may have children whose affect experiences are more differentiated.

It is possible that our inability to differentiate labeling from nonlabeling mothers was due to the fact that we did not obtain the critical dimensions of people who use affect terms. It may be the case that besides verbal fluency, certain types of interpersonal sensitivity and concern with affect experience are characteristics of these people. Here then is another opportunity to explore the socialization of emotions through labeling by distinguishing those who use and those who do not use affect labels.

It is tempting to consider "labeling" mothers and "nonlabeling" mothers as somehow different, yet it must be kept in mind that labeling and nonlabeling pertain to particular situations and emotions. Other situations likely to elicit different emotions might produce a different subset of "labelers" and "nonlabelers." This also is a dimension of socialization to be explored. If people are differentially sensitive to affective moods (e.g., depressives are more sensitive than nondepressives to other peoples' depression), it may be that the mother's own mood state is the critical factor differentiating those who label from those who do not label particular affect states. In the present study the labeling mothers may have been more sensitive to the negative dimensions of emotions than dimensions associated with joy or other positive emotions. Thus, a general sensitivity to affect states may be less important for labeling particular emotions than a selective sensitivity. Although there is little empirical evidence to support this hypothesis, the results of one recent study show moderate correlations between mothers' and infants' emotional expressions, particularly between their displays of anger (Malatesta, 1981; Malatesta & Haviland, 1981).

ATTACHMENT AND MATERNAL AFFECT LABELING

Another issue to be addressed concerns the relationship, if any, between the mother's use of affect labels and the patterning of the infant's emotional expressions in the attachment situation. The reunion episode of the attachment situation in which we observed the mother's labeling behavior towards her distressed infant has been widely used to characterize differences in infants' early social relationships, especially towards the mother. Because this situation is of such importance in the social-development literature, the present results need to be viewed in the context of other work in this area.

Three major types of social relationships emerge when infants are studied in the attachment situation: One is characteristic of children who are avoidant upon reunion with the mother (A children), one of children who are securely attached (B children), and one of children who are ambivalently attached (C children). Each of these attachment classifications is based upon a different patterning of emotional behavior displayed by infants in the attachment situation. (For a detailed description of the classifications, see Ainsworth et al., 1978). It was our hypothesis that affect labeling by the mother during the reunion episode would be related to the kinds of behavior the child exhibited upon reunion, which in turn would be related to the child's attachment classification. If this is correct, we predicted that A children would be labeled "miss me," because A children have been described as avoidant: They do not go to their mothers or show signs of missing them. "Miss me" is actually the mother's way of asking "Didn't you miss me?" in response to the child's behavior that suggests she was not missed. We also predicted that C children would be labeled "angry/mad," because they have been reported to show behaviors of this sort, especially through their desire to be held and comforted and yet at the same time not wanting to be held or comforted. Finally, we predicted that B children would be labeled either "tired/sad" or "scared/upset," because B children did not show signs of either withdrawal from the mothers or anger.

When we applied the attachment classifications to the 29 infants whose mothers used affect labels in the reunion situation, the following results were obtained:[4] Of the eight children labeled "miss me," six were classified as A children, one as a B child, and one as a C child. This finding not only supports our hypothesis but also confirms our belief that the mothers who used "miss me" were in fact responding to children who avoided interacting with them. Of the seven children labeled "angry/mad," five were C children and two were A children, and of the seven children labeled "scared/upset," six were B children, and one was a C child. Again these findings seem to confirm our predictions. Finally, of the children labeled "tired/sad," four were C children, two were A children, and one was a B

---

[4]The children were classified into A, B, and C categories in the standard fashion, except B_1 children were put into the A category, and B_4 children were put into the C category. This reclassification of B_1 and B_4 children was suggested by Connell and Rosenberg on the basis of results from a cluster analysis (Ainsworth et al., 1978). Use of this alternative grouping method results in a more equal distribution of children in the three major classifications. Shiller and Izard (unpublished manuscript) also used this classification procedure.

child. Why mothers of *C* children used this label more than mothers of *B* children (contrary to our prediction) is not known. We suggest, however, that the ambivalent attachment characteristic of *C* children may appear either as anger or as depression (i.e., a tired/sad appearance).

Recently Shiller and Izard (unpublished manuscript) coded videotaped facial behavior of 13-month-old children during the separation episode of the attachment situation using Izard's system for measuring facial expressions (Izard & Dougherty, 1980). Because the children did not directly face the camera much of the time in this situation, a substantial number of their facial expressions could not be coded. Therefore, the findings from this study are limited to those instances when the postures of the children enabled their faces to be coded. Of the faces coded, the three most commonly observed facial expressions were anger, sadness, and interest. The dominant expression was anger, and no fear faces were observed. The absence of fear expressions is somewhat surprising and contradicts our findings as well as the findings of others (e.g., Gaensbauer, Mrazek, & Emde, 1979).

In this study, Shiller and Izard report that *C* children showed similar amounts of anger and sadness, a finding that confirms our results. However, their findings with respect to the emotional expressions of *A* and *B* children do not agree with ours. Whereas Shiller and Izard found anger to be expressed more often than sadness in *both* Groups *A* and *B*, we found Groups *A* and *B* to exhibit dissimilar emotional expressions with few instances of anger observed in either group.

These discrepant results are in part a function of measurement differences: Shiller and Izard measured facial expressions only, whereas we also included postural expressions. The discrepancy is probably due to situational differences as well. Although an attachment paradigm was used in both studies, Shiller and Izard measured infants' emotional expressions during separation from their mothers, whereas we looked at infants during reunion with their mothers. Finally, the measurement system of Shiller and Izard permitted the observer to code more than one emotion in any child, whereas our system restricted the observer to classifying children according to their predominant emotional expression. Although all of these measurement differences could explain the different findings between the two studies, we suspect that the discrepant results are due primarily to the fact that different emotions were expressed during separation and reunion.

The results of the present study underscore the interactive nature of the attachment classification, the emotional expression of the child during reunion with the mother, and maternal labeling. However, even though most mothers in our study labeled the emotions of their children in accord with the behaviors their children expressed, there were several occasions in which the mothers' labeling behaviors contradicted our ratings of the children's general emotional expression. For example, one mother labeled an infant who appeared scared/upset "angry" and another, mother labeled a frightened infant "sad." Such mislabeling of the child's emotional state based on a misinterpretation of that state by the socializing agent has important implications for any model of developmental psychopathology. Because psychopathology may be the consequence of both the characteristics of the child as well as the interpretation of people around the child, evidence of a discrepancy or "mismatch" between these two factors could potentially be used to identify children at risk for later psychopathology. In addition, such discrepancies point to and thus enable us to study the interaction of biological factors and socialization in children's development of emotions.

THE INTERPRETATIONS OF EMOTIONS AND MODELS OF PSYCHOPATHOLOGY

The implications of a socialization of emotions model as it affects psychopathology stand in some contrast to the implications inherent in other models of psychopathology. It is important to highlight the major features of these various models if we are to understand the contributions of each. In conventional models a certain elicitor M is assumed to produce an emotional state N with accompanying expressions and motoric behaviors. For example, M might be a common fear elicitor such as the uncontrollable approach of a stranger. Presumably N, a fear state, becomes, in some one-to-one fashion, a fear experience. In this model it is presumed that state N, fear, is produced by the elicitor whether or not fear is experienced. A fear state may not be experienced if the individual employs a set of defense mechanisms such as suppression, inhibition, repression, or denial. Such might be the case for a 10-year-old boy who does not wish to let others (or even himself) know that he is afraid of an approaching stranger. These defense mechanisms imply that an underlying state N exists even though the individual may be unable to experience N. The defense mechanisms rob the individual of psychic energy and prevent him or her from freely experiencing the underlying emotional state. Implied in these models of psychopathology is a one-to-one relationship between an elicitor and state and between a state and experience. Psychopathology is largely a consequence of the individual's inability to connect the experience to the existing state. Consequently, the role of therapy is to break down the defense systems and allow the subject to experience the underlying emotional state.

This model has, in fact, a strong socialization component inasmuch as the child's particular emotional experience is inhibited or suppressed because of some socialization factor. Nevertheless, the model implies that a particular emotional experience of the child is directly connected to a specific emotional state. However, if we believe that socialization processes *always* intervene between the state and experience, through the attribution or interpretation of others, then an alternative model is necessary. Socialization models, in contrast to biological models, suggest that *experience and state may not be connected in a one-to-one fashion and that the socialization task is to connect them.* That is, socialization is matching what culture expects one to experience with an emotional state as reflected by a set of expressions in a specific situation and in the presence of certain elicitors. In other words, rather than experiencing fear as an automatic consequences of having a fearful state, children may experience fear only to the degree to which they have been socialized (through the interpretation, labeling, and interactive behavior of others) to do so. (Elsewhere [Lewis & Michalson, in preparation] we explore a variety of potentially powerful socialization experiences that, in addition to labeling, may affect the connection between state and experience.)

For instance, if in the early socialization period the child's emotional state (expressed by wary looking and inhibition of activity) in response to the approach of a stranger (an elicitor) is interpreted by the child's social environment as angry rather than fearful, the child would experience anger and not fear. Here, the child's failure to experience fear would not reflect the presence of defense mechanisms such as repression, denial, or suppression but rather would reflect the fact that the child never learned to experience fear under these circumstances. Such a model of the socialization of emotions requires therapeutic practices that are different from those prescribed by more conventional models. Whereas in the biological model the therapist's task is to put the patient in touch with the repressed experience and to release the psychic energy bound up with the defense mechanisms, the therapist's task in the socialization model is one of reeducation. The psychopathology here is not so much a consequence of repression and the dissipation of psychic energy but of the fact that the child, through the mismanagement of a socialization process, has come to experience an inappropriate emotion, A, vis-a-vis the situation. The inappropriateness of emotion A is located in the fact that other members of the social group experience a different emotion under the same conditions and think it inappropriate for the child to experience emotion A. Such children are at risk because of their deviance vis-a-vis others in their social network rather than because of their inability to recover a suppressed or repressed experience.

This model recognizes intergroup differences in socialization processes by which the same stimulus through different meaning systems and socialization practices may result in culturally different emotional experiences. Examples of cultural differences in emotional experiences probably abound. One particular example that comes to mind is a cultural difference in feelings related to personal achievement. In the Western tradition there are elaborate models of competence that emphasize a strong positive emotional experience as the natural consequence of personal achievement. Yet we know that other cultures find it inappropriate to recognize personal achievement because it tends to separate one from the group. Among the Zuñi Indians, for example (according to Benedict, 1934), the individual with undisguised initiative and greater drive than his fellows is apt to be branded a witch and hung up by his thumbs. Consequently, the socialization task for American and Zuñi parents may be quite different and may involve promoting the emotional experience of competence in response to achievement in one case and the emotional experience of shame in response to achievement in the other.

The socialization model does not exclude the role of defense mechanisms in affecting the emotional experience of people. Surely such mechanisms are at work. The present discussion is meant to suggest that socialization factors probably play a more complex role in the emotional life of children and adults than has previously been acknowledged and that they may be responsible for aspects of psychopathology not normally considered. Thus, such considerations should broaden our perspective on the processes involved in emotional development as well as in psychopathology and at the same time allow for the use of other types of psychotherapeutic strategies.

In the study of maternal labeling presented earlier, we found that in general mothers interpreted their children's states and experiences through the combined use of the situation and context and their children's behavior. Their attributions tended to match what our social group would accept as "the true emotional experience." For instance, mothers labeled their children "angry/mad" when the children threw themselves on the ground or threw toys around the room. Nevertheless, mislabeling is a definite possibility and it did occur in several instances in our study. In these cases, the mother's choice of label may have been more a function of *her* feelings than of the feelings of the child.

What are the possible outcomes of such interpretive (labeling) behavior, if the mother's behavior is consistent across many such situations? How will children interpret their own behavior if the behavior of significant others is inappropriate to the behaviors and situations that exist? At least four possibilities can be imagined. First, one might adopt a more biological point of view and answer that children's emotional experiences have a high correspondence to their internal states, independent of the behavior of others. Thus, in those cases in which mothers labeled tired/sad children "angry/mad," according to this view the children would end up feeling tired/sad despite the mother's mislabeling behavior.

A second possibility might require a "mixed-feeling model" in which children's experiences are influenced both by their own states and by the labeling of others. This "mixed feeling" might be a combination of angry/mad (the mothers' label) or tired/sad (the children's state). An analogy to the study of bird songs comes to mind (Marler, 1977). In Marler's study, bird A was raised by bird B with the consequence that the call of bird A was a mixture of the calls of species A and species B. This finding suggests that social experience can act on and alter an underlying biological process but cannot eliminate it. The result is a behavior that is neither due to socialization nor due to biological tendencies. Similarly, children may experience a combined feeling of tired/sad and angry/mad as a consequence of the mother's mislabeling of their emotional state.

The third possibility would be the inhibitory view. Children may really experience sadness even though the mothers label them "angry/mad" but, because of the labeling, sadness is inhibited through some mechanism like repression or denial and the primary emotional experience that emerges into consciousness is anger. Children, according to this model, really are sad. That is, children's behavior expresses their true emotional experience but they have inhibited this sadness through the mothers' socialization and instead feel angry. The task in psychotherapy is to remove the inhibitory effect and allow children to feel their sadness.

A fourth model involves a substitution of experience rather than an inhibition. Through particular socialization processes the child comes to interpret certain emotional states and experiences as anger rather than sadness. There is no inhibition of sadness. The sadness originally associated with the elicitor, mother leaving the room (or sadness associated with any loss), has not been altered through socialization but has been replaced with another experience. The psychotherapeutic technique would involve reeducating these children and teaching them that others experience different emotions in the same situation.

All four of these models may be equally likely or all may be true. The data that exist do not allow us to reject one in favor of another. In light of the fact that the majority of the mothers in our study did not label their children's emotional behavior, we can, in fact, envision other possible models that address the question of how children's emotional states become related to emotional experiences in the absence of maternal labeling. The first model described earlier (the biological model) can be applied to this question as well as to the problem of mislabeling. Recall that in this model the emotional experience is automatically connected to the emotional state and consequently is little affected by either incorrect labeling or the absence of labeling by the socializing agent. The absence of labeling, then, would not produce psychopathology if this model were true.

Another possibility is that if the social environment fails to provide children with appropriate labels for their emotional states, children will be unable to label, or to recognize and thus to experience, their own internal states. Psychotherapy in this case would involve supplying children with affect labels appropriate to their internal states and the circumstances eliciting those states, thereby "creating" a new emotional experience. Thus, the role of the therapist would not be to *reeducate* but to *educate* the child for the first time.

A final possible model states that even though mothers do not label their children's emotional behaviors, they nevertheless still provide an interpretation and evaluation of their children's emotional states through their other, nonverbal responses to their children's emotional behaviors. In other words, children learn to interpret and evaluate (and thus to experience) their emotional states not only through the verbal labels provided by the social environment but also through the nonverbal behaviors of significant others. Indeed, it is possible that children rely on nonverbal behaviors as much as (if not more than) verbal affect labels to connect their emotional states with emotional experiences. In this model, then, the failure of the mothers to label their children's emotional behaviors does not result in psychopathology as long as their nonverbal responses to their children's emotional behavior is appropriate to the underlying emotional state of the child and the eliciting situation.

SUMMARY

In the discussion of the socialization of emotions (presented in more detail in Lewis & Michalson, in preparation), we tried to highlight the fact that the child's social environment plays a critical role in emotional development. From the more simple biologically oriented views of the modulation of arousal states and the differentiation of emotions to highly complex and cognitive views involving interpretation and evaluation of one's own behavior as well as the behavior of others, socialization occurs as a powerful force in the emotional life of children.

In this essay we have chosen to focus on the role of the mother in children's acquisition of a lexicon of specific emotions. People other than the mother are also important socializing agents for emotional experiences (Lewis, 1982). Indeed, different people may actually facilitate different emotional experiences, and different situations more attuned to positive affects may be involved in the socialization of an affect lexicon.

ACKNOWLEDGMENTS

Portions of this chapter were presented at the Symposium on Perspectives on Cognition and Emotion at the Society for Research in Child Development meetings, Boston, April 1981. A more detailed discussion is presented as Chapters 6 and 7 in M. Lewis, & L. Michalson, *Children's emotions and moods: Theory and measurement.* New York: Plenum, in preparation. The research was funded in part by the Carnegie Corporation of New York.

REFERENCES

Ainsworth, M. D. S., Blehar, M., Waters, E., & Wall, S. *Patterns of attachment: A psychological study of the strange situation.* Hillsdale, N.J.: Lawrence Erlbaum Associates, 1978.

Amen, E. Individual differences in apperceptive reaction: A study of the responses of preschool children to pictures. *Genetic Psychology Monographs,* 1941, *23,* 319–385.

Argyle, M. Non-verbal communication in human social interaction. In R. A. Hinde (Ed.), *Non-verbal communication.* Cambridge, Mass.: Harvard University Press, 1972.

Benedict, R. Anthropology and the abnormal. *Journal of Genetic Psychology,* 1934, *10,* 59–82.

Bernstein, B. Social class and linguistic development: A theory of social learning. In A. Halsey, V. Floyd, & A. Anderson (Eds.), *Society, economy, and education.* Glencoe, Ill.: Free Press, 1961.

Borke, H. Interpersonal perception of young children: Egocentrism or empathy. *Developmental Psychology,* 1971, *5,* 263–269.

Cain, W. S. To know with the nose: Keys to odor identification. *Science,* 1979, *203,* 467–470.

Cole, M., & Scribner, S. *Culture and thought: A psychological introduction.* New York: Wiley, 1974.

Darwin, C. R. *The expression of the emotions in man and animals.* London: John Murray, 1872.

Davitz, J. R. *The language of emotion.* New York: Academic Press, 1969.

Edwards, C. P., & Lewis, M. Young children's concepts of social relations: Social functions and social objects. In M. Lewis, & L. A. Rosenblum (Eds.), *The child and its family.* New York: Plenum, 1979.

Ekman, P. Cross-cultural studies of facial expression. In P. Ekman (Ed.), *Darwin and facial expression.* New York: Academic Press, 1973.

Ekman, P., & Friesen, W. V. *Unmasking the face.* Englewood Cliffs, N.J.: Prentice-Hall, 1975.

Ekman, P., Friesen, W. V., & Ellsworth, P. *Emotion in the human face: Guidelines for research and an integration of findings.* New York: Pergamon, 1972.

Feinman, S., & Lewis, M. *Social referencing and second order effects in ten-month-old infants.* Paper presented at the Meetings of the Society for Research in Child Development, Boston, April 1981.

Feshbach, S. Aggression. In P. H. Mussen (Ed.), *Carmichael's manual of child psychology* (Vol. 2). New York: Wiley, 1970.

Freud, S. *The psychopathology of everyday life* (trans. by A. Tyson). New York: Norton, 1960.

Gaensbauer, T. J., Mrazek, D., & Emde, R. N. Patterning of emotional response in a playroom situation. *Infant Behavior and Development,* 1979, *2,* 163–178.

Geertz, C. *The interpretation of cultures.* New York: Basic, 1973.

Geertz, H. The vocabulary of emotion. *Psychiatry,* 1959, *22,* 225–237.

Greif, E. B., Alvarez, M., & Ulman, K. *Recognizing emotions in other people: Sex differences in socialization.* Paper presented at the Biennial Meeting of the Society for Research in Child Development, Boston, April 1981.

Halliday, M. A. K. *Early language learning: A sociolinguistic approach.* Paper presented for the Ninth International Congress of Anthropological and Ethnological Sciences, Chicago, 1973.

Hess, R., & Shipman, V. Early experiences and the socialization of cognitive modes in children. *Child Development,* 1965, *36,* 869–886.

Hochschild, A. R. Emotion work, feeling rules, and social structure. *American Journal of Sociology,* 1979, *85,* 551–575.

Izard, C. E. *The face of emotion.* New York: Appleton, 1971.

Izard, C. E. *Human emotions.* New York: Plenum, 1977.

Izard, C. E., & Dougherty, L. M. *A system for identifying affect expressions by holistic judgments (Affex).* Newark, Del.: University of Delaware, Instructional Resources Center, 1980.

James, W. What is emotion? *Mind,* 1884, *9,* 188–205.

Kagan, J. *On language and emotion.* Paper presented at the Meetings of the Society for Research in Child Development, Boston, April 1981.

Levine, J. Humor and psychopathology. In C. E. Izard (Ed.), *Emotions in personality and psychopathology.* New York: Plenum, 1979.

Lewis, M. Situational analysis and the study of behavioral development. In L. Pervin, & M. Lewis (Eds.), *Perspectives in interactional psychology.* New York: Plenum, 1978.

Lewis, M. *The socialization of emotions.* Paper presented at the Meetings of the Society for Research in Child Development, Boston, April 1981.

Lewis, M. The social network systems model: Toward a theory of social development. In T. Field (Ed.), *Review in human development.* New York: Wiley, 1982.

Lewis, M., & Brooks, J. Self-knowledge and emotional development. In M. Lewis, & L. A. Rosenblum (Eds.), *The development of affect.* New York: Plenum, 1978.

Lewis, M., & Brooks-Gunn, J. *Social cognition and the acquisition of self.* New York: Plenum, 1979.

Lewis, M., & Feiring, C. Direct and indirect interactions in social relationships. In L. Lipsitt (Ed.), *Advances in infancy research* (Vol. 1). New York: Ablex, 1981.

Lewis, M., & Michalson, L. *Affect labelling by mothers during reunion with their one-year-old infants.* Unpublished manuscript, 1981.

Lewis, M., & Michalson, L. *Children's emotions and moods: Theory and measurement.* New York: Plenum, in preparation.

Lewis, M., & Rosenblum, L. A. *Interaction, conversation, and the development of language.* New York: Wiley, 1977.

Lewis, M., & Rosenblum, L. A. Introduction: Issues in affect development. In M. Lewis, & L. A. Rosenblum (Eds.), *The development of affect.* New York: Plenum, 1978.

Lewis, M., & Weinraub, M. The father's role in the infant's social network. In M. Lamb (Ed.), *The role of the father in child development.* New York: Wiley, 1976.

Lewis, W. C., Wolman, R. N., & King, M. The development of the language of emotions: II. Intentionality in the experience of affect. *Journal of Genetic Psychology,* 1972, *120,* 303–316. (a)

Lewis, W. C., Wolman, R. N., & King, M. The development of the language of emotions: III. Type of anxiety in the experience of affect. *Journal of Genetic Psychology,* 1972, *120,* 325–342. (b)

Malatesta, C. Z. Infant emotion and the vocal affect lexicon. *Motivation and Emotion,* 1981, *5*(1).

Malatesta, C. Z., & Haviland, J. M. *Age- and sex-related changes in infant affect expression.* Paper presented at the Meetings of the Society for Research in Child Development, Boston, April 1981.

Marler, P. Sensory templates, vocal perception, and development: A comparative view.

In M. Lewis, & L. A. Rosenblum (Eds.), *Interaction, conversation, and the development of language.* New York: Wiley, 1977.

Pannabecker, B. J., Emde, R. N., Johnson, W., Stenberg, C., & Davis, M. *Maternal perceptions of infant emotions from birth to 18 months: A preliminary report.* Paper presented at the International Conference of Infant Studies, New Haven, April 1980.

Plutchik, R. Emotions, evolution and adaptive processes. In M. Arnold (Ed.), *Feelings and emotions.* New York: Academic Press, 1970.

Plutchik, R. *Emotion: A psychoevolutionary synthesis.* New York: Harper & Row, 1980.

Rotter, J. B. Generalized expectancies for internal versus external control of reinforcement. *Psychological Monographs,* 1966, *80* (No. 1, Whole No. 609).

Scherer, K. R. Nonlinguistic vocal indicators of emotion and psychopathology. In C. E. Izard (Ed.), *Emotions in personality and psychopathology.* New York: Plenum, 1979.

Scherer, K. R. The assessment of vocal expression in infants and children. In C. E. Izard (Ed.), *Measuring emotions in infants and children.* New York: Cambridge University Press, 1982.

Shiller, V. M., & Izard, C. E. *Patterns of emotion expressions during separation.* Unpublished manuscript, 1981.

Shott, S. Emotion and social life. *American Journal of Sociology,* 1979, *84,* 1317–1334.

Sorenson, E. R. Culture and the expression of emotion. In T. R. Williams (Ed.), *Psychological anthropology.* The Hague: Mouton, 1975.

Sroufe, L. A., & Ward, M. J. Seductive behavior of mothers of toddlers: Occurrence, correlates, and family origins. *Child Development,* 1980, *51,* 1222–1229.

Tomkins, S. S. *Affect, imagery, consciousness. Vol. 1. The positive affects.* New York: Springer, 1962.

Tomkins, S. S. *Affect, imagery, consciousness. Vol. 2. The negative affects.* New York: Springer, 1963.

Waters, E., Wippman, J., & Sroufe, L. A. Attachment, positive affect, and competence in the peer group: Two studies in construct validation. *Child Development,* 1979, *50,* 821–829.

Wolman, R. N., Lewis, W. C., & King, M. The development of the language of emotions: Conditions of emotional arousal. *Child Development,* 1971, *42,* 1288–1293.

Wolman, R. N., Lewis, W. C., & King, M. The development of the language of emotions: I. Theoretical and methodological introduction. *Journal of Genetic Psychology,* 1972, *120,* 167–176. (a)

Wolman, R. N., Lewis, W. C., & King, M. The development of the language of emotions: IV. Bodily referents and the experience of affect. *Journal of Genetic Psychology,* 1972, *121,* 65–81. (b)

Zahn-Waxler, C., Radke-Yarrow, M., & King, R. Child rearing and children's prosocial imitations towards victims of distress. *Child Development,* 1979, *50,* 319–330.

Zigler, E., & Child, I. L. Socialization. In G. Lindzey, & E. Aronson (Eds.), *Handbook of social psychology* (Vol. 3). Reading, Mass.: Addison-Wesley, 1969.

III METHODOLOGICAL APPROACHES TO DATA AND ANALYSES

9

Affectivity and Reference: Concepts, Methods, and Techniques in the Study of Communication Development of 6- to 18-Month-Old Infants

Lauren Adamson
Roger Bakeman
Georgia State University

We have just begun a study concerned with how infants develop the capacity to communicate with others about objects during their sixth to 18th months of life. Central to the formulation of this research is the notion that these rudimentary referential skills are not de novo accomplishments. Rather, our working assumption is that these skills should be viewed at least in part as an extension of and an elaboration upon the baby's capacity to engage in reciprocal affective interchanges, a capacity that is amply demonstrated in the first 6 months of life and that we believe is neither lost nor irrelevant as infants and caregivers negotiate new modes and topics of communication during the next 12 months or so.

Recently, the first of our 28 subjects was videotaped in his first of four sessions as he played with objects by himself, with his mother, and with a same-aged peer. This event marks the end of our planning phase, and so, even though we do not yet have any data to analyze and discuss, we do think this is an appropriate time to reflect on several issues we confronted while designing our study. These issues can be divided into three areas: the conceptualization of transitions in early-communication development; the formulation of a suitable observational methodology to explore these transitions; and the deployment of recent technological advances in the service of this methodology. In this chapter, we address each of these areas in turn.

In part one, we briefly review current research concerning how infants communicate with others during their first year and a half of life. Our main conclusion is that even though much is known about the emergence of new communicative skills during this period, we still lack evidence needed for a systematic conceptualization of how new communicative achievements, especially those that involve referencing objects within interactive exchanges, relate developmentally to earlier forms of communication, particularly forms that are central to infants' first face-to-face interactions with adults. We make this presentation, first, to see if this perspective will appear persuasive to others, and second, to provide a context for our subsequent methodological statements.

In part two, we reflect upon observational methodology. Our intent here is not to recommend observational methodology, either in general or in the specific form we use, for all investigations. Rather, we want to suggest why, given our substantive problems, we have chosen our particular approach. To do this, we do not provide a systematic survey of current practice in observational research. For example, we say little about our data analysis. As our project plans progressed, we came to believe that techniques for analyzing the kind of sequential observational data we are collecting are relatively well known and understood, as the work of a number of investigators demonstrates (cf. Bakeman & Brownlee, 1980; Gottman & Ringland, 1981; Kaye & Fogel, 1980). Instead, we delve quite deeply into less explored aspects of observational work: the process of developing behavior codes and the philosophical assumptions that underlie this task.

This emphasis reflects two convictions that were heightened as we developed our study. First, we have come to appreciate more fully that in studies of social development using observational methods, the coding schemes used are absolutely central to the conceptualization and success of the project. It is at this point of data capture that the researchers express their basic understanding of the observed events. Second, our past experience developing and using different coding schemes now impresses us as less than satisfactory. Previously, we had made little effort to develop coherent ideas about what coding schemes are and what they should do when placed in the context of observational research. In short, we feel we have lacked a theory about coding schemes that could guide their development, use, and interpretation.

Lack of an explicit theory need not, of course, be a fatal flaw for a study such as ours. After all, most of us speak reasonably well although we would perform poorly if we were asked to explicate the complex rules guiding what we say. Even so, we suspect that a more articulate statement about what we can expect a coding scheme to be and do can potentially reduce confusion surrounding its implementation. In our initial attempt to be self-reflective about our formulation of a coding scheme, we have found ourselves increasingly influenced by the work of the philosopher Stephen C. Pepper. We therefore present some of his basic notions as a prelude to our efforts to document the course of early-communication development.

In part three, we turn briefly from theory to practice and describe the combination of video and computer equipment we use for coding videotapes. Many researchers avoid videorecording because they fear that coding videotapes may consume vast quantities of time. This is a reasonable concern, but it is one that may be lessened because of recent technological advances. To demonstrate how video and computer technology can assist in making the coding task relatively simple and efficient, we sketch the system we have recently assembled and are now using.

CONTINUITY AND DISCONTINUITY IN EARLY-COMMUNICATION DEVELOPMENT

Until quite recently, psychologists have tended to view the newborn and the 2-year-old human being almost as if they were members of two different species. The former was considered an essentially asocial organism whereas the latter, recent master of the symbol, seemed to be the new arrival into the human community. The gap between the two grew even wider when, inspired by Chomsky's insights concerning the complexity of our linguistic competence, researchers attempted to unravel the mysteries of language acquisition by dissecting the rich verbal productions of 2- and 3-year-old children.

This dichotomy has become increasingly untenable. Since the 1960s, very young infants have been acquiring a new reputation, one praising their competence as organized social actors. The behavior patterns they perform are now commonly considered to have communicative significance within the context of their first social interactions with adults. Gradually during the 1970s, the communicative aspects of early-language performance also received attention as the image of the 2 year old's achievements underwent radical revision. Difficulties in characterizing linguistic competence through the analysis of syntactic relationships led developmental psycholinguists to consider both word meaning and contextual information. This expanded focus raised questions about the nature of language itself and spurred interest in linguistic theories such as Fillmore's consideration of case and Searle's of speech arts. We can clearly see the impact of this widening perspective on language reflected in recent language-acquisition research. Investigators now seek to understand not only how children develoop intricate formal linguistic competence, but also how they come to use language as a form with a function, as communication intentionally employed to share meaning with others.

An analysis focused on the *continuous* development of communicative processes during infancy is consistent with these profound changes in our images both of the young infant and the young language user. Such a view would highlight and deliberately examine how each new communicative accomplishment relates developmentally to prior communicative achievements. Within such a conceptual scheme, older infants' language use does not mark the beginning point of communication development; it is viewed rather as just one manifestation (albeit a very powerful one) of their developing capacity to convey and to comprehend intentional, meaningful messages. Nor are infants' first referential gestures the first indications of their capacity to direct a listener's attention to a specific topic; rather such gestures are a new manifestation of a process of attention modulation that has been developing during even earlier social exchanges.

This perspective is not intended to dismiss or gloss over discontinuities that obviously occur as infants develop new communicative skills. Infants may indeed be initially unable to perform acts that are intentionally communicative, and when they can, they may no longer rely on the same means of sharing information with others that they used prior to the advent of these acts. Moreover, infants' first communicative achievements may not remain intact and essentially unaltered as new communicative means and goals emerge. Yet, even in the light of significant qualitatively new communicative performances, it is still important to seek the roots of these performances within a foundation provided by prior communicative performances if the process of communication development is to be fully appreciated.

There appear to be two interrelated ways to conceptualize how a currently developing form of communication is rooted in earlier forms of communication. One is to note parallels between the structure of the two forms. This approach is often used when researchers who study the young infants as they interact with adults forecast the developmental course of their subjects' rudimentary communication skills. For example, parallels between the turn taking apparent in the play dialogues of infants and their caregivers and young children's conversational skills as they alternately act as listener and speaker have been suggested by researchers (Stern, 1977; Tronick, 1980) who are impressed by analogy of form. Language researchers also stress continuities in this way when they note that many of the pragmatic aspects of language use and many of the early semantically based syntactic relationships expressed by the young child may be observed in an analogous form using different actions during the prelinguistic period of infancy (cf. Bruner, 1974/75).

The second way to view continuities of early-communication development is to focus on the process of transformation of early-communicative structures. In this view, analogy of form becomes less important because what is sought is a principle of development that explains how earlier forms of communication are altered as new modes of communication develop and how these altered, earlier-developing forms support the use of newly developing ones. Several developmental theorists have attempted to articulate how such continuities might best be understood. For example, psychodynamically oriented theorists often stress how emotional aspects of early-communication experiences provide the foundation for later communicative acts. René Spitz (1972) provides an excellent exemplar of this position when he describes how the early affective reciprocity of mother and infant provides the infant with an invaluable "fundamental education," one that leads towards an understanding of a coherent interpersonal world necessary for referential communication.

Cognitive-structuralist theorists also endorse this general perspective while striving to illustrate how overarching developmental principles integrate continuity and discontinuity in the process of early symbol formation. Foremost among these theorists are Werner and Kaplan (1963) who begin their extensive discussion of symbol formation with an account of how a foundation of social activity provides the critical elements for the emergence of referential communication. They contend that the infant's first actions relevant to symbolic communication are sensorimotor-affective behavior patterns that are embedded within an intimate "primordial sharing situation" with an adult. Here the infant is unable to communicate *to* the other person because he or she has yet to differentiate the medium and topic of communication and the roles of speaker and listener. Yet the infant can share affective information *with* the other person and as he or she does, he or she develops actions that will later function to serve true, symbolically based communication. (See Langer [1970] for a discussion of Werner's treatment of continuities and discontinuities in development. Also see Vygotsky [1978] for a similar perspective).

Recently Bullowa (1979) elaborated upon Werner and Kaplan's view by detailing how elements central to early social exchanges, such as attention to another person and the display of affectivity, gradually become the context for new communicative content. Bullowa (1979) expressed this point with the following illustration:

> What is content at one time becomes context later. I suspect that this has a developmental sequence.
> This may be illustrated with data from a study on the development of pointing (Murphy, forthcoming). Infants and toddlers at nine, fourteen, twenty and twenty-four months were video taped while on their mother's laps sharing picture books . . . . At nine and fourteen months infants pointing and vocalizing were not well integrated with each other. Frequency of vocalizing at the same time as pointing reached a peak at twenty months and then consisted mostly of naming, whereas the twenty-four-month-olds and their mothers were looking "more earnestly" at individual pictures and defining more details . . . . What interests me in this developmental sequence is the way in which manual pointing developed within the context of shared visual attention and then was overtaken by vocalization wich became naming of the objects looked at, and, when language came in, whole objects became contexts for their parts in turn. *What had been content had moved from central focus to periphery, from figure to ground* [p. 10, emphasis added].

An approach as Bullowa's might lead to an integrative analysis of both the continuous and the discontinuous aspects of early-communication development. Continuities can be conceptualized both by abstracting parallels of form across different communicative actions and by relating these forms to each other developmentally by charting how the use of older forms of communication is systematically altered as new forms of communication emerge. Discontinuity is also respected because this analysis does not entail merging all communication systems into a single form that initially contains all the critical aspects of communication.

Despite the appeal of such an approach to early-communication development, there are still several weaknesses in our understanding of how early forms of communication evolve into later forms. One major weakness is that we do not have sufficient empirical information with which to evaluate such notions.

Typically, descriptions of communication development during the first year and a half of life seem to emphasize discontinuity at the expense of continuity. Three phases are usually demarcated. The first and last phases represent two extreme ways of structuring the relationship between the "medium" of communication and the main "topic" of the exchange. In the first—the "affective-reciprocity" phase—the communication medium and topic are essentially merged. An adult–infant face-to-face interaction in the first 4 to 5 months of the infant's life thus seems to involve primarily the regulation of mutual attention and affectivity while the dyad seems to share messages about "how I feel and how I feel about your feelings." Although terms vary for the overall characterization of this phase, Trevarthen's (1977) label of "primary intersubjectivity" is particularly well suited to conveying the merging of medium and topic that occurs as the interactors share affective information using affective expressions without implying the infants are aware of the differentiation of self from partner. In contrast, the third phase—the "linguistic-referencing" phase—is characterized by the differentiation and coordination of linguistic medium with referential and expressive topics, which is evident as the infant begins to speak during the latter half of the second year. Bates, Camaioni, and Volterra (1975) term this the "locutionary phase" to emphasize how the infant and other can now convey intended messages with referential value using verbal propositions.

It is the second or "nonverbal-referencing" phase that concerns us most. Within the framework of its surrounding phases, this is a transitional phase that can be viewed as the period during which the gradual differentiation and coordination of communicative medium and topic occur. By about the infant's sixth month, adult–infant pairs begin to display concern for objects and events external to the interactive process itself. Gaze patterns, vocalizations, and gestures increasingly serve the referential function of introducing a new topic for discussion, a new message that *"that* thing over there is what I want to communicate about, to comment on." Using Trevarthen's terminology (Hubley & Trevarthen, 1979), this phase is one of "secondary intersubjectivity" in which the earlier "interlacing of subjective perspectives" is linked to the "objects about which the subjects converse [p. 73]" (see also Trevarthen & Hubley, 1978).

So far, we can only speculate about how these three phases are developmentally interrelated. Partly, this seems due to the division of labor among different groups of psychologists. Researchers concerned with the onset of communication per se focus primarily on the earliest months of infancy, on the phase of "affective reciprocity." Those probing the onset of language-related skills search most commonly during the middle portion of the nonverbal-referencing phase for the first clear indications of referential skill. Moreover, descriptions generated by these two research groups often highlight the content of communication during the interactions they analyze and so, different aspects of social interaction receive attention. These differences are discussed further when we review current research; for the moment we merely want to point out that the structuring of social interaction when the infant is between 1 and 5 months and 9 and 13 months of age is relatively well described whereas far less attention has been given to the beginning and to the end of the nonverbal-referencing phase. Yet in order to evaluate if and how phases of early-communication development are related, we need to understand what occurs during the observational voids that now bracket the salient middle period of the nonverbal-referencing phase.

These voids may, of course, be little more than pauses as far as communication development is concerned. Perhaps infants periodically shift their interest away from communication with other people and towards concerns relating to other developmental domains such as motor development. But, in line with the theoretical perspectives mentioned previously, it seems more plausible that significant communication progress is occurring. Despite the apparent lack of new formal modes of communication, the infant and partner may be transforming their earliest system of communication to allow for new modes of sharing meaning and new topics of communication. To chart such a developmental pattern, we would need to look more closely for changes in how the infant and the partner are coordinating their current modes and topics of communication and not focus exclusively on the infant's use of new gestures and vocalizations.

In summary, in order to trace communication development as a continuous progression across phases that contain qualitatively different modes of communication, we must follow the same aspects of communicative interactions forward from the end of the affective-reciprocity phase through the subsequent nonverbal-referencing phase. Our task is to describe if and how the form and function of these aspects become transformed. This approach would allow us to evaluate if indeed the earlier-developing phenomenon of "primary intersubjectivity" is the developmental precursor of the phenomenon of "secondary intersubjectivity." Moreover, it would also permit a new view of how the emergence of linguistic referencing alters the earlier interactive processes that have evolved over the entire infancy period.

To suggest how this might be accomplished, we need first to review briefly the current picture of how infants interact with adults. As this sketch reveals, there is now considerable evidence concerning the use of new communicative means as adults and infants begin to communicate about objects in their immediate environment. In contrast, we do not yet have a clear image of how the adult and infant transform their earlier system of modulating visual attention and affective expressions as they begin to communicate referentially.

When infants are less than 6 months of age, most researchers concerned with social-interaction skills focus on describing the subtle interplay of caregiver and infant attention and affectivity. Typically, face-to-face exchanges have been videotaped as the adult "plays" with the infant during brief periods when no specific caregiving tasks are being performed. These exchanges are then analyzed in detail to document both the specific actions of the infant and mother and the temporal course of mother and infant attention and expressiveness.

Gaze regulations by the infant appear to establish the cyclical framework of such face-to-face interactions (Brazelton, Koslowski, & Main, 1974; Stern, 1974). Within phases of the interaction in which the infant is gazing at the mother, there appear moments of mutual sharing that involve the continual meshing of infant and caregiver expressions of arousal and affectivity. For example, Brazelton, Tronick, and their colleagues (Brazelton et al., 1974; Brazelton, Tronick, Adamson, Als, & Wise, 1975; Tronick, Als, & Adamson, 1979) argue that by the infant's third month, the caregiver and infant have begun to establish a system of reciprocal regulation of affective displays such that both are actively contributing to the structure of the interaction. Stern (1974, 1977) describes how exquisitely the mother works to maintain an optimal level of infant arousal within the constraints of the infant's endogenous arousal cycles and how sensitive the infant is to the mother's expressive activity. Trevarthen (1977, 1979) focuses on the fine-grained coordination between the mother's expressive movements and her infant's rudimentary prespeech actions and vocalizations as the caregiver and infant share a dance of expressions and excitement.

What happens to affective regulation of the mother–infant interaction during the middle of the first year of the baby's life? By about the infant's fifth or sixth month, the system of affective reciprocity seems to be consolidated (Kaye & Fogel, 1980) so that the infant and mother can rapidly and smoothly enter into face-to-face exchanges. Whereas Kaye and Fogel (1980) conclude only that now the infant is taking initiatives independent of the mother's elicitations, others like Tronick (1980) see this consolidation as persuasive evidence that the mother and infant can now readily exchange messages about their current affective states within interactions that essentially involve reference to the interaction itself. At about the same time, however, it becomes increasingly difficult to sustain such "topicless" conversations. The enface situation—the staple of the research just described—becomes very difficult to maintain because the infant frequently refuses to look at the mother and away from objects (Fatouti-Milenkovic & Uzgiris, 1979; Kaye & Fogel, 1980; Trevarthen & Hubley, 1978). Young babies (particularly by their third or fourth month) seem well equipped, indeed designed, to both elicit and engage in face-to-face affective games with adults (e.g., Schaffer, 1977; Watson, 1972). Yet they typically cannot attend to adult acts that are directed towards gaining mutual attention to an object (Clark, 1978; Trevarthen, 1977). In contrast, the 6 month old, now well schooled in the process of affective sharing, appears to devote less time to maintaining a shared context as he or she eagerly pursues the object world. Even when the mother modulates the movements of an object or of parts of herself to complement the infant's interest, the baby does not appear to acknowledge this assistance.

This seeming rupture of the structure of affective reciprocity constrains the delightful interplay of mother and infant while they are involved with objects. Nevertheless, the infant and mother are moving towards a new communicative possibility. As the child seeks beyond the boundaries of the established communicative routines of face-to-face play, the potential for referencing—for incorporating objects from outside the interaction into its matrix as "content"—is gradually emerging.

We can cull from the literature a fairly extensive picture of the changes that now ensue in how mothers and infants exchange messages. Over the next 6 months, infants become effective referencers. At first, they may display this skill by merely switching their gaze back and forth between their mothers and objects (Newson & Newson, 1975). Later, they can be observed elaborating upon the possibilities suggested in this gaze-modulation pattern as they follow a mother's gaze (Scaife & Bruner, 1975) and point (Murphy & Messer, 1977), call her attention to interesting objects by pointing (Murphy, 1978; Leung & Rheingold, 1979), and coordinate vocalizations with looking back and forth between a mother and a desired object (Harding & Golinkoff, 1979). By about 13 months of age, infants appear to have mastered many nonverbal forms of communicating a wide array of referential messages and have begun to display early forms of verbal reference (cf. Bates, 1979; Greenfield & Smith, 1976; Sugarman-Bell, 1978).

222   ADAMSON AND BAKEMAN

In these studies, the infant's referential actions were recorded as the babies were interacting with adults. Yet information concerning the interrelationship between adult and infant communicative actions is rarely retained. Bruner (1974/75), in reviewing early reports of some of these investigations, applauded the researchers' expanded view of communication but still expressed concern that their work "concentrates almost exclusively on the formal aspects of language without due regard for the uses to which language is put in different contexts [p. 258]." To study this interactional basis of referential communication, Bruner suggests that we make explicit what researchers often leave implicit: the mother's actions as the infant performs new communicative coordinations.

In pursuing this suggestion, researchers join a growing group of psychologists who are primarily concerned with how infants perform communicative actions, which might have relevance to later language performances (cf. Lock, 1978). They typically observe a small sample of mother and infant pairs intensively to document the development of specific "joint action routines" (Bruner, 1975) or "communicative structures" (Clark, 1978) such as "giving and taking" and interactional "picture book reading." From such observational work come richly detailed descriptions of a rather narrow segment of infant–mother interactions.

In summary, two complementary approaches to the development of nonverbal-referential communication have dominated current research. On the one hand, the infant's progress in mastering the formal means of nonverbal reference is studied. Here the infant's growing comprehension and use of intentional referential-behavior patterns is observed and the process through which the baby refines and coordinates person- and object-directed actions is highlighted. On the other hand, a more functional view of the mother–infant communication system is presented. Rather than abstracting the infant's referential actions from the on-going interaction, researchers now observe how they are embedded within brief portions of mother–infant interaction that contain repetitive game-like sequences. Here the mother's vital role in supporting the infant's new formal means of communication becomes highlighted because in these game-like segments, the mothers seem to provide a repetitive structure into which the infant can insert new actions that the mother then sensitively interprets as she completes what she construes to be the infant's nascent intentions (cf. Ryan, 1974).

Certainly both approaches are important to a conceptualization of early-communication development. Yet, as currently conceived, these approaches are nevertheless insufficient. So far, they do not speak clearly to the issue of how a communicative system incorporating referential actions is related to the earlier, affectively based communicative system. Rather, researchers seem motivated more by the desire to root later linguistic development in preverbal-referential exchanges. This has led to glances "backwards" from language, to a selective treatment of nonverbal-referential communication such that what appears most important are those actions that seem most similar to later language performances.

We believe that a third approach is needed, an approach that supplements these "backward-looking" analyses with a "forward-looking" one. Such an approach would provide a fuller characterization of the communication capacities of infants from 6 to 18 months of age, for it would increase our attention to the process of current communication and to the gradual emergence of new topics and means of reference. Affective reciprocity may indeed fade into the context of later-developing referentially based interactions. But in describing the affective and attentional regulation of these new exchanges, we may better discern how mother and infant modulate their ongoing interactions as they negotiate these new forms and topics of communication.

AFFECTIVITY AND CONTEXT

In line with this contention that we need a "forward" analysis of early-communication development in order to test the claim that there are continuities between phases of interaction in infancy, we have begun a series of observations that we hope will permit us to describe the process through which new means and topics of communication develop within mother-infant interactions soon after the consolidation of a system of affective reciprocity. Our study design specifies that we observe 28 infants four times each at 3-month intervals. Half of our subjects will begin the series at 6 months of age, the others at 9 months. Sessions will be conducted in each infant's home and will include 10-minute videotaped episodes of the infant playing with objects while alone, with the mother, and with a same-aged peer.

The rationale for this design is fairly straightforward. We need data with which to characterize how, during the course of a typical interaction, the infant modulates affective expression and attention—two elements central to the affective-reciprocity phase of communication—as he or she develops new referential skills. Viewing the infant within different contexts—alone, with the mother, and with a peer—will hopefully aid this analysis by providing information about how the infant behaves separately from and in concert with an adult partner.

This simple statement of rationale, however, masks some very difficult problems. These can be suggested by posing what at first blush might seem to be rather superficial questions: Assuming that we do obtain the observations we seek, what will we do with them? How will we digest over 50 hours of videotaped interactions? What is it that we are looking at and for anyway? Coming to terms with such anxiety-provoking questions demands that we focus on the process of data coding. And, as we indicated in our introductory comments, we are coming to view data coding not as an isolated exercise but as a critical link between conceptualization and methodology. Our substantive problem presented in the first part of this chapter does, of course, lead us to define data codes relating to such behavior patterns as affective expression and referential actions. Yet before we outline this data-coding system, we take a rather long path towards it to explore more fully how our conceptualization of the process of communication development might influence our selection of specific methodological procedures.

We have selected Stephen C. Pepper as our guide. His classic work *World Hypotheses* (1942) first attracted our attention as we were mulling over the question: How do we conceptualize infants as we watch them interacting with objects and people in their world? Essentially, Pepper answers that when we approach any novel phenomenon, we begin to understand it first by metaphor. We start to make sense of the phenomenon by treating it as if it were like some other phenomenon with which we are more familiar. This second phenomenon thus supplies our "root metaphor." Subsequently we refine and articulate the categories implied in this metaphor. Not all root metaphors stand up under the pressures of cognitive refinement but historically those few that have provided us with reasonably precise bases for understanding a wide range of phenomena. Pepper calls these major systems of understanding "world hypotheses." Each provides a relatively autonomous framework for explanation by defining its own criteria for obtaining and organizing information. Pepper identifies four adequate world hypotheses, three of which we consider shortly.

Pepper's influence can be discerned in several contemporary accounts of developmental theories. It is now quite common, for example, to divide developmental perspectives into two metaphorical bins, usually labeled "the mechanical mirror" and "the organic lamp" (Langer, 1969), and then to discuss their contrasting procedures for defining and researching developmental questions (Kuhn, 1978; Reese & Overton, 1970). A central distinction often drawn in such presentations is between organicism's synthetic (or holistic) and mechanism's analytic (or elemental) approach to phenomena.

To our chagrin, neither of these metaphors fully captures our intuitive feel for how we view infants during social interactions. In large measure, our approach is consistent with the synthetic aim of organicism for we set as our goal the description of the structure of social interactions and we have good cause to believe that this structural analysis will not be fully successful if we isolate the infant's actions from the entire matrix of the on-going interaction (cf. Tronick et al., 1979). Yet we also sense that we might best obtain a grasp on the complexity of the infants' and mothers' activity if we could detail the minute changes in their behavior patterns, a tactic often thought most consistent with the analytic stance of mechanistically oriented psychologists.

With this sense of unease, we sought out Pepper. He presents a wealth of intriguing comments germane to how we image infants in interactions with others, but we trace here only one argument that struck us as particularly helpful in clarifying what we hope our coding schemes might retain from our videotapes.

We pick up Pepper's presentation as he reflects upon the ways in which adequate world hypotheses differ from one another. First he notes the familiar synthetic versus analytic split that seems to set organicism and mechanism so at odds in developmental psychology. But then he contends that this is not the only relevant divider. Equally central is whether or not the hypothesis has at its root a notion that there is a single order underlying all phenomena. Those that do Pepper labels "integrative" and he includes in this category both mechanism and organicism. In Pepper's (1942) words, "for these two theories, the world appears literally as a cosmos where facts occur in a determinant order, and where, if enough were known, they could be predicted, or at least described, as being necessarily just what they are to the minutest detail [p. 143]."

This integrative stance may not be fully appropriate when conceptualizing how infants develop early-communication skills. Variations in infant behavior during social interactions do occur, for example, when an infant interacts with different people who differ in their communicative capacities and goals. Analytically, such variability may be regarded as produced by both systematic effects and mere "noise." Such a view does not preclude a single integrative explanation. Yet, when approached from such a vantage point, researchers are also making a conceptual commitment to a claim that there is a universal process that underlies communication development despite evidence of variations. This in turn has often led to a search for a single developmental pathway and a single view of the communication skills the infants must bring to bear if certain communication functions, such as reference, are to occur. But, as the recent work of Katherine Nelson (1979, 1981) and others suggests, there may be periods during early-communication development when different infants seem to focus on different aspects of a new communication system so that to adequately describe the process of communication development, we may need to imagine diverse ways in which infants may achieve the same endpoint—in Nelson's case, linguistic referencing.

Perhaps we still could abstract a common developmental sequence through a series of typical social-interaction patterns that might characterize how all infants develop referential communication. But to do so we may have to step back to gain a sweeping synthetic overview of the developmental course or we may need to focus narrowly on only a few commonly shared elements. In either case, we might be forced to delete from consideration some of the seemingly most interesting or potentially meaningful aspects of the interactions we study. Pepper (1942) summarizes this problem as follows: "by wishing perhaps too hard to get everything into one determinant order, they [mechanism and organicism] have to deny the reality of a good many things [p. 145]."

There are alternatives, however. In contrast to the integrative perspectives we commonly try to apply to the study of new phenomena, Pepper suggests that for some purposes reality is viewed dispersively. That is, we derive categories of understanding based on metaphors that lead to no single set of rules or laws, but that nonetheless allow us to capture the essence central to whatever we are observing. One such dispersive root metaphor Pepper discusses is "the dynamic, active historical event." This metaphor, he suggests, provides the basis for a "contextualist" world hypothesis. It shares with organicism a commitment to dealing synthetically with phenomena but it diverges from organicism because it entertains the notion that there may be novel or multiple ways in which phenomena are ordered. (For an analogous argument emerging from the psychometric tradition, see Meehl, 1978).

A contextualist perspective allows for diversity by focusing attention on the *quality* and the *texture* of dynamic events. Because these are categorical or absolute terms, Pepper claims he cannot define them directly but can illustrate them by example. He does so by pointing to a sentence; the notion of quality is roughly analogous to "meaning" and the concept of texture to the "words" and "grammatical relations." Quality and texture are therefore inseparable. Pepper (1942) writes: "The quality of a given event is its intuited wholeness or total character; the texture is the details and relations which make up that character or quality [p. 238]." Yet even though quality and texture are intertwined, we can set out to attend to them separately. When we do so, however, a paradox seems to result. In observing an event's quality, we tend to lose sight of the organization of elements that make up its texture. And conversely, when we notice texture intently, the qualities are not noticed.

Pepper's description of the antagonism between the analyses of meaning and of structure seems quite apropos the experience of many researchers who code videotaped social interactions. The closer one notices the specific action patterns, the more one may sense the fading of the event's meaning. Yet narrative description of the event's quality in turn do not lend themselves readily to the analysis of the units and the relationships between units that contribute to the event's texture.

Nevertheless, it would be misleading to identify quality with narrative reports or rating scales and texture with detailed behavioral codes. At least within the contextualist framework, the separations are not so neat; events are enmeshed in the historian's seamless web. Pepper (1942) suggests that this web contains both meaning and structure simultaneously in the following way:

> . . . what is analyzed is categorically an event, and the analysis of an event consists in the exhibition of its texture, and the exhibition of its texture is the discrimination of its strands, and the full discrimination of its strands is the exhibition of other textures in the context of the one being analyzed—textures from which the strands of the texture being analyzed gain part of their quality. In the extended analysis of any event we presently find ourselves in the context of that event, and so on from event to event as long as we wish to go, which would be forever or until we got tired [p. 249].

It appears, then, that we begin by selecting elements of an event and we then try to describe these elements. But, as soon as we relate these elements to each other, we must get involved once more with the event itself. We must decide which strands of the texture to abstract from the context and we can only do so based on our understanding of the quality or meaning of the strands within context.

Once again, Pepper speaks to our experience as observers of early social interactions. How indeed can one select which textural strands to follow? When does one expect to learn more about the meaning of an event by multiplying strands or by tracing them more minutely in time? When can we legitimately call off our search?

The researcher, posed for action, may be made somewhat impatient by Pepper's prose. The problems he presents sound familiar enough, but what does he suggest we do to solve them? And, how does any of this affect what a researcher actually does while sitting in front of a video monitor? Pepper does not, of course, answer such questions directly. But he does offer some hints we think might be helpful.

First, Pepper urges us to be quite self-conscious about the "world hypothesis" (and its underlying root metaphor) we bring to whatever we are studying—in our case, early-communication development. Currently, we believe we may gain insight into the process of early communication by approaching the phenomena of infant–caregiver interactions as if they were dynamic historical events unfolding moment by moment and month by month. We find this image particularly attractive for two reasons. First, it alerts us to the somewhat untidy nature of the social life of infants as they develop communication skills. The context of the infant's interactions vary enormously and we are not yet in a position to dismiss these variations as mere "noise" that disturbs our view of a single path towards mature referential communication. Second, it suggests that descriptions both of the quality (context) and the texture (content) of social interactions are needed if we are to fully characterize these events.

Pepper assists in this effort by clarifying the relationship between different methodological approaches to the analysis of interactive sequences. Perhaps because of the inherent antagonism of attending simultaneously to textural details and the quality of events, researchers seem divided over how best to document the changing ways in which infants engage in communicative interchanges. Some investigators seem to act like historians who write narratives. For example, Bruner (1975) and Clark (1978) describe the interaction of infants and their mothers by attending to a particular form of meeting between interactors—those rare but highly ritualized game-like sequences—and by describing changes in the format of these meetings that seem most central to the future evolution of such events. That they find this data much more compelling than data derived from more systematic methods indicates to us the strength of the contextualist's emphasis on the synthetic or holistic quality of dynamic events.

But narratives are not satisfying to many other researchers. They seem to be a necessary first step but, as questions about the textural organization of the interaction become articulated, so too does the impetus for formulating more analytic coding schemes. In addition, we suspect that at least implicitly a mechanistic viewpoint underpins many of the microanalytic coding schemes currently in use; we know that such a view underlies some of our own past work. These schemes soon seem to take on a life of their own as researchers shape them to stress actions and reactions, cause and effect, and strive for analytic "completeness." This does not mean that they are inherently inferior (or superior) to narrative approaches. But microanalytic schemes do seem to us to often rest on a different conceptualization of the phenomenon under study than the conceptualization motivating narrative reports. Instead of embedding descriptions of the details of an event into its overarching context, they demand that context be minimized, that it be treated as a covariate or background variable. If an "ideal" microanalytic scheme were formulated, it would, we believe, reveal the plan that underlies the workings of a "machine" by displaying how elements of behavior are arranged to form a larger unit regardless of the context of the machine's activity.

As we have been emphasizing, this is not necessarily an undesirable approach as long as the method is consistent with our conceptualization of the system we hope to understand. If it is not consistent, then we may just be falling back on analyzing details for details' sake. Pepper does explicitly warn of this potential pitfall of loosening the link between conceptual commitments and methods of investigation. He summarizes this advice in the form of the maxim (Pepper, 1942): "eclecticism is confusing [p. 104]." We understand this to mean the following: Once we make a commitment to understand a phenomenon within the framework provided by one world hypothesis, we must be very cautious when we try to switch orientations to draw on the advantages of another world hypothesis. If we do attempt to pick and choose our methods from several views simultaneously, these methods become empty procedures, for they have lost contact with our underlying conceptualization of the phenomenon. In short, by attempting to fuse world hypotheses, we often end up confused.

Can one avoid the perils of eclecticism when working within a contextualist framework? Despite the attraction of narratives as one way of recognizing both the intertwining of quality and textural details within an event and the enmeshing of events within the context of other events, we agree with researchers who do not wish to abandon more systematic procedures. Particularly when events seem to repeat themselves, if not in every detail, at least in general elements and the organization of these elements for a large number of people, we think we gain insight into these events by searching for repeated order using systematic methods of data coding that produce demonstrably reliable information about these events, information that can then be viewed independently from a linear, narrative description of the event.

The application of such systematic methods must, however, be tailored to suit our contextualist aims of discerning the quality and texture of dynamic events. This recognition may not lead us to do anything startlingly different from what others have done, but at this point, we do think we can abstract from Pepper's analysis two useful, practical morals. First, we think we should be unapologetically selective when deciding which textural elements to code. In other words, we must strive not for exhausting completeness, but for working hypotheses concerning which aspects of an interaction might be most critical to the organization of the dynamic events we observe. Second, we must try not to lose sight of the context in which these textural elements are embedded. Context may, and often does, qualify the meaning of any particular textural detail and so, to understand this detail, we must be aware of the overall character of the event in which it occurs.

Let us now briefly describe the first few coding schemes we are developing as a way of demonstrating how Pepper's morals influenced us as we began constructing our coding system. Ultimately this system will consist of a number of different coding schemes. These we regard as falling into two interrelated groups, those concerned primarily with the textural elements or the content of the interaction and those primarily concerned with the quality or the context of the interaction. Five schemes are described here. The first two code textural elements that we think are important from the very beginning of the age period we are studying; the second two schemes focus on textural elements that we think will emerge at some point during the period from 6 to 18 months as infants gradually master referential-communication skills. The fifth scheme focuses essentially on the context of the interaction.

As we argued previously, the modulation of affective expressions appears to play a major role in the structuring of mother–infant interactions prior to the onset of referential communication, and so our first scheme codes affective expressiveness. However, we need to define affective expressiveness carefully, because this term has several possible meanings (cf. Lewis & Rosenblum, 1978), some of which are tangential to our interests. Our concern, for example, is not with determining what the "primary" emotions are (cf. Izard, 1978), or with documenting the development of specific affective expressions (cf. Sroufe, 1979). Rather, we are concerned with the modulation of affectivity viewed simply as "hedonic tone" ranging alone a continuum from displeaure to pleasure. Such an approach to affectivity is consistent with the views of Stechler and Carpenter (1967) and Emde (Emde, Kligman, Reich, & Wade, 1978), whose works suggest that the negative to positive dimensional property of emotional displays can be observed by the infant's second or third month. Others suggest that affective tone will retain its early significance through the life cycle, that it remains the most salient feature of any emotional display (as indeed it may be when judging almost any event; cf. Osgood, Tannenbaum, & Suci, 1957).

Our second scheme codes the "topic" of the interaction. Here we seek to document the time of occurrence of a shared focus or topic between the infant and the partner and we wish to note if this topic appears to be predominantly an interpersonal ritual or game or if it is an object such as a toy. Moreover, we will also instruct coders to specify if possible which interactor initiated the joint topic and how this initiation was apparently conveyed to the other person.

Application of these first two schemes should allow us to explore hypotheses concerning the relationship between the expression of affectivity and the engagement in joint topics. We hypothesize, for example, that during the earlier months of social interaction, the occurrence of positive affective tone and joint topics will coincide whereas later they may not, because affectivity will no longer be simultaneously the topic and means of communication. As affectivity begins to serve a secondary function in primarily referentially focused interactions, we expect that affectively charged events will become briefer or more punctuation-like and that they will not occur at the same time—but will precede and follow—joint engagement with objects.

The third scheme is designed to document the use of nonverbal-referential actions—that is, of attempts by one person to direct and maintain attention of another person to something or to the self. The fourth concentrates specifically on the use of vocalizations that serve either this referential function or that appear to be used to comment upon a referenced object.

We expect that as our work proceeds, we will need to elaborate upon these and other coding schemes. This may happen if our coders are not able to assess reliably the appropriate code for an event; it also will occur as we gain greater familiarity with the development of referential communication such that new textural elements impress us as critical to the description of the texture of an interaction. What will remain constant is the basic format of applying different coding schemes successively to the same data base. This strategy allows us to document the various strands of the event's texture and supplies us with data in a form suited both to abstracting regularities in the relationship between different strands and documenting how these regularities change developmentally.

Apart from textural elements, we are also concerned with the context of our subject's behavior. At the simplest level, just dividing our observations according to the condition (alone, with mother, with peer) in which our subjects are observed defines context. However, here context is a predefined notion and although we do think it important to observe our subjects while alone and with a same-aged peer in order to understand the events that occur while they are interacting with an adult, we are not satisfied that this gross division fully captures the way context may influence or qualify textural elements. To do this, we must define another level of context, one that divides the stream of observed action into different "interactive states" that are not under our direct control. Thus the fifth scheme we are formulating consists of a set of mutually exclusive codes that exhaustively characterize the infant's current engagement with people and/or objects. These "interactive states" are quite reminiscent of codes often used in peer-interaction research, which describes how children seem engaged with various objects and people. They are also consistent in aim with the priority assigned to gaze or attention modulation by the research cited previously involving early mother–infant face-to-face interaction.

We purposely chose the term "interactive state" to bring to mind some of the same sensibilities that led researchers studying newborns to the concept of "state of arousal." As in such research, we think that the meaning of an event in the infant's surroudings depends in part on the infant's current involvement with that event. For example, if a mother smiles and manipulates a toy, the infant's apprehension of her behavior may depend greatly on whether or not he or she is attending primarily to her, to the object, or to both simultaneously. There is a second way that our notion of "interactive state" parallels that of "state of arousal." Both are concepts that may be best systematized by relying heavily on the judgment of observers. If coders can judge the state of the infant directly with a high degree of reliability, we think that their judgments are no less (and perhaps, they are more) adequate than assignment of state based on the resynthesis of a series of more microcodes if the primary function of documenting states is to qualify more specific descriptors of the elements observed.

The value of a primarily "contextual" code such as "interactive state" has yet to be demonstrated in research concerning communication development. It is our hope, however, that our data-coding scheme will be helpful in evaluating the usefulness of such contextual variables. If it turns out that our description of the interrelationship between various strands of communicative behavior—of affective expression, topic, nonverbal reference, verbalizations, and such—is not altered by the information gained from documenting the state in which these activities occur, then we have gathered no support for the idea that context defined from the subject's perspective is critical to our understanding of development of social-interactive events. Yet it is our suspicion that textural elements will be related to each other in different ways within different interactive states and that communication development will involve alterations in the patterning of such states as well as the relationship of elements within states. If such is indeed the case, then Pepper's guidance in exploring the interrelationship between our conception of interactive events and our methodology will not have lead us astray.

INSTRUMENTATION

This general approach to coding would prove pragmatically impossible if we did not have a way to synchronize data from our coder's many runs through the videotapes. Whatever coordination is present between data from different runs should emerge from the data and should not be the product of the coders' own syntheses as they scan the videotapes for relevant observations.

Actually, a multiple-pass approach to coding videotapes is desirable, just from the standpoint of easing the coders' work. It allows us to break up the task into small and coherent chunks. But there is an additional advantage. With each pass, we merge new information with the old, and gradually accrete an ever-richer and more detailed data base. Given the advantages, it is somewhat surprising how few investigators have adopted this strategy. We think the major reason is that synchronizing data from different runs has not been all that easy to do technically.

We have put together a system that consists almost entirely of commercially available equipment, that makes synchronization of different runs easy, and that simplifies the coders' task in other ways as well. We suspect that this kind of system will tempt more people to do the kind of work that only a few brave pioneers, like Kaye and Fogel (1980), are doing now. Such a system could be put together in more than one way. What we would like to describe now is the way we have done it.

The coder needs to do two things: search the videotape for points when a momentary behavior occurs or when a duration behavior begins or ends, and record the appropriate code and its associated time. Searching in our system is accomplished with the aid of an editing video cassette recorder. These devices were developed for broadcasters and producers who need to edit videotaped material rapidly and efficiently. They allow the user to move forward and backward, at varying speeds, searching for a particular point, all the time maintaining a picture. With our particular model (a JVC CR-8200U), the user manipulates a large knob. In the middle position, the frame is frozen; moving the knob clockwise gradually increases the speed forward, from slow motion through real time to a maximum of about five times real time. Moving the knob from its extreme clockwise position counter clockwise gradually slows down the motion, freezes it at the midpoint, and then begins to move it ever faster backward. In this way, the user can "home in" on the exact point of interest.

Once a coder locates such a point, he or she simply enters the appropriate code on a keyboard. The system takes care of all the rest, including recording the associated time; this frees the coder to search immediately for the next point. This is possible because each frame on the videotape (there are 30 frames per second) has associated with it a unique time code. This time code (the hours, minutes, seconds, and frame number since the time code generator was initialized by the camera operator) is put on one of the two auditory channels at the same time the video signal is recorded. In our case, we record the baby and the interactive partner with two cameras. Rather than merging the signal from these two cameras on one tape with a special-effects generator, we record on different cassettes. But the VCR's are yoked to the same time-code generator, so codings from either cassette can be snychronized.

On playback, a time-code reader visually displays the current time code, and also makes signals representing those digits available for an external device. In our case, this is essentially a microcomputer, a solid-state digital recording device designed to collect observational data. The only custombuilt part of our system is an interface that allows the recording device to read the time code. This could be dispensed with if we were willing to have our coders enter the time code into the recording device themselves, but we think it important to relieve coders of all clerical work, leaving them free to concentrate on the coding task itself.

We recognize a substantial debt to those researchers who have worked out ways to systematically code behavior recorded on videotapes. Often their efforts have been heroic and their investments in time extraordinary. But we think it is *now* possible to make that task almost routine, and to require of coders that they concentrate on manageable chunks of the coding task, and only that.

CONCLUSION

At the beginning of this chapter, we said that it would consist of three parts so that the conceptual, methodological, and technological aspects of our research could be discussed in turn. In closing, we want to comment briefly on just how arbitrary this division really is; the issues addressed are in fact tightly interconnected.

This interconnection is perhaps clearest when technology is related to methodology. After all, we could never expect to actualize a research plan for which the requisite techniques are unavailable. Yet the interconnection between conceptualization and methodology strikes us right now as even more compelling. We have argued that the approach one takes to a problem should fuse (and not confuse) theoretical and methodological orientations. By rooting our work in the contextualist world hypothesis, we hope to have found a productive way to reflect upon the bridge between conceptual and methodological concerns, a way that may allow us to look more closely at the quality and texture of social interactions.

If there is any moral we draw from our reflections on the interconnections of conceptualization and methodology, it is probably this: Research methodology, at any detailed level, cannot be yanked off the shelf and plugged into a conceptual hypothesis. It needs to be carefully fitted, in all its details, to the conceptualization at hand. We think we are doing this now more thoroughly than we have previously. In a few years, we hope our colleagues will tell us whether the effort worked and whether it was worthwhile.

ACKNOWLEDGMENTS

The work reported here was supported in part by a grant from the National Science Foundation (BNS–8012068).

REFERENCES

Bakeman, R., & Brownlee, J. R. The strategic use of parallel play: A sequential analysis. *Child Development,* 1980, *51,* 873–878.

Bates, E. *The emergence of symbols: Cognition and communication in infancy.* New York: Academic Press, 1979.

Bates, E., Camaioni, L., & Volterra, V. The acquisition of performatives prior to speech. *Merrill-Palmer Quarterly,* 1975, *21,* 205–226.

Brazelton, T. B., Koslowski, B., & Main, M. The origins of reciprocity. In M. Lewis, & R. L. Rosenblum (Eds.), *The effect of the infant on its caregiver.* New York: Wiley, 1974.

Brazelton, T. B., Tronick, E., Adamson, L., Als, H., & Wise, S. Early mother–infant reciprocity. In M. A. Hofer (Ed.), *Parent–infant interaction, CIBA Foundation symposium*

33. New York: Associated Scientific Publishers, 1975.

Bruner, J. From communication to language: A psychological perspective. *Cognition,* 1974/75, *3,* 255-287.

Bruner, J. The ontogenesis of speech acts. *Journal of Child Language,* 1975, *2,* 1-19.

Bullowa, M. Introduction. Prelinguistic communication: A field for scientific research. In M. Bullowa (Ed.), *Before speech: The beginning of interpersonal communication.* Cambridge, Eng.: Cambridge University Press, 1979.

Clark, R. A. The transition from action to gesture. In A. Lock (Ed.), *Action, gesture, and symbol.* London: Academic Press, 1978.

Emde, R. N., Kligman, D. H., Reich, J. H., & Wade, T. D. Emotional expression in infancy: I. Initial studies of social signaling and an emergent model. In M. Lewis, & L. A. Rosenblum (Eds.), *The development of affect.* New York: Plenum, 1978.

Fatouti-Milenkovic, M., & Uzgiris, I. The mother–infant communication system. *New Directions for Child Development,* 1979, *4,* 41-56.

Gottman, J. M., & Ringland, J. T. The analysis of dominance and bidirectionality in social development. *Child Development,* 1981, *52,* 393-412.

Greenfield, P. M., & Smith, J. H. *The structure of communication in early language development.* New York: Academic Press, 1976.

Harding, C., & Golinkoff, R. The origins of intentional vocalizations in prelinguistic infants. *Child Development,* 1979, *50,* 33-40.

Hubley, P., & Trevarthen, C. Sharing a task in infancy. *New Directions for Child Development,* 1979, *4,* 57-80.

Izard, C. E. On the ontogenesis of emotions and emotion-cognition: Relationships in infancy. In M. Lewis, & L. A. Rosenblum (Eds.), *The development of affect.* New York: Plenum, 1978.

Kaye, K., & Fogel, A. The temporal structure of face-to-face communication between mothers and infants. *Developmental Psychology,* 1980, *16,* 454-464.

Kuhn, D. Mechanisms of cognitive and social development: One psychology or two? *Human Development,* 1978, *21,* 92-118.

Langer, J. *Theories of development.* New York: Holt, Rinehart & Winston, 1969.

Langer, J. Werner's comparative organismic theory. In P. Mussen (Ed.), *Carmichael's manual of child psychology* (Vol. 1, 3rd ed.). New York: Wiley, 1970.

Leung, E. H., & Rheingold, H. L. *The development of pointing as a social gesture.* Unpublished manuscript, University of North Carolina, 1979.

Lewis, M., & Rosenblum, L. (Eds.). *The development of affect.* New York: Plenum, 1978.

Lock, A. (Ed.). *Action, gesture, and symbol.* London: Academic Press, 1978.

Meehl, P. E. Theoretical risks and tabular asterisks: Sir Karl, Sir Ronald and the slow progress of soft psychology. *Journal of Consulting and Clinical Psychology,* 1978, *46,* 806-834.

Murphy, C. Pointing in the context of a shared activity. *Child Development,* 1978, *49,* 371-380.

Murphy, C., & Messer, D. Mothers, infants and pointing: A study of gesture. In H. R. Schaffer (Ed.), *Studies in mother–infant interaction.* London: Academic Press, 1977.

Nelson, K. The role of language in infant development. In M. Bornstein, & W. Kessen (Eds.), *Psychological development from infancy: Image to intention.* Hillsdale, N.J.: Lawrence Erlbaum Associates, 1979.

Nelson, K. Individual differences in language development: Implications for development and language. *Developmental Psychology,* 1981, *17,* 170-187.

Newson, J., & Newson, E. Intersubjectivity and the transmission of culture. *Bulletin of the British Psychological Society,* 1975, *28,* 437-446.

Osgood, C. E., Tannenbaum, P. H., & Suci, G. J. *The measurement of meaning.* Urbana, Ill.: University of Illinois, 1957.

Pepper, S. *World hypotheses.* Berkeley: University of California, 1942.

Reese, H., & Overton, W. Models of development and theories of development. In L. Goulet, & P. Baltes (Eds.), *Life-span developmental psychology: Research and theory.* New York: Academic Press, 1970.

Ryan, J. Early language development: Towards a communications analysis. In M. Richards (Ed.), *The integration of a child into a social world.* Cambridge, Eng.: Cambridge University Press, 1974.

Scaife, M., & Bruner, J. The capacity for joint visual attention in the infant. *Nature,* 1975, *253,* 265–266.

Schaffer, H. R. (Ed.). *Studies in mother–infant interaction.* London: Academic Press, 1977.

Spitz, R. Fundamental education: The coherent object as a developmental model. In M. Piers (Ed.), *Play and development.* New York: Norton, 1972.

Sroufe, L. A. Socioemotional development. In J. Osofsky (Ed.), *Handbook of infant development.* New York: Wiley, 1979.

Stechler, G., & Carpenter, G. A viewpoint on early affective development. In J. Hellmuth (Ed.), *Exceptional infant* (Vol. 1). Seattle: Special Child Publications, 1967.

Stern, D. Mother and infant at play. In M. Lewis, & L. Rosenblum (Eds.), *The effect of the infant on its caregiver.* New York: Wiley, 1974.

Stern, D. *The first relationship.* Cambridge, Mass.: Harvard University Press, 1977.

Sugarman-Bell, S. Some organizational aspects of preverbal communication. In I. Markova (Ed.), *The social context of language.* Chichester, Eng.: Wiley, 1978.

Trevarthen, C. Descriptive analyses of infant communicative behavior. In H. R. Schaffer (Ed.), *Studies in mother–infant interaction.* London: Academic Press, 1977.

Trevarthen, C. Communication and cooperation in early infancy: A description of primary subjectivity. In M. Bullova (Ed.), *Before speech: The beginning of interpersonal communication.* Cambridge, Eng.: Cambridge University Press, 1979.

Trevarthen, C., & Hubley, P. Secondary intersubjectivity: Confidence, confiding and acts of meaning in the first year. In A. Lock (Ed.), *Action, gesture, and symbol.* London: Academic Press, 1978.

Tronick, E. The primacy of social skills in infancy. In D. Sawin, R. Hawkins, L. Walker, & J. Penticutt (Eds.), *Exceptional infant* (Vol. 4). New York: Brunner/Mazel, 1980.

Tronick, E., Als, H., & Adamson, L. Structure of early face to face communicative interactions. In M. Bullowa (Ed.), *Before speech: The beginning of interpersonal communication.* Cambridge, Eng.: Cambridge University Press, 1979.

Vygotsky, L. S. *Mind in society.* Cambridge, Mass.: Harvard University Press, 1978.

Watson, J. Smiling, cooing and "the game." *Merrill-Palmer Quarterly,* 1972, *18,* 323–339.

Werner, H., & Kaplan, B. *Symbol formation.* New York: Wiley, 1963.

10 The Moral Philosophy of Microanalysis

Kenneth Kaye
Northwestern University Medical School

The microanalysis of videotape, film, or digital event recordings of naturally occurring behavior can be more than a method of research. It can appear to be a political act—that is, taking sides in a controversy of broad ideological proportions.

Microanalysis involves (1) the exploration of relationships among events *within* sessions, as opposed to counting how many times predefined categories occur and comparing those counts across sessions or across experimental conditions; and (2) taking the passage of time into account, either in terms of sequential units or in continuous real time. Although some of us are by temperament more inclined to this sort of work than are others, no one would claim that it can stand alone or that it obviates the necessity for "macro" kinds of case studies on the one hand, or for experimental design on the other.

Before we had videotape and computers, when coding, tabulating, and counting were costly and time consuming, investigators were under more pressure to plan their analyses in advance and to limit themselves to testing prior hypotheses. Our work today is more exciting and more revealing. However, the value of microanalysis is limited by the lack of a clear set of principles governing its use. We must begin to do something no one has yet done: to devise a set of procedures for using these tools without deceiving ourselves or our readers about the amount of fishing—casting, reeling in, casting again—that we have done.

The topic of this book is a field of study in which the need for methodological principles is particularly acute. Of all the areas of psychological research, none requires more subjectivity than the study of affect; and in the lifespan there is no period that raises more complex issues about the subjectivity of the observer than does infancy (Kaye, 1982).

To a certain extent, the problem is a basic paradox in the nature of coding. Science is simplification; the reduction of chaos to order; recasting the unknown in terms of the known. The process of coding, our particular type of simplification, is *not-seeing*. The challenging part of learning to be a good coder is learning to *not-see* most of what is happening and to see only certain categories of things. One has to ignore the differences within categories, trusting one's intuition that the gross category is important. We do this first between the videotape and the coding sheets or the keyboard; then we do it again between the computer disk and the printout, and again between the printout and the published article.

In fact, by positioning the camera and zooming in on only a portion of the scene, we commit ourselves to not-seeing most of what is in the room. This process is merely continued as we define each coding category. "Smiling" commits us to not-seeing a dozen variations in smiles that our eyes and minds are perfectly capable of seeing, indeed beg to see; but we learn to shut them out. We commit ourselves to a guess about a class of smiles we think might be equivalent, at one level, ignoring the ways in which every smile is different. (This, in fact, is exactly what the parent has to do in coding the infant's expressions and what the infant has to do in coding the world.)

The paradoxical aspect of all this selectivity is that its goal is to discover relationships we did not know about before. We want to see as much as possible: If we have to narrow our vision, we want to be able to open it up again, refocus, and try narrowing it in a different way. One of the things I hope to do in this chapter is to share two techniques that I have found to be helpful in this process. However, I want to do that in the context of a first attempt at some principles to guide the use of all such techniques in microanalytic research.

SIX PRINCIPLES FOR MICROANALYSIS

The first principle is that *methodology is only the handmaiden of hypothesis*. The servant must not be allowed to become master. There is no best way to do research in general. On the contrary, when hypotheses are stated more and more specifically, they lead inevitably to the design of procedures for their own confirmation or disconfirmation.

The second principle is that we must try to *hypothesize a process*. It is not enough for the microanalyst to have an idea that certain events are somewhat "related" or even that one is contingent upon another. We need to hypothesize a mechanism, or several alternative mechanisms, by which the occurrence of one type of event might affect the occurrence of the other.

In other words, the exploratory goals of microanalysis do not permit us to by-pass the necessary theoretical work, a priori. Just as an oil exploration crew knows what it is looking for and has reasons for sinking test wells in particular areas, the explorer for behavioral contingencies had better have reasons, not just intuitions.

As I prepared to list the different kinds of relations one might hypothesize between two categories of events A and B, I realized with horror that I could list as many as 1152 different hypotheses, based upon the $4 \times 4 \times 3 \times 4 \times 3 \times 2$ classification scheme shown in Table 10.1. Furthermore, that scheme is far from complete. It merely indicates the most basic alternative kinds of things we might mean when we say of some domain of interaction, "Behavior A has an effect upon behavior B." Even without embellishing the classification, the number of possibilities is much larger than 1152 because polynomial combinations of the different kinds of effects are possible for any A and B. I refer to some of the distinctions in Table 10.1 when illustrating, later, some microanalyses from our own work.

TABLE 10.1
Classification of Microanalytic Hypotheses

Effect of:	1. Discrete *occurrence* of event A.
	2. Continual, ongoing *state* of A ("behavioral context")
	3. *Parameter* of the A series, as a *continuous* variable
	4. *Parameter* of the A series, as a *threshold*
Effect on:	1. Discrete *occurrence* of event B
	2. *Parameter* of B (e.g., rate, stochastic probability of occurrence as a function of time since A, etc.)
	3. *Structure* of series B (periodicity, clustering, etc.)
	4. *Resetting* clock on which B depends
Mechanism:	1. *Physical* (e.g., A is a push; B is a fall)
	2. *Neurological* (e.g., orientation to a sound)
	3. *Conventional* (a learned signal-response contingency)
Closure:	1. *Direct* (A is the actual cause of B)
	2. *Mediated* (A affects Q, which affects B)
	3. *Correlated* (A and B are both affected by Q)
	4. *Subset* (A is only a subset of the class of events that affect B, or A only affects a subset of B)
Rule:	1. *Obligatory response*, optional signal
	2. *Obligatory signal*, optional response
	3. Obligatory *response and* obligatory *signal*
Roles:	1. *Symmetrical* (person 1's A affects person 2's B as 2's A affects 1's B)
	2. *Asymmetrical* (different effects of person 1 upon person 2 than of 2 upon 1)

The third principle is a heuristic: *Begin with departures from randomness.* It is a good idea to think about behavior B as a series of events in time, and to begin by asking whether they occur randomly—that is, as a Poisson process—and if not, how they differ from a random series of occurrences. A Poisson process means that the probability of a B occurring at any point in time is independent of when the last B occurred. The discrete events B are, in short, independent of each other, which means that they must also be independent of any nonrandom events. A Poisson process has zero autocorrelation (see Gottman, Chapter 12, this volume); the frequency distribution of intervals between B's is exponential, positively skewed; and the log-survivorship function (plotting on the Y axis the number of intervals longer than each duration plotted on the X axis) is a straight line with negative slope. The latter two results are mathematically equivalent, and are always true when the autocorrelation is zero at all time lags (though the converse need not be the case).

If the B series is random, then it is either unrelated to any behavior A, or it is closely related (a direct consequence) while A itself is a Poisson process.

If the B series deviates from a Poisson process, the first question is how; the second question is whether A is one of the things responsible for that departure from randomness. These questions take us back to the stage of hypothesizing a process (principle 2) and devising a method appropriate to that hypothesis (principle 1). Chapter 12 of this volume deals with one way of approaching the question, how much of B's nonrandom structure is accounted for by the structure of A? In a time series, the observation at each point is a continuous variable, such as the daily temperature or the price of wheat. A point process can be translated into a continuous variable rate, either by averaging over a moving window large enough to include several events, or by taking the reciprocal of each interval from one occurrence to the next. Time-series analysis is a powerful way of allocating the relative roles of intrinsic structure versus interactive effects, but by translating the analysis into a regression problem it can take us away from the specific alternative forms the interactive effects may take.

Fig. 10.1 illustrates the test of an hypothesis directly involving the issue of randomness versus clustering. B, in this case, is a heterogeneous category of infants' facial expressive behaviors while being held face to face in their mothers' laps. Such expressions had been found to cluster into "runs" or "turns," and we wondered under what conditions they did so. If they were indeed intentionally communicative, the clusters of expressions should occur when the babies were attending to their mothers' faces. If they were a matter of conversational turn taking, the infants' facial expressions should cluster together when the mothers were relatively quiet, during the pauses in their own expressive behavior to the infants. The first of these hypotheses was only slightly confirmed for the 6-week-old infants, more clearly confirmed for the 13-week and 26-week infants: The log-survivorship function changed from a straight line to a sagging one, with a break at about the

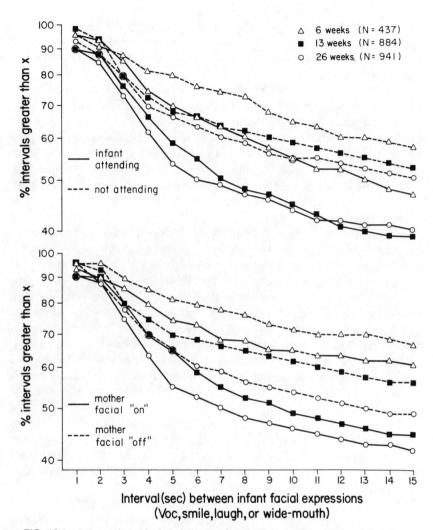

FIG. 10.1   Log-survivorship functions showing the organization of infants' facial expressions in face-to-face sessions with their mothers, deviating from a Poisson process. *N* of mothers and babies = 47. (Data from Kaye & Fogel, 1980.)

point of the 5-second intervals. This means that there were more expressions within 5 seconds of each other than would have been found by chance, given the average rate with which such expressions occurred. The difference between the two conditions, attending to the mother versus not attending, was significant at 13 and 26 weeks. (In this case, to capture the interaction of the three independent variables, we used a repeated-measures analysis of variance, with the proportion of intervals less than 5 seconds as the dependent variable.)

The second hypothesis was disconfirmed. In fact, the opposite was the case: Infant facial expressions clustered together while mothers were making faces at them, not while mothers were pausing. Again, the effect increased with age.

Now let us proceed to my fourth principle: *Use the right baseline.* Microanalysis is an attempt to fabricate an experimental design within observational data that one was unable to subject to an actual controlled experiment. An experimental manipulation is always preferable; it is just not always possible without distorting the phenomena in which one is interested. A smile presented upon the investigator's cue, for example, may not have the same effect upon a child's or parent's behavior as smiles in the real world have. Our job, therefore, is to organize the data as if the events *A* constituted trials in an experiment.

The baseline problem has two parts: One is the decision as to which two (or more) circumstances to compare. In the foregoing example, the hypotheses involved the effects of various states (e.g., attending to the mother) upon the structure of a series (the organization of facial expressions in time). The next example involves the effect of discrete events, the onset and offset of mothers' jiggling their babies during feeding, upon the likelihood of occurrence of another discrete event, the babies' resumption of sucking. The "experimental" condition is therefore the moments immediately following jiggling, and the baseline or "control" condition consists of moments when the babies have paused from sucking but when the mothers have not jiggled.

This raises the second part of the baseline problem: The two conditions have to be comparable in terms of some starting point in time. In this case, the question is whether the jiggling makes the baby start sucking sooner. Sooner from when? Because the question has to do with effects on the duration of the pause in sucking, all conditions have to be compared as a function of time since the beginning of the pause.

The resulting *contingency function,* a conditional probability as a function of time, is shown in Fig. 10.2. Functions of this kind have been used for some time in other fields, for example in comparing the effects of chemotherapy upon life expectancy as a function of time since the onset of cancer. Fig. 10.2 shows that jiggling itself suppresses the likelihood of a new burst of sucking, but that the cessation of jiggling accelerated the burst, even above what its likelihood would have been had the mother not jiggled at all.

An explanation of exactly what is plotted in Fig. 10.2 will allow the reader to translate this technique into his or her own research questions involving conditional probabilities. Notice that transitional or Markov probabilities are of no interest here: We already know that the next thing the baby is going to do after pausing is to start sucking again. The question is whether the mother's jiggling has any effect on how long it will be before the sucking

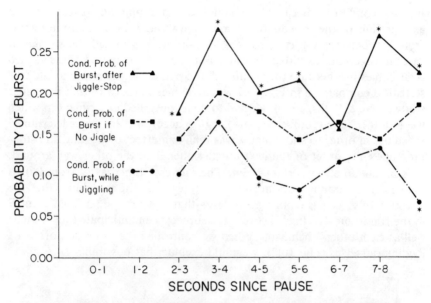

FIG. 10.2   Contingency functions showing conditional probability of a burst of suck-ing (end of the pause), as a function of time since onset of the pause, depending on mothers' jiggling. N of mothers and babies = 52, N of pauses = 1814. (From Kaye & Wells, 1980.)

resumes. This effect is expressed as the conditional probability of a burst, within any 1-second interval. (The analysis begins in the third second of the pause because intersuck intervals of less than 2 seconds were not defined as pauses). Of all those pauses that have lasted x seconds, what proportion will end in the next 1-second interval, and is this likelihood affected by whether the mother has jiggled? After $x + 1$ seconds, a smaller number of pauses re-main for consideration, because some have already ended. For any 1-second interval, Fig. 10.2 shows the pauses divided into three conditions: those in which the mother had not yet jiggled and the infant had not yet resumed sucking; those in which she was jiggling; and those in which she had previously started and stopped jiggling. Each point represents bursts per op-portunities to burst at that point in time.

In practice, one chooses the interval to be plotted along the X axis, then has the computer find all the latencies from the starting event to the condi-tional (A) and/or the terminal event (B), sort them into piles determined by the interval to be used, and compute (by arithmetic on the contents of those piles) the proportions for each point. These proportions can then be com-pared, at any point on the X axis, by a simple chi-square test. The asterisks in Fig. 10.2 show where the conditional probability of a burst under one of the two jiggling conditions was significantly different from the baseline no-jiggling condition. Because the conditions are mutually exclusive, the assumptions of the chi-square are met even though the cases do not come from independent subjects, so long as nothing has biased the sorting of cases into conditions along the way. For example, if mothers had jiggled their babies just because they could tell the pause was not going to end, the statistical comparison in Fig. 10.2 would be meaningless. In that particular study (Kaye & Wells, 1980), we had to do a controlled experiment in which we fed the babies ourselves and jiggled according to a predetermined schedule, in order to show that it was really an effect of jiggling and stopping upon the onset of the next burst, rather than the other way around. This brings up an important point: The fact that time passes from left to right in these graphs does not necessarily exclude the possibility that the direction of effects is from right to left—that is, from the terminal event B to the condition A. This is because the subjects can anticipate their own as well as each others' behavior. When we controlled the onset and offset of jiggling ourselves (Fig. 10.3), we could exclude that possibility.

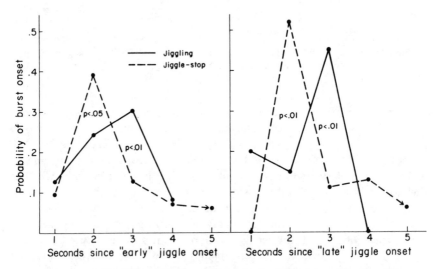

FIG. 10.3 Conditional probability of a burst of sucking, depending on the experimenter's jiggling: (1) 2 seconds after the onset of the pause; (2) 4 seconds after the onset of the pause. N of babies = 12, N of pauses = 899. (From Kaye & Wells, 1980.)

The choice of intervals on the X axis is important. They have to be: (1) a simple unit, like seconds or weeks; (2) large enough so that at least 10 cases (e.g., "opportunities to burst") occur in each interval under each condition (otherwise one will not get anything like smooth curves); (3) larger than one's confidence interval, based on reliability studies, for how close together in time two events can be and still allow one to be sure that they occurred in the order in which they appear (Kaye, 1980); and (4) otherwise as small as possible.

A fine point: One might decide to exclude all cases from the analysis whose latencies from A to B were less than the reliable confidence interval. Similarly, with time-sampled data, it might be wise to exclude cases in which both events occurred during the same interval. If so, then the data should only be excluded from that time onward; everything that happened (or did not happen) up to the moment the given condition became true should still be retained in the baseline data, to prevent bias.

Fig. 10.4 shows a variation of this technique, a contingency function both forward and backward from the onset of a pause, showing how it doubles the likelihood of a mother's jiggling.

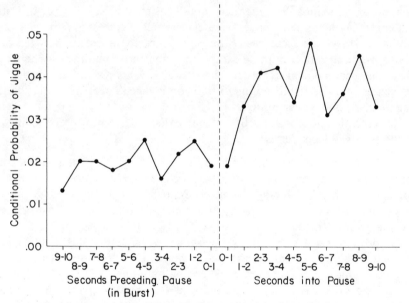

FIG. 10.4   Contingency function forward and backward from a target event. $N = 52$ mothers and babies, 1814 pauses. (Data from Kaye & Wells, 1980.)

My fifth principle is one that I need not belabor, because it is commonly known even though it is commonly violated: *Exploratory findings must be confirmed in a second sample.* It is reasonable to reject all manuscripts submitted for publication, and all dissertations submitted for doctoral degrees, whose results consist of nothing more than behavioral relationships found through exploratory microanalysis without confirmatory analysis. The fact that B is "significantly" contingent upon A does not test how fortuitous might be the finding of that particular contingency, among all the hypotheses explored, among all the different kinds of *A* and *B* analyzed, in that particular sample. However, if it is fortuitous it will not emerge again in a new corpus of data.

The obvious exception to that last statement brings me to my sixth and last principle: *Always suspect artifacts.* The time to dwell on possible spurious relationships in the data is not after the analysis has been done, as an attempt to account for only those results that are unfriendly to our theory. The time is before designing the study, especially before designing the procedures of observation and coding.

Perhaps the most difficult kinds of artifact to avoid are those having to do with the reification of categories. We tend to assume that those behavioral units we can identify and code independently are independent acts in the subjects' repertoires of behavior. If, in fact, they are neurophysiologically linked to other acts, and if (as must always be true to some extent) the boundaries around our categories fail to correspond to the actual units of behavior, we can easily find significant contingencies between our categories that reflect nothing except our poor understanding of where the psychological boundaries actually are between events. Or the confusion can have the opposite result: failing to find contingencies because of our inadequate definition of categories.

More avoidable types of artifact include three different ways of failing to code events independently:

1. Both series of events, *A* and *B*, are coded by the same coder at the same time. When an *A* and a *B* occur in close proximity, the coder misses one or the other, producing a spurious exclusivity. Alternatively, by only a few unconscious coding errors, the coder introduces an hypothesized regularity into the data.

2. Both series are coded by the same coder, but at different times. Nonetheless the coder biases the data because he or she cannot help watching both kinds of events even while coding only one.

3. Two different coders are employed for *A* and *B*, and are kept as unaware as possible of one another's work. But the coder of the baby's facial expression keeps the audio on and is unconsciously biased by the mother's vocalizations, and the coder of the latter keeps the video visible and is biased by the baby's face.

My students and I have regrettably discovered many other means of introducing artifacts into microanalysis, and it is likely that the reader will independently rediscover them. Although it is obviously preferable to think about the possibility of artifacts in advance, the specific results of each study are an occasion for checking back to rule out artifacts before publication.

INTERPRETATION VERSUS EXPLANATION

Not all of my colleagues feel comfortable about the attitude implied by the foregoing principles. Some, I think, hearing Goethe's (1808) lines:

> Mysterious in the light of day,
> Nature will not be denied her veil,
> And what she does not make manifest to your spirit
> Cannot be forced from her with levers and screws [p. 188].

assume the converse, that whatever Nature does make manifest to their spirit must be true and must be defended *against* levers and screws. Their main rhetorical weapon is the assertion that human minds and social relations transcend science. This is not the place to refute that controversial assertion, but I do want to devote the remaining discussion to at least raising the issue. It is of concern to all developmental psychologists, but microanalysis especially forces us to come to terms with it.

One of the themes of my own work has been that even though parents naturally overinterpret expressive-looking acts in young infants, psychology ought to guard against doing so. It is one thing for a mother to say to a father, "He says, 'Who are you?'," when the baby seems to be making a quizzical face. It is quite another thing for psychologists to talk that way when our purpose is to discover when and how the infant actually comes to use gestures with meaningful intent (Kaye, 1982). Yet some authors claim that human thought and communication are beyond the domain of what they consider to be hard-nosed science. Rather than imposing systematic procedures to test the validity of interpretations of events, they would treat the interpretations themselves as data, arguing that acts between human beings are always, by definition of their humanity, meaningful gestures. Harré (1974) wrote:

> I shall assume that all forms of social behaviour have the same level of sophistication, and indeed that human beings are unable to perform in a socially unsophisticated way [p. 16].

This troubles me because I should have thought it was an investigable question, not something to be assumed; and it seems to me that the evidence on young infants shows that it takes them some time, with adults playing an important role, before their social behavior becomes sophisticated in any sense of the word.

Elsewhere in the same article Harré castigates what he calls "outmoded positivistic ideas about what science is [p. 14]." Trevarthen (1977) takes up the same theme:

> I believe that a different kind of research, less analytical *at the start* is a necessary complement to experiment in scientific study of intelligence, especially for the early developmental stages when great impressionability of memory is controlled by

innate forms of action. This alternative method attempts to capture regular patterns in spontaneous action and tailors experimental intervention to what is discovered . . . . The essential difference resides in an emphasis on generative or structural and functional complexity in the subject who thus becomes a free-acting agent [p. 229].

This "alternative method" sounds like just the kind of methods I have discussed previously, including lip service to confirmatory analysis. Yet we find in Trevarthen's studies only the conclusions from his observations, illustrated by anecdote and by selected photographs and drawings, without any attempt to test hypotheses.

I am not ready to be classed among those who reduce psychology to the "behavior of organisms" or those who allow similarities across species to blind them to the more important qualities that make humans unique. We do need theories of *human* development. The issue, as I see it, is whether those theories ought to be tested by traditional rules of evidence or whether the rules should be suspended when we turn our lenses upon our own species. On that issue I take a conservative view. Innovative, painstaking observation and analysis of parent–infant interaction is possible within the format of ordinary scientific investigation; we have neither the need nor the right to suspend the rules.

A great deal has been written in philosophy and in the theory of literary criticism about *interpretation*. This referred originally to the interpretation of texts, such as the Bible; thence it was applied to analysis and criticism of literature in general, thence to a theory of symbolic meaning. It is not a big leap from there to interpretations about the mental and social life of babies. But must we leave the realm of science altogether, in favor of "hermeneutics" (Heidegger, 1962), whenever we study our own species? Enmeshed in this question is the problem of what we mean by "study." Are we trying to make plausible sense out of individual cases, or are we trying to explain processes common to all? I argue that the latter is our goal. Interpretation, by itself, may be the goal of idiographic analysis but is never sufficient for explanation.

I see our present tension, then, as the same one that has existed in psychology since the 19th century (Allport, 1962) between idiographic and nomothetic research. The proper goal of one is to interpret a particular event in depth without reducing it to a mere instance of categories already known. The proper goal of the other is to generalize about a whole set of things, by adequately sampling them. The biggest difference between the two approaches is in the relationship between the data that must be presented and the prior beliefs of the intended audience. One can show that something exists by demonstrating one instance of it, so long as the reader agrees that it is an instance. That depends on his or her prior belief that what is asserted is possible. If I point to a clam opening and shutting, and say, "This clam is communicating with its fellows," your acceptance of the proposition depends on your belief in the more general proposition "clams can communicate." In no way could my one clam, or even thousands of clams doing the same thing, be taken as proof that what we are seeing is communication. However, the converse is true: A prior belief that this form of communication exists will usually function as sufficient basis for acceptance of the particular instance.

A nomothetic approach is required when the communication abilities of clams are precisely what the audience doubts. The prior beliefs that the audience must share with the researcher are beliefs about procedures for identifying communication (or whatever the behavior in question is) when it exists.

Within the work of one investigator or a group of like-minded investigators, these two modes of questioning can coexist quite peacefully. But between two authors whose theories are at odds (for example, myself and Trevarthen), different predilections towards idiographic versus nomothetic arguments tend to drive them further apart and make fruitful dialectics impossible. The nomothete regards the idiograph as an unscientific storyteller; the idiograph regards the nomothete as a pseudoscientific reductionist. One says, "Let us see your data." The other replies, "Data lie; look at my videotape." "But your videotape is not representative; I don't see the same things in my videotape." "Because you have blinded yourself."

A long-standing version of this debate has to do with psychoanalytic interpretation. An interpretation is offered about the meaning of a person's behavior, about the symbolic meaning of a dream, or about something the patient says during a session. The most important evaluation of the analyst's interpretation comes from the patient. If the case is written up, the interpretation will also be evaluated by a different audience: the readers. In both cases, the validity of the interpretation is measured only by its success in eliciting recognition from the patient or colleague. So it is *doubly* idiographic: It does not have to be true *of* people in general, and it does not have to be true *to* people in general. Still its acceptance is not an arbitrary matter. Psychoanalytic interpretations only appear plausible to those of us who are already prepared to believe that all aspects of human behavior, including unconscious acts, are intentional and significant. The psychoanalytic literature, which is almost entirely in the form of case studies, does not convince anyone who is skeptical about the basic principles of psychoanalytic psychology.

The same is true of illustrative cases as evidence about the development of affective expressions in infants. Consider the following interpretation of a 7-month-old child who had been left with his grandparents for 2 weeks (Mahler, Pine, & Bergman, 1975):

When his mother returned, he at first had a rather severe crisis of reunion, crying unconsolably for quite a while and not allowing her to either feed him or put him to sleep. However, by the next day he was his old smiling and tranquil self. This reaction to brief separation, which is peculiarly specific to mother–infant reunions in the second half of the first year, might be understood metapsychologically in terms of the split that still exists in the internal part-images of the mother. This split is easily activated by such brief absences; the mother of separation must be reintegrated as the "all good" symbiotic mother so as not to hurt or destroy the good object [p. 67].

Whatever the authors may mean by "metapsychologically," they obviously make some controversial assumptions about what goes on in the 7-month-old's mind. I wish only to point out that a report of this kind cannot possibly be considered data in support of such assumptions. That is essentially the criticism I have made elsewhere of the blanket applications of notions of "systems" and "intersubjectivity" to the young infant (Kaye, 1982). Whether we accept those interpretations depends on our prior beliefs about gesturing by infants; anecdotes and photographs are not evidence.

In summary, it is not sufficient for an investigator to fall back upon the familiar excuse "this is an exploratory study," as though that were to sanction any and all informal, inspired, or intuitive manifestations of the spirit. Microanalysis, properly understood, belongs to nomothetic science.

ACKNOWLEDGMENTS

Research described in this chapter was funded by a grant from the Spencer Foundation.

REFERENCES

Allport, G. The general and the unique in psychological science. *Journal of Personality,* 1962, *30,* 405–422.

Goethe, J. W. von. *Faust,* Part I. New York: D.C. Heath, 1954. (Originally published in German, 1808.)

Harré, R. Some remarks on "rule" as a scientific concept. In T. Mischel (Ed.), *Understanding other persons.* Totowa, N.J.: Rowman & Littlefield, 1974.

Heidegger, M. *Being and time.* London: SCM Press, 1962. (Originally published in German, 1927.)

Kaye, K. Estimating false alarms and missed events from inter-observer agreements. *Psychological Bulletin,* 1980, *88,* 458–468.

Kaye, K. *The mental and social life of babies: How parents create persons.* Chicago: University of Chicago Press, 1982.

Kaye, K., & Fogel, A. The temporal structure of face-to-face communication between mothers and infants. *Developmental Psychology,* 1980, *16,* 454–464.

Kaye, K., & Wells, A. Mothers' jiggling and the burst-pause pattern in neonatal sucking. *Infant Behavior and Development,* 1980, *3,* 29–46.

Mahler, M., Pine, F., & Bergman, A. *The psychological birth of the human infant.* New York: Basic Books, 1975.

Trevarthen, C. Descriptive analyses of infant communicative behaviour. In H. R. Schaffer (Ed.), *Studies in mother–infant interaction.* London: Academic Press, 1977.

11 Young Infants' Hand and Finger Expressions: An Analysis of Category Reliability

Thomas Edward Hannan
Purdue University

Anecdotal accounts of infants under 3 months of age have suggested that the activities of the hands and fingers may be systematically organized in the sense that there are regularities in the timing of display of particular manual behavioral acts in relation to affective states (Papousek, 1978; Trevarthen, 1977). The fingers appear to cycle between differing forms of activity, and the tempo of these changes appears to be associated with the overall activity level of the infant (Trevarthen, 1977). Tightly clenched fingers may reflect states of anger or distress, whereas loosely curled fingers may reflect states of engagement (Papousek, 1978).

Any attempt to validate this speculation depends on the ability to transform infant hand and finger movements into data types suitable for statistical analysis. Such transformations depend on the subjective interpretations of observers in assigning the appropriate category of behavior to the perceived movement. It is not clear from the recent descriptive accounts whether discrete hand and finger movements can be reliably detected from the flow of continuous manual activity.

Although ultimately we may be most concerned with the "meaning" of the expression to the infant, or the possible correlation of specific manual expressions to specific emotional states, the issue of category reliability must first be solved. The scope of this chapter is restricted to the question: Are there methods available that would allow infant hand movements to be reliably coded into discrete expressions?

Probably the most thorough attempt to evaluate reliability of early infant body movements has dealt with movements of the infant's face—particularly movements of the mouth and eyebrows. The majority of the recent work is based on the detailed evaluations of adult facial expression pioneered by Ekman and his associates (e.g., Ekman & Friesen, 1975). The result of these investigations was the introduction of a reliable and valid method of coding adult facial movements, the Facial Action Coding System or FACS (see Ekman & Friesen, 1978). The FACS is a system of coding facial behavior designed to note changes in individual muscles of the face. Assignment of a specific emotional expression results from a detailed analysis of which facial muscles were active at a given moment.

The validity of applying a system of categorizing adult facial behavior to assessments of infant facial expression has been established in a number of recent studies. Oster and Ekman (1977) demonstrated that the facial "atlas" of the FACS was an exhaustive representation of all infant facial movements. Further, Izard, Huedner, Risser, McGuinnes, and Dougherty (1980) found that adults could accurately identify states of infant affect while viewing photographs of the infant's facial expression.

The techniques for coding facial expression have been successfully used with videotaped recordings of infant faces as well. Oster (1978) analyzed interobserver reliability by coding videotaped sessions of two infants using the FACS, and then having a second naive observer repeat the process on the same time sequences. Detection of facial changes and assignment of the category of facial movement was judged to be quite good. Percent of agreement ranged between .74 and .95, and the average time error for onset and offset detection between the coders was less than 1 second. More recently, Gaensbauer, Mrazek, and Emde (1979) coded expressions of facial affect utilizing descriptions based on the FACS. Coders identified the category of affect and assigned it a value on a 9-point scale reflecting the perceived intensity of affect. Ratings of facial affect were made at 30-second intervals. A subset of the data was recoded by a second trained observer, with agreement within 1 intensity point on the scale, ranging from .84 to .98. A third trained, but naive observer coded six of the 40 infants once more. These ratings were compared with those of the first observer and similar percent of agreement was found.

The problems encountered with describing and classifying facial expressiveness are somewhat analogous to the problems of assessing hand activity. In both cases, a specific expression is a composite of a number of individual movements. Facial expressions are determined by the coordination of movements of the eyebrows and mouth, whereas hand expressions would seem to rely on the coordination of individual fingers. However, not all of the hand and finger movements of young infants have parallel counterparts in adults. It may not be readily apparent to adult observers when one movement has ended and another has begun, nor would it seem as easy to assign an affective meaning to what adult observers may feel are discrete expressions. The coding of individual components of the face and the structuring of these elements into emotional expressions is facilitated by the fact that facial movements project clearly distinguishable affective features in adults and young infants (cf. Ekman & Friesen, 1975; Izard et al., 1980).

Even so, the methodologies employed in studies of facial expression serve as useful models for approaching the study of hand and finger activity. The work with facial expressions suggests attention to the following methodological issues: First, a coding system should be developed that is able to detect behavior changes in real time. Hand and finger movements are dynamic and fluid in their nature. If they are not examined as real-time events, there is no way to determine if observed expressions are more than just the observer's teleological structuring of random movements. Second, the catalogue of infant hand movements must be exhaustive and possess the ability to detect fine-grained differences through the use of subcategories or intensity measures. Because we really do not wish to make prior assumptions about which movements will constitute an expression, it seems best to try to detect all possible movements, and then construct expressions from these components. This approach is similar to the very early attempts by Ekman and Friesen to identify components of facial expression rather than the expressions themselves.

In line with the concerns outlined so far, the present study was intended to ask the following questions: (1) Could discrete expressions of the hands and fingers be detected from the flow of continuous hand activity? and (2) Could descriptions be developed that accurately described these expressions?

METHODS AND PROCEDURES

The data for this investigation are part of a longitudinal assessment of the development of emotional expression and attachment in four parent–infant dyads (see Fogel, 1981, and Chapter 2, this volume). Prospective participants were contacted soon after birth and invited to participate in the study. No attempt was made to control for SES factors or parity. Two of the four dyads were selected for this analysis. Each mother was multiparous and both came from middle-class backgrounds. Both infants were considered to be normal, full-term infants; one infant H. was female, the other infant J. was a male.

Each dyad visited the lab once a week for the first year of the infant's life. During the first 12 weeks, each of these sessions was divided into two segments—an infant-seat condition and a lap condition. The data for the current analysis were based only on the first condition. The seat condition was chosen because it afforded the clearest opportunity to observe both of the infant's hands. In the seat condition, the infant was placed in an infant seat, mounted on a projection table at a height allowing for face-to-face interaction with the mother while she was standing. The taping began with a

60-second baseline in which the infant was left alone, after which the mother entered and spent 5 minutes of nonstructured interaction with the infant. Aside from the limits of the time interval, no further experimental manipulations were enforced. Mothers were instructed simply to "chat with your baby" in a normal manner. For infant H., the length of the 12 sessions ranged between 2 minutes and 7 minutes with a mean length of 5.5 minutes. For infant J., the length of the 12 sessions ranged between 5 minutes and 7.5 minutes with a mean length of 6.5 minutes.

Two Sony video cameras were employed for the data collection; one focused exclusively on the infant's whole body and one focused on both interactants. The signals from each camera were mixed with a Sony special-effects generator. An ODETICS digital timer was added to the mixed signal and the result was a split-screen record of the on-going interaction. The cameras were hidden from view by a screen that surrounded the infant at a radius of 10 feet. The recording equipment was contained in an observation booth adjacent to the experimental "living room." The recorded interactions constituted the raw data for analysis.

The nature of the questions outlined for this study required a method of videotape transcription that would be a continuous recording of all hand movements of the infant. A method of coding was designed that allowed even the most subtle movements or changes to be coded by categories in real-time (see Table 11.1). The digital timer allowed the coding of onset and offset times as categories of behavior were observed.

The coding was done by four teams of coders composed of two observers each. A team was assigned to one member of the two mother–infant pairs. These teams of coders observed each of the sessions, transcribing units of time and action. Any change in the on-going flow of movement in the activities of the hands signaled one coder to pause the tape, while the other coder recorded the time of onset (and thus the offset of the previous movement); together, the coders then decided on the category of behavior observed. During the coding periods, the tape was run at normal speed. However, coders were encouraged to rewind the tape and reobserve a segment of time if they were initially unsure of either the decision that a change had occurred, or how they coded the event.

For purposes of reliability assessment, a subset of 50% of the total number of sessions was selected at random (this constituted six of the 12 seat-condition segments for each infant). For these six sessions, the length ranged from 2 minutes to 7 minutes with a mean length of 5.8 minutes for infant H., and 5 minutes to 7.5 minutes with a mean length of 6.3 minutes for infant J. Each of these subset sessions was completely recoded by a different coding team. The reliability coding of the hands and fingers was done approximately 1 year after the original coding took place.

TABLE 11.1
Descriptions of Hand and Finger Coding Categories

FINGER CURLING	Fingers flexing and unflexing 1. Fingers repetitively "drumming" 2. Alteration of index and other finger extensions
INDEX-FINGER EXTENSION	Other fingers curled; index finger extended 1. Towards mother 1. Bent finger 2. Towards object 2. Straight finger 3. Other 3. Moving finger
OTHER THAN INDEX-FINGER EXTENSION	Any other single finger extended, other fingers curled 1. Towards mother 1. Bent finger 2. Towards object 2. Straight finger 3. Other 3. Finger moving
FINGERS SPREAD	Sustained extension of all fingers 1. Close together 1. Moving 2. Web-like 2. Static 3. Claw-like 4. Bye-bye
FIST	Tightly curled fingers, thumb behind fingers, knuckles standing out
FINGERS TO THUMB	Tip of finger touches tip of thumb forming a circle 1. Index finger 2. Middle finger 3. Ring finger 4. Little finger
CURLED FINGERS	Fingers loosely bent inward, curled under
HAND CLASP	Two hands clasping one another 1. Static 2. Moderate movement of fingers 3. Rapid movement of fingers
HANDS TOGETHER	Hands touch or brush one another, not a clasping of the hands 1. Static 2. Moderate movement of fingers 3. Rapid movement of fingers
WRIST FLEX	Bend of hand at wrist 1. Up 2. Down
GRASP	Clasping or grabbing at specified object 1. Self 2. Object 3. Mother 4. Own clothing 5. Seat 6. Mother's clothing

A number of methods of estimating reliability are currently available (for a review, see Hollenbeck, 1978). Each method involves some measure of percent of agreement between two coders. However, in this analysis the focus was on the flow of activity across time, and how observers perceived the differences. We would want to know: (1) Can observers reliably decide that one type of movement had ended and another begun? and (2) Can observers agree on what to call the events that they decide are discrete movements? In short, we would want to know how accurately we can recreate an extended segment of time as a series of categories of action. However, the relative density of the number of possible movements would be expected to be variable across sessions. Some sessions may have very few changes, whereas others may involve rapid change from moment to moment. Because the probability of finding agreement differs as a function of this density, the estimate of reliability should have a measure of agreement in real time, and an adjustment for the probability of chance agreement as a function of density; percent of agreement measures alone do not suffice.

Kaye (1980) has suggested a procedure that allows computation of an estimate of reliability (given as the value $p(r)$ in Kaye's formula) for a given segment of time. This value is sensitive to a number of factors not tested by a percent of agreement measure: specifically, the onset/offset detection agreement within a prespecified time tolerance, the duration of the event, the application of category labels, and the session length. Each of these factors can contribute to errors of "missed events" or "false alarms"; $p(r)$ is a function composed of estimates of each of these error factors either directly or indirectly, as well as agreements and disagreements.

The agreement measure in Kaye's procedure requires a method of estimating category agreement and onset time detection agreement. Each original and recoded transcript for a given sessions can be visually represented as three parallel vertical vectors: one event or time column and two category columns. To measure the reliability of a session, an intercepting X axis began at the first entry and passed through all events (time) and all categories (movements). To constitute an agreement or "match," both the onset times and the categories indicated had to agree. Because of the probability that time would not be totally in agreement to .01 seconds for any event, a maximum tolerance of 2 seconds was set as being acceptable interteam time error. At each intercepting point, the degree of interteam time error (the differences between the original onset time and the recoded onset time) was measured and a + or − scored to indicate whether there was category agreement or not.

RESULTS

The initial attempts at estimating reliability yielded disappointing results, with estimates well below .60 for each session examined. Visual inspection of the original and recoded transcripts for each session indicated that two factors might be interacting to influence the results. The first factor was the agreement on the detection of change, or the alignment of onset and offset times for the paired transcripts. The second factor was the agreement between transcripts on the category applied to like-identified events. Were the nonmatches a result of missed events, "false alarms," or the misapplication of category labels?

At this stage, reliability analyses were restricted to infant H., with the intention of using infant J. as a replication. The decision was arbitrary and was made to simplify the task of exploring what was leading to such low reliability estimates.

The first step was to test whether onsets and offsets were being detected. If one just looks at agreement between coders on when a change is detected, a binomial test can be constructed that asks whether the distribution of matches and nonmatches are drawn from the same population. Computation of the binomial probabilities for each session indicated that the number of matches were significantly greater than nonmatches in only three of six sessions ($p < .05$). Of the three sessions in which the number of matches did not differ from nonmatches, the missed events tended to be of a shorter duration than the identified events (i.e., either instantaneous or lasting less than 3 seconds).

The next step involved testing whether there was agreement on the application of category labels. For each session, a matrix was constructed and each category of behavior occupied a place along an X and a Y axis. An event-by-event analysis was performed by comparing the original coded event (the tally mark on the X axis) and the recoded event (the tally mark on the Y axis). Agreements fall on the diagonal, whereas disagreements fall on either side. Hollenbeck (1978) has described this method for use in computing Cohen's Kappa; however, in this instance the matrix method was employed simply to examine which labels were misapplied.

Category mismatches were usually the result of confusing two very similar categories (e.g., the category a *claw-like finger spread*—the fingers spread at the knuckles, but curling inward at the ends of the fingers—and the category *fingers curled*—the fingers loosely bent inward), and variations of the same category (e.g., *finger curling type 1* and *finger curling type 2*). However, a third type of error was detected that could not be dismissed by either of these explanations.

A number of the errors detected involved agreement on onset time, but with vastly different category labels applied (e.g., *fist* and *finger curling*). In these cases offset times never agreed, and quite often there would be a series of brief (i.e., less than 3-second) events identified by one coding team, but not the other. By looking for the next onset agreement, these series of events could be compared to the other transcript as if it were one event. It appeared that the most common pattern of mismatch of events involved the code *finger curling*—a category applied to cyclic or rythmic flexions and extensions of the fingers—and a series of short duration (i.e., 3- to 5-second) events that could be perceived of as single events, or one event with frequent variations.

Based on these diagnostic assessments, the following tentative hypotheses were constructed: Event duration seemed to account for many of the identified mismatches. Therefore, elimination of brief events should improve the probability of identifying an event. However, in some cases a series of brief events may represent a larger event; therefore, there should be some method of recategorizing these brief events into larger units. Finally, to account for category-label misapplication, similar categories should be grouped into a smaller number of supraordinate categories.

To test these hypotheses, the following manipulations were performed on the original and recoded transcripts for each of the six sessions. First, events coded as instantaneous (having no clearly discernible onset or offset—in other words, those events considered too brief to even have a duration) were eliminated. Second, there was an elimination of all "brief" events (events having a duration of less than 3 seconds). This figure was chosen because inspection of mismatched categories indicated consistently that events less than 3 seconds long were not reliably detected. If the brief event occurred as the first event in a series of brief events, a new category was assigned to the whole string in the following manner: The onset time of this newly derived event was the onset of the first event in the series, and the new offset time was the onset time of the next event lasting more than 3 seconds. These newly created events were reclassified based on the content of the brief events contained within it. Finally, there was a collapsing of all the original category labels into the six supraordinate categories presented in Table 11.2.

The results of reliability estimates based on these transformations were much more encouraging. The average reliability for all six sessions was .96 for the right hand and .95 for the left. The mean time error for the right hand was .53 seconds (low 95% C.I. = .48 seconds, high 95% C.I. = .58 seconds), and for the left hand it was .96 seconds (low 95% C.I. = .89 seconds, high 95% C.I. = 1.03 seconds).

As a test of the validity of the decision to manipulate the original and recoded transcripts by collapsing and eliminating events, a third coding team recoded all the 12 sessions for both infants. This team was given only the category definitions listed in Table 11.2, and they were also instructed to ignore events less than 3 seconds in duration. This team was not aware of which sessions had served as the basis for previous reliability assessments. The assumption was that if indeed the previous manipulations actually represented the infant's movements, then the use of the newly derived coding categories should produce virtually the same transcript of events as the adjusted, original transcripts.

TABLE 11.2
Descriptions of Derived Hand Categories

FINGER CYCLING

Any degree of movement by the fingers; rhythmic tapping movements, rhythmic curling of the fingers, etc.

FINGERS CURLED

Fingers bent inward either loosely or in a fist. Includes any variation on this theme (i.e., movements including "other than index-finger extensions" or "claw-like" movements). The crucial element is the lack of activity in the fingers.

INDEX-FINGER EXTENSION

Any clear, sustained extension of the index finger. Other fingers will be most likely bent inward. However, if the extension is straight and clearly visible, any other static form of the fingers is okay. Index finger may be bent or slightly moving. The crucial element is the sustained extension of the one finger.

GRASP

The hands/fingers are either held by the mother or grasping something other than the infant's own hands and fingers. Note: If the activity is of the direction infant grasp, then this category should be used; if the direction is of the form "mother grasp," use only if it obscures the view of the infant's movements.

CLASPING

Any clasping or the mutual contact of the hands or fingers; may include wringing of the hands. If hands or fingers simply brush one another or make any haphazard contact, do not use this category.

SPREAD

All fingers fully extended and spread apart in a "starfish" fashion. There is no other movement of the fingers.

Criteria:

1. Each movement must last 3 seconds or longer.
2. When looking at an interval, try to define it by its overall nature. For example, if during a segment there is a momentary pause or slight variation lasting less than 3 seconds, ignore it.

Comparisons of the transcripts of the third coding and the original adjusted transcripts replicated the previous findings. Average reliability for the right hand was estimated to be .96, whereas the average reliability for the left hand was estimated to be .98. The mean time error was .70 seconds for the right hand (low 95% C.I. = .44 seconds, high 95% C.I. = 1.20 seconds), and 1.01 seconds for the left (low 95% C.I. = .82 seconds, high 95% C.I. = 1.20 seconds).

As a replication of the validity of employing these transformations, the same procedures were performed on the second infant J. The results of these two analyses are presented in Table 11.3.

To assess whether the coding categories had an equal likelihood of being detected, percent of agreement measures were derived for each category across the six sessions for both infants. For infant H., only four of the six categories of behavior were displayed during the six sessions: *finger cycling, fingers curled, index-finger extension,* and *grasp.* For the right hand, the

TABLE 11.3
Reliability Estimates for the Second Infant

A. *Reliability Estimates with Adjusted Transcripts*

Session	Left Hand p(r)	Right Hand p(r)
1.	.95	.95
2	.98	.99
7	.96	.94
9	.94	.96
11	.94	.93
13	.96	.98

Mean time lag	= .77 seconds	1.14 seconds
Low C.I.	= .69 seconds	.93 seconds
High C.I.	= .85 seconds	1.35 seconds

B. *Reliability Estimates Comparing the Original Transcripts with Adjustments and the Third Coding Using Derived Hand Categories*

Session	Left Hand p(r)	Right Hand p(r)
1	.93	.96
2	.98	.99
7	.96	.96
9	.96	.96
11	.94	.93
13	.96	.98

Mean time lag	= .68 seconds	.96 seconds
Low C.I.	= .66 seconds	.85 seconds
High C.I.	= .70 seconds	1.07 seconds

percent of agreement measures were .96, .95, .93, and .86, respectively; for the left hand, .95, .96, .99, and .92, respectively. For infant J., there were also only four categories observed: *finger cycling, fingers curled, grasp,* and *clasp.* For the right hand, the percent of agreement measures were .97, .95, .93, and .95, respectively; for the left hand, the values were .95, .96, .88, and .95, respectively.

DISCUSSION

Support was presented for the hypothesis that certain categories of hand movements could be described and reliably coded as real-time units. The stability of these derived coding categories is seen in the consistency of reliability across session. There were no apparent systematic changes in the estimates of session reliability for either infant and there did not appear to be a disproportionate number of errors in any of the categories of behavior. The six categories of behavior described in Table 11.2 represent clear-cut distinctions between one type of hand activity and the next, and the categories are exhaustive of all possible hand movements observed across a 12-week span of time for both the infants.

The initially low reliability estimates appear to have been the result of the difficulty each team had in distinguishing instances of rapid moment-to-moment change and the fine-grained differences between individual hand categories, using the original coding categories. Unlike the behaviors of the eyes, brows, and mouth, the fingers are often rapidly changing from one movement to another. Clearly detectable pauses between these changes seldom occur, and when they do, they are hard to detect reliably. Very short duration behaviors may be seen as unique events or simply as variations on a larger theme of activity—for example, *index-finger extensions* occurring with slow and brief alternations of flexions and extensions. One team chooses to describe such events in broader categories, whereas the other chooses a more narrow application of categories in creating events within the stream. With little consensus to guide the knowledge of the exact nature of an "at-rest" category, let alone a moving category, duration probably becomes an important parameter used by coding teams during their transcriptions. Duration affects the detection of event change as well as the application of category labels.

The current investigation was intended to develop a method of coding hand movements in real time. Although we acknowledge that the original coding categories could not accurately describe each single, unique finger movement in the same detail as has been accomplished for the face, the codes that were derived roughly describe a finite number of discrete patterns that individually could become a focus of concern. As such, they provide a useful starting place to begin to ask questions relating to the temporal or sequential occurrence of each category during social or nonsocial interaction.

One hypothesis is that differing emotional states may be associated with the discrete categories given in Table 11.2. Papousek (1978) has presented his anectdotal evidence that the fist or tightly clenched hand is most often associated with states of distress, whereas loosely clenched fingers reflect states of engagement. Trevarthen (1977) has argued that the *index-finger extension* (or what he terms a "point") occurs most during changes in the ongoing flow of dyadic interaction, whereas the repetitive flexing and extending of the fingers occurs during states of heightened arousal. Further explorations of the hand behavior of infant H. and infant J. (Hannan, 1981) have revealed that the category *index-finger extension* (or "point") is correlated with the infant's percent of time looking at some object or the mother, the percent of time that the mouth is at rest, and the percent of time that the eyebrows are relaxed. Analysis of the probability of cooccurrence between the *index-finger extension* and the previous categories mentioned indicated a greater-than-chance likelihood of these categories' occurring together. This evidence would seem to provide support both for Trevarthen's view that *index-finger extensions* may be more likely to occur during changes in the on-going flow of infant–mother interaction, and for an hypothesis of a relationship between finger movements and specific observable states of emotion.

One can also derive developmental hypotheses based on these hand expressions. Unlike facial behavior, where the number of expressions may increase (Oster, 1978), some of the hand expressions would be expected to either cease to be displayed or to become reorganized into new behaviors as development proceeds. *Finger cycling,* for example, is not a common activity for the older child, but *index-finger extensions* have been suggested to be the forerunner of pointing (Fogel, 1981). *Grasping* becomes more differentiated over time (see Bower, 1974), and the *spread* may become reorganized into activities of usage not readily apparent in the early months of life. For example, Fogel (1981) suggests that *finger spread* may later become organized into a more complex behavior that can function as a social signal. In this case, the inclusion of the *finger spread* with an extended arm and the palm of the spread directed forward is employed as a gesture meaning "wait" or "stop."

The issue of category reliability has been given this much attention because further investigations will be totally dependent on the strength of the coding process. To attempt to analyze the behavioral flow of infant hand movements requires that the reduction from three-dimensional behavior to two-dimensional parameters be done as accurately as possible. A method of coding and reliability testing is provided that seems to satisfy this need.

ACKNOWLEDGMENTS

This study was part of the author's Ph. D. dissertation and was funded in part by a grant from the National Science Foundation (BNS–77–14524) to Dr. Alan Fogel, and by a grant from the Agriculture Experiment Station to Purdue University. I wish to thank the mothers and their infants for their cooperation, and to acknowledge the assistance of Glenn Diamond, Wanda Temm, Pravish Singh, Theresa Hawkins, and Lisa Bradfueher. In addition, I would like to thank Dr. Alan Fogel for providing me with the data used in the present study and for the helpful comments made during the preparation of this manuscript.

REFERENCES

Bower, T. G. R. *Development in infancy*. San Francisco: W. H. Freeman, 1974.

Ekman, P., & Friesen, W. V. *Unmasking the face: A guide to recognizing emotions from facial clues*. Englewood Cliffs, N.J.: Prentice-Hall, 1975.

Ekman, P., & Friesen, W. V. *Manual for the facial action coding system*. Palo Alto, Calif.: Consulting Psychologists Press, 1978.

Fogel, A. The ontogeny of gestural communication: The first six months. In R. Stark (Ed.), *Language behavior in infancy and early development*. New York: Elsevier, 1981.

Gaensbauer, T. J., Mrazek, D., & Emde, R. N. Patterning of emotional response in a playroom laboratory situation. *Infant Behavior and Development*, 1979, *2*, 166–178.

Hannan, T. E. *Infant "pointing" behavior in the first three months of life*. Doctoral dissertation, Purdue University, 1981.

Hollenbeck, A. R. Problems of reliability in observational research. In G. P. Sackett (Ed.), *Observing behavior, Volume 2: Data collection and analysis methods*. Baltimore: University Park Press, 1978.

Izard, C. E., Huedner, R. R., Risser, D., McGuinnes, G. C., & Dougherty, L. M. The young infant's ability to produce discrete emotion expressions. *Developmental Psychology*, 1980, 132–140.

Kaye, K. Estimating "false alarms" and missed events from interobserver agreement: A rationale. *Psychological Bulletin*, 1980, *88*, 458–468.

Oster, H. Facial expression and affect development. In M. Lewis, & L. A. Rosenblum (Eds.), *The development of affect*. New York: Plenum Press, 1978.

Oster, H., & Ekman, P. Facial behavior in child development. In A. Collins (Ed.), *Minnesota symposia on child psychology* (Vol. 11). Hillsdale, N.J.: Lawrence Erlbaum Associates, 1977.

Papousek, H. Keynote Address, International Conference on Infant Studies, Providence, R.I., 1978.

Trevarthen, C. Descriptive analysis of infant communicative behavior. In H. R. Schaffer (Ed.), *Studies of mother-infant interaction*. London: Academic Press, 1977.

12 Time-Series Analysis of Social-Interaction Data

John Gottman
F. Thomas Rose
Gwendolyn Mettetal
University of Illinois

This chapter reviews time-series methods for analyzing continuous bivariate time-series data of the sort obtained by Tronick, Als, and Brazelton (1977). In this situation two graphs are obtained over time, one representing the second-by-second involvement of the mother with her baby, and a second representing the involvement of the baby with the mother. This is called bivariate time-series data. Similar data sets are often obtained in other fields; for example, in political science one series may be yearly USA military expenditures and the other series yearly USSR military expenditures, or in economics one series may represent inflation and the other may represent the prime lending rate.

Brazelton, Koslowski, and Main (1974) provided an excellent description of the cyclicity and rhythmicity they believe characterizes the interactive flow between mother and infant. They wrote:

> When the infant was interacting with his mother, there seemed to be a constant cycle of attention (A), followed by withdrawal of attention (W)—the cycle being used by each partner as he approached and then withdrew and waited for a response from the other participant. In the mothers and infants we observed, this mode of attention seemed to exist on several levels during an interaction sequence. If she responds in one way, their interactional energy builds up; if another, he may turn away. The same holds true of her response to his behavior. In order to predict and understand which behavioral cluster will produce an ongoing sequence of attention, one must understand the affective attention available in each member of the dyad. In other words, the strength of the dyadic interaction dominates the meaning of each member's behavior. The behavior of any one member becomes a part of a cluster of behaviors which interact with a cluster of behaviors from the other member of the dyad. No single behavior can be separated from the cluster for analysis without losing its meaning in the sequence. The effect of clustering and of sequencing takes over in assessing the value of particular behaviors, and in the

same way the dyadic nature of interaction supercedes the importance of an individual member's clusters and sequences [pp. 55–56].

In Brazelton's laboratory the behavior of the mother and infant are recorded by two cameras positioned so that one camera captures a frontal view of the mother, the other a frontal view of the infant. The two images of the mother and infant are then merged with a split-screen generator and an electronic time-code generator. This recording procedure greatly facilitates slow motion and/or frame-by-frame scoring of a mother's and infant's nonverbal behavior. Brazelton and his associates organized behavior into dimensions that vary in terms of affective and attentional involvement. Each level of attentional and affective involvement is assigned specific behavior referents.

In the area of mother–infant interaction, two major concepts have been important in the literature. One concept is the *cyclicity* of the infant's attention and excitement and the *synchronicity* of the mother's involvement in the play. It has been suggested by Brazelton and his associates that "cycling together" is an index of a mother who is sensitive to her baby's cycles of inattention and does not continue to stimulate the baby at such times. Thus, synchronicity or cycling together has been proposed as an index of the quality of the relationship and, potentially, as an index of the amount of pleasure that the play can hold for both people.

A second concept that has been proposed as an index of the relationship, particularly as an index of the infant's social development, is *bidirectionality* (Bell, 1968). An interaction in which social influence is reciprocal has been proposed as an index of intersubjectivity—that is, of the two people sharing a phenomenological world of emotional interaction.

This chapter addresses these concepts in a technical manner. No equations are used. Instead the methods are discussed conceptually and through visual means. This chapter is intended as an introduction to both the kinds of conceptual and statistical analysis that is now possible in the 20th century, after nearly 200 years of mathematical invention. To make the discussion concrete, we conducted a single-subject longitudinal study of the play of a mother with her infant daughter. After a brief description of the methods of this ministudy, we return to a technical discussion of the issues of *cyclicity and synchronicity* and then the issue of *bidirectionality*. This chapter is clearly introductory. More detail is available in Gottman's (1981) *Time-Series Analysis: A Comprehensive Introduction for Social Scientists.* The data discussed in this chapter were analyzed using programs from the Gottman–Williams computer packages (Williams & Gottman, 1981).

METHODS

The mother we videotaped is a Caucasian, middle-class, primaparous female in her early 20s. Her infant was delivered full term and was a normal, healthy infant girl. Taping took place in our laboratory located in the psychology building at the University of Illinois. Our laboratory is decorated with carpet, drapes, a table and chairs, and bookcases, and has the appearance of a comfortable living room. Two cameras are positioned behind the bookcases and are operated by remote control from an adjacent room. Although the cameras are unobtrusive, the mother knew that she was being taped. Three microphones are placed around the room in unobtrusive locations and ensure high-quality sound reproduction.

At the beginning of each session, the mother was met by members of our research staff who gave her the opportunity to ask any questions about the taping and attempted to allay any concerns that she may have had about her and her infant's performance. Once both mother and infant were comfortable, we gave the mother the simple instructions to play with her infant, left them alone in the room, and began taping. Initially we attempted to film the couple with the infant sitting in an infant seat but the infant found the seat so aversive that we modified our original procedures. We decided to lay the infant supine on a table in the room and positioned the mother's chair so that she would be parallel and shoulder to shoulder with her infant's body and facing in the direction of the infant's face. This still permitted the full observation of both the mother and the infant's behavior. Minor adjustments were made in the coding system we employed to preserve the integrity of the system yet reflect changes in the body position of the mother and infant relative to each other. In later sessions it was possible to tape the infant in the infant seat, and so we returned to our original procedures. During these later sessions, the infant seat was positioned 1 1/2 feet in front of the mother so that both infant and mother were facing each other.

A common problem faced by researchers working with human infants is that changes in the infant state necessitate frequent interruptions in the data-collection process. Whenever the infant required changing or feeding we stopped filming and resumed again when both mother and infant were comfortable. Our objective was to record 15 minutes of positive social play; often this required as much as 1 1/2 hours of laboratory time.

Mother and child visited our laboratory for the first time when the infant was 9 weeks old. Thereafter, they were videotaped in 2-week intervals for the following 2 1/3 months. In total we had a six-session record of the development of social interaction between this mother–infant dyad from the ninth to the 19th week of the infant's life.

The format of the videotape record of the behavior of our mother–infant dyad was very similar to that of Brazelton and his colleagues. One camera captured the behavior of the mother; the other camera captured the behavior of the infant. Both images were fed into a split-screen generator and recorded on tape mixed with an electronic digital frame counter/timer. There are 60 frames per second; the equipment permits a frame-by-frame or slow-motion observation of the dyad's interaction for microanalysis of their behavior.

From each taping session we randomly selected two 5-minute segments for scoring. The coding system we employed was the Bates (1981) laboratory revision of the Tronick laboratory system. The Bates system organizes infant nonverbal behavior into seven dimensions—body position, facial expressions, direction of gaze, hand movements, head orientation, vocalizations, and limb movements—and mother nonverbal behavior into six dimensions—body position, facial expressions, direction of gaze, hand movements, head orientation, and vocalizations. Each dimension represents an ordinal scale of levels of affective and attentional involvement to which there are assigned specific behavioral referents. Scale values range from 1, representing the least involvement, to 4, 7, or 9, depending on the dimension, representing the greatest involvement.

One trained observer coded the couple's behavior in random order of sessions, scoring all dimensions once every second for all sessions. A second trained coder using the same coding strategy scored 1-minute samples from each session to check for reliability. Intercoder reliability was calculated as the percentage of agreement on each 1/10-second interval, and exceeded 85% for all sessions. These reliabilities were 97% for the baby's data and 97% for the mother's data for the 9-week session and 96% and 99% for the baby's and mother's data for the 13-week session. We also computed correlation coefficients for these data on the summed variables that were used to create the time series. For the 9-week session these correlation coefficients were .80 for the baby's data and .75 for the mother's data. For the 13-week session these correlations were .62 and .83 for the baby's and the mother's data, respectively.

We collapsed the nonverbal dimensions into one variable. We summed the six mother variables to create one time series for the mother and summed the seven baby variables to create one time series for the baby.

CYCLICITY AND SYNCHRONICITY

One fact has been clear in time-series analysis for at least a century: Patterns cannot usually be detected by visual inspection. The recognition of this fact is critical. Also critical is the quantitative analysis of data rather than intuitive, albeit influential, conclusions based on anecdotal reports by investigators. It is not uncommon for researchers who study social interaction to comment on the periodicity and cyclicity of social behavior, and to sense intuitively the need for analytic methods to detect these patterns. In fact, cycles and synchronicity are particularly interesting to researchers of parent–infant interaction. However, researchers have tended to be frustrated in summarizing their data, and instead they have relied on metaphors that create a *veneer* of time-series language. For example, Condon and Ogston (1967), using slow-motion film, undertook the frame-by-frame microanalysis of 15 minutes of the dinnertime interaction of a father, mother, and son. They wrote:

> We are dealing with ordered patterns of change during change, which exhibit rhythmic and varying patterns in the temporal sequencing of such changes. Metaphorically, there are waves within waves within waves, with complex yet determinable relationships between peaks and the troughs of the levels of waves, which serve to express organized processes with continually changing relationships [p. 224].

This bewildering array of metaphor is an excellent intuitive prologue to spectral time-series analysis methods.

Waves within Waves within Waves

There is an important distinction that needs to be made in the discussion of cyclicity. Some cycles are extremely regular. The periods of oscillation of these cycles are more or less fixed and determined; this is called *deterministic* cyclicity. The motion of a well-constructed pendulum is such a cycle. If a pen is attached to an oscillating pendulum, and it marks on a uniformly moving sheet of paper, the motion described would be the *sine wave* illustrated by Fig. 12.1. More complex deterministic oscillations are

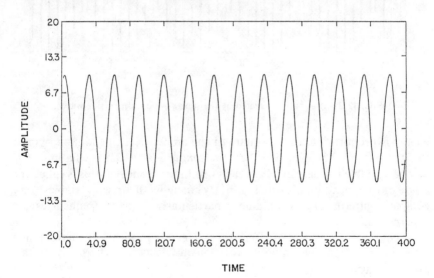

FIG. 12.1   A sine wave.

possible by the superposition of the other cycles. This is physically possible by attaching a second pendulum to the base of the first. An example of a pattern that can be obtained by superposing two sine waves is the beat pattern, illustrated by Fig. 12.2. In the beat pattern, a faster wave oscillates within the envelope of a slower wave. Extremely elaborate patterns are possible by adding more cycles. Two variables need to be considered in the creation of these patterns. Consider the case of two pendulums attached to one another. The first variable is the energy of each pendulum—that is, how hard each pendulum is shoved when it starts out. It turns out that this

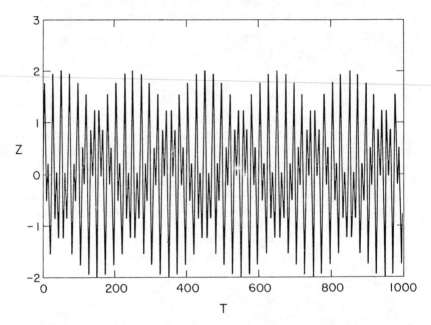

FIG. 12.2   Beat pattern created by the superposition of two sine waves.

energy is proportional to the square of the amount each pendulum swings; the amount of the swing is called the *amplitude* of the oscillation. The second variable is where in its arc each pendulum is shoved; this is called the *phase* of each pendulum's oscillation. By changing these two variables, very complex patterns can be obtained, particularly if many frequencies are superposed.

Of course, the problem of interest is the reverse problem: We have a time series and wish to determine its component cyclicities. The study of this problem has a long history.

In the early 20th century, very precise astronomical measurements became possible for the first time. For example, Whittaker and Robinson (1924) observed the brightness of a variable star on 600 successive days. The problem they had was that their data were obscured by atmospheric disturbances. Thus, random error, or *noise*, obscured or masked their data. This noise was not trivial. So the problem they had was how to detect the deterministic cycles in brightness that were masked by the noise. They applied an old method that worked very well for them. They discovered that their data could be fit very well by two components cycles; like the two pendulums, this variable star turned out to be a binary star. Whittaker and Robinson's success caused great excitement.

Unfortunately, their methods were a complete failure for most other data. Furthermore, it turned out that what was necessary mathematically to deal with most people's data was a conceptual revolution about cyclicity. This revolution can now be summarized very simply. Most data are not made up of deterministic (fixed) cycles masked by noise. Most data are made up of cycles that are not deterministic at all. In fact, the components of most data are cycles that meander randomly in amplitude and phase around some mean values and with some statistical distributions. In other words, most cycles are *nearly periodic*. This transition from determinism to probabilism was an important breakthrough in being able to analyze data for component cyclicity. To understand the mathematics, we need to introduce a new mathematical tool.

This new tool is called the *spectral density function*. The spectral density function measures the amount of energy in each cycle. The usual way to represent this is by a graph. The X axis of the graph measures the *frequency* of the potential cycles in the data. Frequency is related to the time that it takes for the cycle to repeat. In the case of the pendulum, it is related to the time for a full swing of the pendulum; actually, the frequency is the *reciprocal* of the period of oscillation. If you imagine a graph with a set of time points, the fastest frequency is one that goes above the mean and then immediately below the mean. It thus repeats every two time points (i.e., this is the peak-to-peak interval); the fastest frequency is thus $1/2 = 0.5$. The slowest frequency is obtained by a cycle of infinite period, so that the slowest frequency is 0.0. All our graphs of the spectral density function's X axis therefore go from 0.0 to 0.5.

On the Y axis is a plot of something related to the amount of energy in each cycle. Remember that this is related to how hard each pendulum was shoved, which is proportional to the square of the amplitude of its oscillation. The beat pattern of Fig. 12.2 had two component cycles of equal amplitude, and the spectral density of the beat pattern is illustrated in Fig. 12.3. Notice that we have two sharp spikes. This is obtained by deterministic oscillations.

Nondeterministic oscillations have a *band* of cycles represented so that their spectral density functions do not have peaks that are as spiked. They are smeared out a bit around a peak.

What would the spectral density function of the beat pattern look like if noise obscured the pattern? First, what do these look like? Fig. 12.4 il-

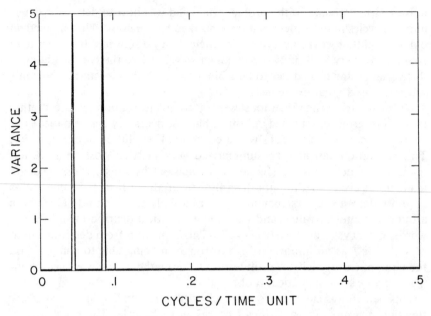

FIG. 12.3   Spectral density function of the beat pattern.

lustrates that the beat pattern may not be recognizable if it is obscured by noise. But the spectral density function of these data shows the two

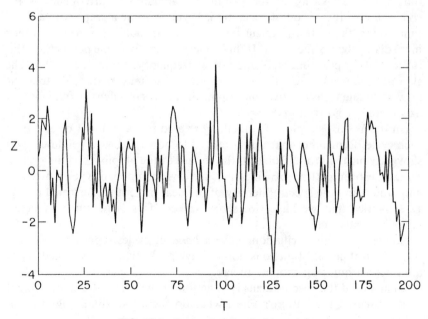

FIG. 12.4   Beat pattern masked by noise.

characteristic spikes (see Fig. 12.5). This is clearly a useful function. However, notice that there is an elevation to the spectral density function throughout the frequency range. This is because the spectral density of noise should theoretically be a straight line. All oscillations are potentially present to equal degrees. If we kept adding noise to the data, this background line would rise in power and eventually obscure the peaks. .

At this point let us consider the analysis of one set of data.

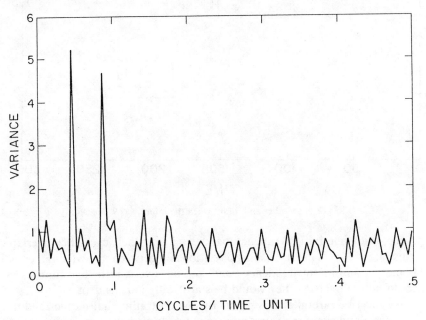

FIG. 12.5   Spectral density function of the beat pattern obscured by noise.

Cyclicity

We begin with a data set from the first session. The data are plotted in Fig. 12.6. The spectral density functions for the mother and infant are plotted in Fig. 12.7. Note the horizontal line of dots. This represents the theoretical spectral density if the data were noise. If the confidence interval (dashed line) around the estimated spectral density function (solid line) excludes this horizontal line, then the peak is statistically significant at $p < .05$. This is true for these data. Furthermore, there is only one peak. Note, however, that the peaks include a band of frequencies. These data are not deterministically periodic. For the baby (Fig. 12.7a) the frequencies up to .073 are significant; beyond this, the dashed line meets or is below the dots. For the mother (Fig. 12.7b) the range is narrower, from zero up to .043. We can conclude that the baby's and mother's behavior are both significantly

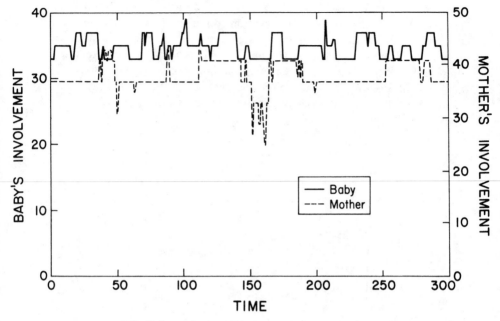

FIG. 12.6   Mother and infant when the infant was 9 weeks old.

cyclic, with one basic frequency band, and that their cyclicities overlap. This fact is critical in establishing a relationship between the two time series: If mother and infant frequency bands did not overlap, the two time series could not be related—they would be statistically independent.

We must be careful at this point. By demonstrating that mother and infant cycle and share the same frequency bands we have *not* demonstrated that they are synchronous or related. To demonstrate synchronicity we need to examine two other functions: the *coherence spectrum* and the *phase spectrum*.

Synchronicity

The concept of synchronicity needs to be expanded as follows: Suppose we have two tuning forks that are attached to resonant chambers. Suppose we strike one tuning fork that we know vibrates in a band of frequencies around middle C. We now measure the sympathetic resonant activity of the second tuning fork. What are the possibilities? If the second tuning fork responds at all, we need two numbers to describe its response—how much it responds, and how rapidly it responds. The "how much" measures how much energy is transmitted and the "how rapidly" measures the lag or phase of this response. Thus we need two concepts to operationalize the notion of synchronicity.

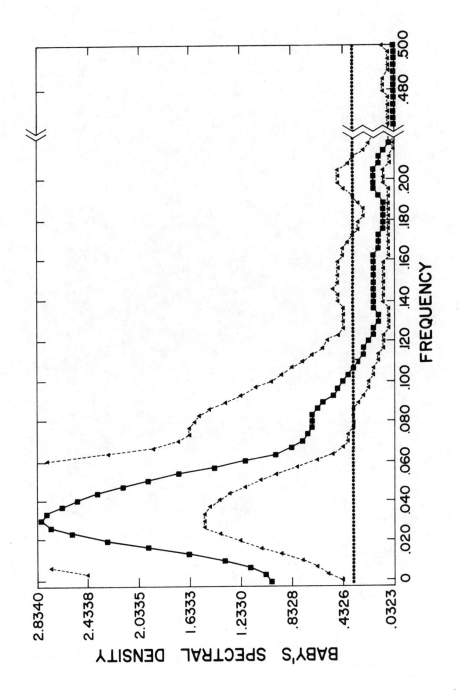

FREQUENCY

BABY'S SPECTRAL DENSITY

2.8340 2.4338 2.0335 1.6333 1.2330 .8328 .4326 .0323

0 .020 .040 .060 .080 .100 .120 .140 .160 .180 .200 .480 .500

277

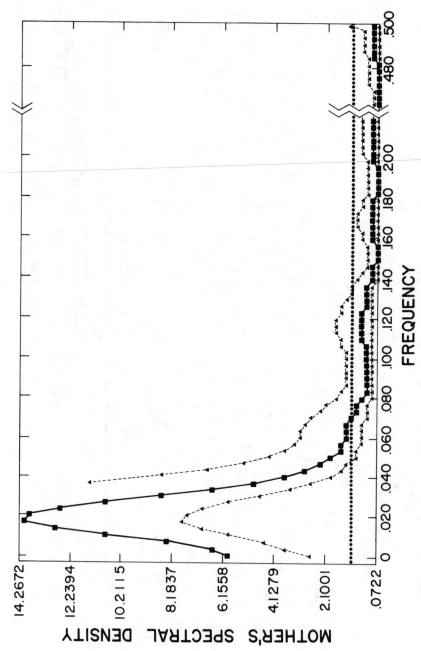

FIG. 12.7   Spectral densities of the data in Fig. 12.6.

Now let us ask the question whether the mother's data in Fig. 12.6 are related to the baby's data. We know that they share a range of frequencies so we actually have a *set* of tuning forks for which we measure the response (the baby's). We need two numbers at each frequency to describe this "input–output" relationship.

These two functions are called the coherence and the phase. At each frequency we assess the *coherence*, which assesses the maximum amount of linear association, and the *phase*, which measures lead–lag relationship. It is essential to realize that we are interested in these two numbers only across frequency bands that are statistically significant. In our case this would be the overlap between mother and infant—that is, from zero frequency to .043. The coherence is like the square of the correlation coefficient, and it varies between zero and one.

It also turns out that it makes no sense to examine the phase if the coherence is not at least significant, and preferably sizable. This is because the confidence interval on the phase is proportional to one minus the coherence divided by the coherence. If the coherence is high (near one), the confidence interval on the phase (which assesses lead/lag) will be small. If the coherence is near zero, the confidence interval on the phase will be large.

For our data, the coherence is not significant in the frequency ranges that the mother and infant share (see Fig. 12.8). It thus makes no sense to interpret the phase.

One Month Later

Let us consider the data from a tape made 1 month later (Fig. 12.9). Once again the data are cyclic. For both mother and infant there are significant elevations of the spectral density function (see Fig. 12.10). Note, however, that the oscillation is far more complex. This is exemplified, in part, by a wider band of frequencies for which the spectral density function is significant. For the mother the range extends to .80; for the baby it extends up to .097.

If we now examine the coherence spectrum within the common band of frequencies, we note that it is significant, particularly from frequencies from .027 to .047 (see Fig. 12.11). Because the coherence is significant within this band, we are safe in examining the phase spectrum. If it is negative, this means that the mother leads the baby, or that the baby is able to respond to her mother.[1] The amount of time lag is actually minus the phase divided by 2π times the frequency (see Fig. 12.12). For example, at frequency of maximum coherence, .033, the phase is $-.48$, so that the

---

[1] A negative phase means that the first series entered into the analysis (the x series) leads the second. In our example the mother's series was first. This is, of course, arbitrary.

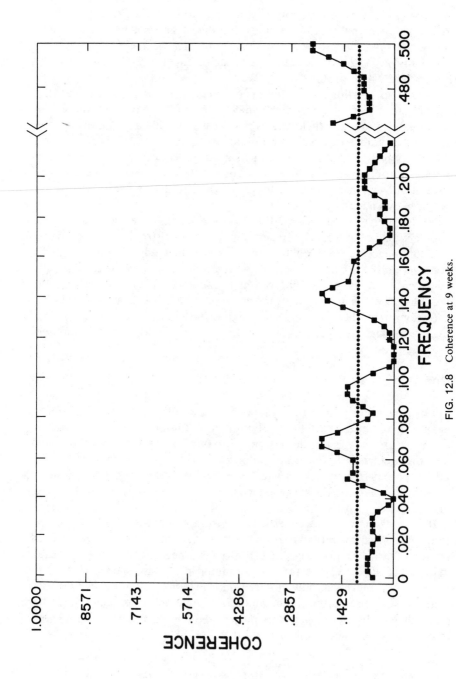

FIG. 12.8   Coherence at 9 weeks.

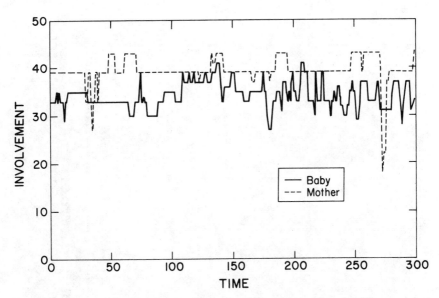

FIG. 12.9   Mother and infant when the infant was 13 weeks old.

estimated time lag is $+.48/2\pi$ $(.033)$ $= 2.32$ seconds at that frequency. We would thus be led to conclude that, at 2 months of age, the baby and mother have become coherent and that the baby is responding to the mother. Note, however, that the confidence interval around the phase spectrum estimate is only reasonably narrow in the frequency range depicted in Fig. 12.12.

Possibilities and Limitations

The amazing fact is that *this entire analysis is applicable regardless of whether the data are cyclic or not.* This is true because of a famous theorem by Fourier (1822/1978) that proved that *any* reasonable set of data can be approximated to any degree of accuracy by a sum of independent cyclic functions. Do not be concerned if this amazes and surprises you; it did the same to Fourier's contemporaries. In fact, although Fourier's theorem is true, he proved it incorrectly and it took a century for some of the best mathematical minds to correctly prove it. (If you would like to learn more about this, see Gottman [1981].) Hence, whether or not one is interested in cyclicity, the issue of the *relationship* between the mother's and the infant's series can be approached in the identical way.

There are, however, two inherent limitations to the analyses discussed so far in this chapter. The first limitation is that the data must have a property called *stationarity.* Stationary data vary about a fixed mean, and have constant spectral density function throughout the data. This restriction is not

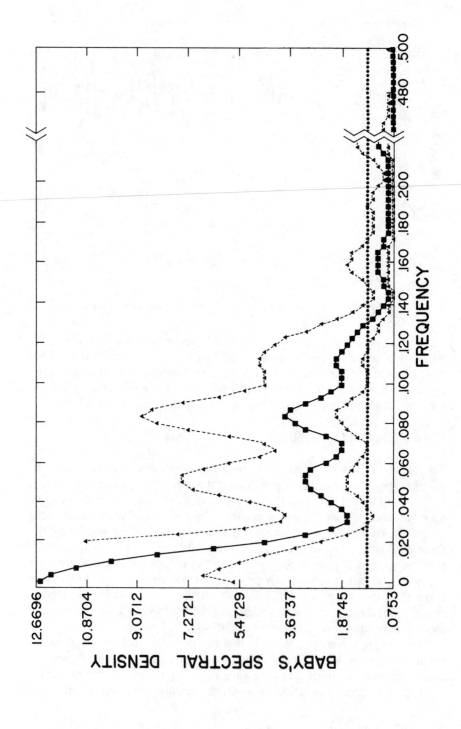

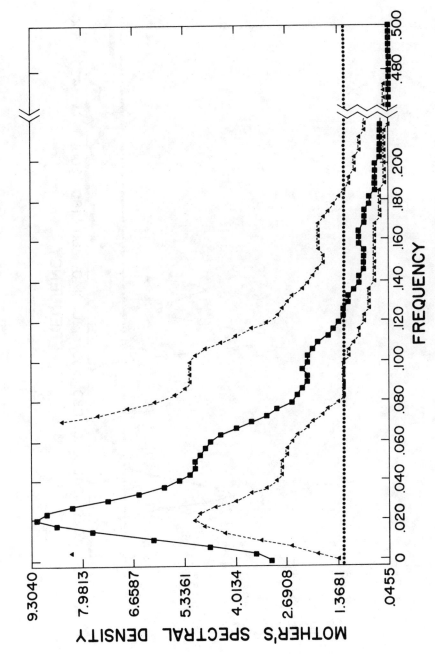

FIG. 12.10 Spectral densities of the data in Fig. 12.9.

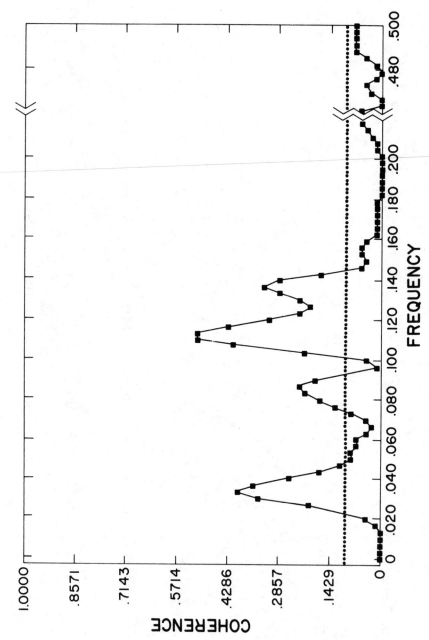

FIG. 12.11   Coherence at 13 weeks.

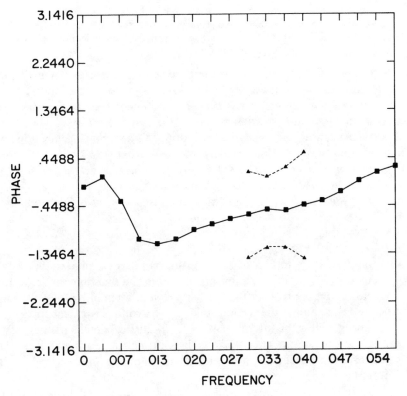

FIG. 12.12   Phase spectrum for the data in Fig. 12.9.

usually a serious problem; however, space does not permit a discussion of what to do if the data are not stationary. Two alternative approaches are discussed in detail in Gottman (1981); one approach is to model the non-stationarity and the other is to transform the data. These approaches can be complimentary. An illustration of the transformation approach is given in Gottman and Ringland (1981) in which data by Tronick et al. (1977) were differenced (i.e., the rate of change of the data were analyzed) to eliminate nonstationarity. To summarize, we must assume that the data are stationary or deal with the nonstationarity by modeling it, or transforming the data so that the transformed data are stationary. Stationarity is thus usually not a serious problem. The second limitation is that it is difficult to make confident inferences about cross-correlation between the two time series without controlling for autocorrelation in each series. Spurious relationships between two time series can be obtained simply because each of the time series is predictable, to some extent, from its past. This point about autocontingency has been made before. Sackett (1980) wrote:

The basic issue of autocontingency has not been addressed by students of social interaction. Unfortunately, autocontingency does effect the degree to which cross lag dependencies can occur. In some instances, apparent cross contingencies may be a total artifact of strong autolag functions [p. 330].

The point has also been made in the time-series literature. For example, Jenkins and Watts (1968) showed that: "very large cross covariances, all of them spurious, can be generated *between* two uncorrelated processes as a result of the large autocovariances *within* the two processes [p. 338]."

To make a causal inference of association, this autocontingency must be removed from the data. Conceptually this means that we may conclude that *the mother influences the baby (M → B) if the mother's data account for variance in the baby's data over and above the variance accounted for by the past of the baby's data.* This leads to a discussion of bidirectionality.

Bidirectionality

Using the previus definition of social influence, it is possible to write two equations for the possible relationships between the two time series. In the first equation, we control for the mother's past in attempting to test the inference $B → M$, and in the second equation, we control for the baby's past in attempting to test the inference $M → B$. Statistical details of these tests are discussed in Gottman (1981) and in Gottman and Ringland (1981). Briefly, a stepwise procedure is employed. In testing the inference $M → B$, for example, models are successively fit that go back into the past of the baby's series one, two, three, and so on, time units, and back into the mother's past one, two, three, and so on, time units. Finally the best model is selected and compared to a model with no terms from the mother's series—that is, the model with cross-regressive and autoregressive terms is compared to a model with only autoregressive terms. The spectral analyses can be used to suggest start-up values for how far to go back into the past. There are clearly four possibilities: (1) no relationship ($M ⇸ B, B ⇸ M$); (2) the baby influences the mother ($M ⇸ B$, but $B → M$); (3) the mother influences the baby ($M → B$, but $B ⇸ M$); and (4) bidirectionality ($M → B$ and $B → M$).

Table 12.1 summarizes the two analyses for the 9-weeks data. The important statistic to examine in this Table is the comparison of Model 2 with Model 3. The top half of Table 12.1 relates to the $B → M$ inference. Model 2 has two autoregressive mother terms (under column A) and six cross-regressive baby terms (under column B). The autoregressive Model 3 has only the two autoregressive terms. In "2 vs. 3" on the Table the statistic Q is distributed as chi-square with 6 degrees of freedom. The Z statistic is the standard normal deviate for this chi-square. If this Z score is greater than 1.96, the result is probably significant at $p < .05$, which is the case here, so

TABLE 12.1
Bidirectionality Analysis for the Mother-Infant Dyad at 2 Months

Model	A	B	SSE	$T\,LN(SSE/T)$
1	10	10	630.775	230.314
2	2	6	663.467	243.502
3	2	0	710.615	261.420
4	10	0	680.176	249.994
5	0	0	382555.000	1902.718
1 vs. 2 Q = 13.188			12 = DF Z = .243	
2 vs. 3 Q = 17.918			6 = DF Z = 3.440	
3 vs. 4 Q = 11.426			8 = DF Z = .857	
				$B \rightarrow M$

Model	C	D	SSE	$T\,LN(SSE/T)$
1	10	10	272.897	11.634
2	9	1	280.142	18.473
3	9	0	284.621	22.612
4	10	0	284.469	22.474
5	0	0	313691.000	1850.919
1 vs. 2 Q = 6.839			10 = DF Z = -.707	
2 vs. 3 Q = 4.140			1 = DF Z = 2.220	
3 vs. 4 Q = .139			1 = DF Z = -.609	
				$M \rightarrow B$

that we may conclude that $B \rightarrow M$. Similarly, by examining the lower half of Table 12.1, we can conclude that $M \rightarrow B$. Thus, even at 9 weeks this dyad was bidirectional. However, it is important to be precise in the language we use to describe these relationships. If we are actually interested, as Tronick et al. (1977) were, in how the mother and baby are *changing* together, we must analyze rates of change of these data (see Gottman & Ringland, 1981).

Table 12.2 is a similar analysis for the data at 13 weeks. Note that Z scores for the "2 vs. 3" model comparison are also significant. Also note that although the Z scores for the $B \rightarrow M$ inference have not increased, they have increased developmentally for the $M \rightarrow B$ inference. The developmental change from 2 to 3 months for this dyad is the baby's responsiveness to the mother and/or the mother's ability to get her baby to respond to her. Hence the influence in the dyad was still bidirectional at 3 months.

If we refer back to the spectral time-series analyses we can add that the baby's and mother's behavior have also become more complex. More cycles are added to their behavior, and these now include rapid as well as slow oscillations. Note that the mean levels of involvement in the play are not very different from Fig. 12.6 and Fig. 12.9, but the frequency content of the data become markedly different.

TABLE 12.2
Bidirectionality Analysis for the Mother-Infant Dyad at 3 Months

Model	A	B	SSE	T LN(SSE/T)
1	10	10	1023.202	365.635
2	9	5	1030.747	367.766
3	9	0	1086.913	383.153
4	10	0	1086.835	383.132
5	0	0	451182.000	2131.426

1 vs. 1	Q = 2.131		6 = DF Z = -1.117	
2 vs. 3	Q = 15.387		5 = DF Z = 3.285	
3 vs. 4	Q = .021		1 = DF Z = -.692	

$B \rightarrow M$

Model	C	D	SSE	T LN(SSE/T)
1	10	10	869.980	318.591
2	8	1	894.658	326.703
3	8	0	921.930	335.411
4	10	0	913.874	332.866
5	0	0	341648.000	2050.780

1 vs. 2	Q = 8.112		11 = DF Z = -.616	
2 vs. 3	Q = 8.708		1 = DF Z = 5.450	
3 vs. 4	Q = 2.545		2 = DF Z = .272	

$M \rightarrow B$

SUMMARY

Two issues were addressed in this chapter: (1) cyclicity and synchronicity of mother–infant interaction; and (2) bidirectionality of mother–infant interactions. The spectral density function was designed to the analysis of cyclicity. In the past 60 years, this work has been extended from deterministic cycles to deterministic cycles masked by noise and finally to nondeterministic (or almost periodic) cyclicity. Synchronicity can be studied by the coherence and phase spectrum; the coherence measures linear association at each frequency and phase measures lead–lag relationship. Furthermore, the data need not be cyclic to employ the coherence and phase for the assessments.

The major limitation of these methods is that they do not control for autocorrelation within each series (i.e., each series' predictability from its own past) in inferring cross-correlation between the series. To accomplish this analysis, the time-domain procedure of Gottman and Ringland was discussed.

Analysis of mother–infant interaction data obtained at 2 and 3 months demonstrated that, for this dyad, the interaction becomes more complex with age by adding faster cycles and that the baby becomes more responsive to the mother.

Two points need to be made: First, the methods proposed in this chapter demonstrate that *conceptual* clarity in this field can be gained by a thorough working knowledge of time-series concepts. These methods have been developed over the last 200 years; they have been successfully applied in other sciences; there is no point in reinventing the wheel, particularly with such vague metaphors as "waves within waves within waves," nor is there much point in employing incorrect statistical procedures. These data are painstaking to gather so why not get the most out of our analyses of them? Second, this chapter is clearly only an advertisement for time-series analysis. The interested reader is urged to further reading (Gottman, 1981). A set of computer programs designed for the beginner in this area has been written and is currently available (Williams & Gottman, 1981).

ACKNOWLEDGMENTS

This chapter was supported, in part, by an NIMH Research Scientist Development Award 1K02MH 00257 to the first author.

REFERENCES

Bates, J. *Revision of the Tronick scoring system for mother–infant interaction.* Unpublished laboratory manual, Indiana University, Bloomington, Indiana, 1981.

Bell, R. W. A reinterpretation of the direction of effects in studies of socialization. *Psychological Review,* 1968, *75,* 81–95.

Brazelton, T. B., Koslowski, B., & Main, M. The origin of reciprocity: The early mother–infant interaction. In M. Lewis, & L. Rosenblum (Eds.), *The effect of the infant on its caregiver.* New York: Wiley, 1974.

Condon, W. S., & Ogston, W. D. A segmentation of behavior. *Journal of Psychiatric Research,* 1967, *5,* 221–235.

Fourier, J. *La theorie de la chaleur.* Paris: Didot, 1822. (Translated by Alexander Freeman as *The analytic theory of heat.* Cambridge, Eng.: Cambridge University Press, 1978.)

Gottman, J. *Time-series analysis: A comprehensive introduction for social scientists.* New York: Cambridge University Press, 1981.

Gottman, J., & Ringland, J. The analysis of dominance and bidirectionality in social development. *Child Development,* 1981, *52,* 393–412.

Jenkins, G. M., & Watts, D. G. *Spectral analysis and its applications.* San Francisco: Holden Day, 1968.

Sackett, G. P. Lag sequential analysis as a data reduction technique in social interaction research. In D. Sawin, R. Hawkins, L. Walker, & J. Penticuff (Eds.), *Exceptional infant* (Vol. 4). New York: Brunner/Mazel, 1980.

Tronick, E. D., Als, H., & Brazelton, T. B. Mutuality in mother–infant interaction. *Journal of Communication,* 1977, *27,* 74–79.

Whittaker, E. T., & Robinson, G. *The calculus of observations.* New York: D. Van Nostrand, 1924.

Williams, E., & Gottman, J. *Time series analysis computer programs for social scientists.* New York: Cambridge University Press, 1981.

Author Index

Subject Index